About Island Press

Island Press is the only nonprofit organization in the United States whose principal purpose is the publication of books on environmental issues and natural resource management. We provide solutions-oriented information to professionals, public officials, business and community leaders, and concerned citizens who are shaping responses to environmental problems.

In 2001, Island Press celebrates its seventeenth anniversary as the leading provider of timely and practical books that take a multidisciplinary approach to critical environmental concerns. Our growing list of titles reflects our commitment to bringing the best of an expanding body of literature to the environmental community throughout North America and the world.

Support for Island Press is provided by The Bullitt Foundation, The Mary Flagler Cary Charitable Trust, The Nathan Cummings Foundation, Geraldine R. Dodge Foundation, Doris Duke Charitable Foundation, The Charles Engelhard Foundation, The Ford Foundation, The George Gund Foundation, The Vira I. Heinz Endowment, The William and Flora Hewlett Foundation, W. Alton Jones Foundation, The John D. and Catherine T. MacArthur Foundation, The Andrew W. Mellon Foundation, The Charles Stewart Mott Foundation, The Curtis and Edith Munson Foundation, National Fish and Wildlife Foundation, The New-Land Foundation, Oak Foundation, The Overbrook Foundation, The David and Lucile Packard Foundation, The Pew Charitable Trusts, Rockefeller Brothers Fund, The Winslow Foundation, and other generous donors.

Urban Development:
The Logic of Making Plans

Urban Development:
The Logic of Making Plans

Lewis D. Hopkins

ISLAND PRESS

WASHINGTON COVELO LONDON

ISLAND PRESS is a trademark of the Center for Resource Economics.

Library of Congress Cataloging-in-Publication Data

Hopkins, Lewis D.
  Urban development : the logic of making plans / Lewis D. Hopkins.
    p. cm.
Includes bibliographical references and index.
  ISBN 1-55963-852-4 (cloth : alk. paper) — ISBN 1-55963-853-2 (paper : alk.
paper)
  1. City planning. 2. City planning—Evaluation. 3. Social choice. I. Title.
  HT166 .H663 2001
  307.1'216—dc21

                                                              2001002229

British Library Cataloguing in Publication data available.

Printed on recycled, acid-free paper   ✳

Manufactured in the United States of America
10 9 8 7 6 5 4 3 2 1

To my parents,
their vision of what the world could be,
their precision in acting to achieve it,
and their commitment to community.

Contents

List of Figures

List of Tables

List of Games

Preface

Urban planning is used loosely to refer to intentional interventions in the urban development process, usually by local government. The term "planning" thus subsumes a variety of mechanisms that are in fact quite distinct: regulation, collective choice, organizational design, market correction, citizen participation, and public sector action. Plans, more narrowly defined, have logic and functions that are distinct from each of these other mechanisms, but related to each of them. The objective of this book is to set out the logic of how plans work and how they relate to other types of intentional actions in urban development. Clarity about how plans work leads to more reasonable expectations of what plans can accomplish and more careful choices about when to make plans, about what, for whom, and how.

I have been trying for a long time to figure out how plans for urban development work and how to make them. My parents encouraged this interest so that I am one of those unusual persons who was interested in planning by junior high school and even had some clue what it was. I grew up in Lakewood, Ohio, in a neighborhood built about 1905 in the style of Riverside, Illinois, with a public access footpath through our block and recreation areas owned in common by a homeowners' association. Within a few short years I saw the end of streetcars, the shift from taking the bus to downtown Cleveland to shop and see baseball games or to downtown Lakewood for music lessons, to taking a car in the opposite direction to suburban shopping malls and outlying services. I wrote junior high civics papers, about the Erieview redevelopment proposal and a letter in opposition to the new highway that cut our neighborhood in half.

These ideas were further shaped by the full breadth of the University of Pennsylvania of the late 1960s, where I was enrolled at various stages in architecture, landscape architecture, and planning programs. As dissertation adviser and through twenty-five years of continuing discussion, Brit Harris has developed and defended the argument that despite complexity, indeed because of it, plans are worth making. Bruce MacDougall, Ian McHarg, Russell Ackoff, Klaus Krippendorf, Seymour Mandelbaum, Tom Reiner, Ann Strong, and other faculty and students at the University of Pennsylvania influenced my thinking.

One of my criteria for assessing potential faculty colleagues has been: Could we reach a productive disagreement and a focused idea of how to investigate it? Over my twenty-eight years at the University of Illinois at Urbana-Champaign, this criterion yielded substantial collaborations on ideas related to this book with Downey Brill, Peter Schaeffer, Doug Johnston, Alex Anas, Kieran Donaghy, Gerrit Knaap, and Varkki George. The University of Illinois Research Board provided small grants over the years at key points that enabled these collaborations before they could attract outside funds. Ten years of work with Gerrit Knaap on the question, "Does planning matter?" have been particularly pertinent to my arguments here. I have discussed plans with colleagues Len Heumann, Andy Isserman, John Kim, Ken Reardon, and Louis Wetmore in working on curriculum and co-teaching courses. Al Guttenberg engaged in many discussions and read an early version of the entire manuscript, and Clyde Forrest and Daniel Schneider kept me from at least some errors in their specialties. Dick Klosterman, Jon Liebman, Zorica Nedovic-Budic, Rob Olshansky, Eliza Steelwater, and Bruce Williams helped create the intellectual environment of a department in which I could thrive. Bob Riley brought me to Illinois originally in landscape architecture and helped me learn how to take advantage of the full scope of this university.

Students in my classes and former students have read evolving versions and engaged these ideas critically. Shih-Kung Lai has commented extensively on successive versions and tried them in his courses at National Chung Hsing University in Taiwan. Alexandra Ortiz helped in working out many numerical examples of planning situations involving uncertainty. Several student teams worked with Illinois towns on planning-assistance projects, which also served as tests of some of these ideas. I thank the City of Taylorville for letting me use graphics from a recent such project by Matthew Gebhardt, Allison Laff, and Sathya Ponnuswamy. Paul Hanley provided useful information and feedback on wastewater treatment examples. I also benefited from being an outside reader of Emily Talen's dissertation on the effectiveness of plans.

Ernest Alexander read thoroughly and thoughtfully an earlier version and provided specific suggestions for focusing, abandoning, or improving particular arguments. Island Press editor Heather Boyer pinpointed opportunities to frame the arguments and make them more accessible to a broader readership.

Local examples from Champaign and Urbana result from conversations with Lachlan Blair, April Getchius, Bruce Knight, Dennis Schmidt, Libby Tyler, and Steven Wegman. Phoenix examples result from many presentations by and discussions with Joy Mee and John McNamara; Cassandra Ecker provided the issues and forces sketch from a Phoenix community meeting. The Lexington examples derive from the excellent resources of the library at the University of Illinois at Urbana-Champaign. Dijon Duncan created the final graphics so that despite diverse sources they all communicate specific ideas effectively when fitted to a page in a book.

I wrote some of this book while teaching geographic information systems in the Central Department of Geography at Tribhuvan University as a Fulbright Senior Scholar, which explains the examples from Nepal. I thank Professor Mangal Siddhi Manandhar for the invitation that made it possible, and Professor Sudarshan Tiwari for inviting me to work with the new planning program. Don Miller and Tim Nyerges arranged a visiting scholar stopover at the University of Washington where I wrote and went through "demountainization" from 28,000-foot to 14,000-foot peaks before returning to central Illinois.

After a major canoeing mishap early in our relationship, my wife Susan and I spent many weekends with the Buck Ridge Ski Club learning whitewater canoeing from excellent teachers, which explains my use and elaboration for twenty-five years of the whitewater canoeing metaphor in chapter 2. Susan's thoughtful willingness to consider living in Philadelphia, Urbana, Sheffield (England), and Kathmandu and her creativity in making a life in each place for herself and us has enabled me to pursue this work. She also made sure that our sons survived my preoccupation with plans, though Joshua's current work as rocket engineer and Nathaniel's in counseling psychology have more to do with the ideas presented here than might first seem evident. Examples and ideas from many discussions with my family, including my siblings and their spouses, about group processes, decision making, environmental policy, law, and Lexington, Kentucky, can be found woven into the text.

In thanking others for their contributions, I am not claiming that any of these people agree with what I say here. Indeed, they are noted in part because they disagreed productively as these ideas were emerging. I am confident that each will continue to disagree with some of it. This only means that there is more to be done to figure out how plans work. I hope what follows at least makes clear the many opportunities for continuing, productive disagreements.

I

Plans for Urban Development:
Why and How?

Making most development decisions one by one—with the focus on process, without benefit of something called a plan—is to forget why the field exists.
—Allan B. Jacobs (2000), "Notes on Planning Practice and Education"

To the northwest of Champaign, Illinois, Interstate 74 leads to the small town of Mahomet ten miles away. The city of Champaign, the village of Mahomet, Champaign County, and private landowners recognize opportunities for urban development in this corridor. Each knows that the results of the decisions it makes will depend on what others do and when. A private landowner wants to develop a parcel as low-density residential halfway between Champaign and Mahomet now, but this would preclude a future interstate highway interchange and the industrial and commercial uses that could be associated with it. If Mahomet zones for industrial along its end of the corridor and Champaign zones for residential, the results may not be what either intended. If developers can bargain to annex either to Champaign or to Mahomet, the municipalities will have less leverage than if they agreed to annexation boundaries so that a developer can bargain with only one municipality.

All these actors were making plans and trying to learn about each other's plans. The city of Champaign, the village of Mahomet, and the county jointly hired a planning consultant (Chicago Associates Architects and Planners) to work with the three governments, the current residents of the corridor, and some developers in the area. The focus of this plan was on general patterns of expected land use, potential for major infrastructure such as a new interstate interchange, and agreement on which areas would be annexed eventually to which municipality. Is such joint planning in these cir-

cumstances, by these parties, for these aspects of urban development typical or surprising? Should it have been done differently?

The purpose of this book is to present a coherent set of explanations that make sense of the planning we observe and justifications for prescriptions about when and how to make plans. Under what circumstances should plans be made, by whom, and about what aspects of urban development? How should such plans be made? These fundamental questions are answered implicitly every day in the practice of planning.

Why was the Mahomet Corridor Plan made by these participants in this situation? Three public jurisdictions formed a voluntary group to make a plan that was useful to them jointly. Resistance to and costs of forming such groups can be overcome if one of the members is significantly larger than the others and able to cover a large share of the costs of the joint activity. The city of Champaign played this "leader" role. This leader-follower behavior is one explanation that makes sense of when such groups are likely to form. The members of the group agreed on a joint planning effort, but each still had distinct interests and goals and each retained authority over its own decisions. They could share professional planning services because much of what each wanted to know was based on the same information, and each benefited from this information without decreasing its value to the others.

Why did this plan address just the Mahomet Corridor as its geographic scope? The plan addressed one chunk of potential urban development, a corridor along an interstate highway connecting two communities that were gradually growing together. Rather than addressing all of any one jurisdiction, all of the growth areas of the three jurisdictions, or all of one function such as transportation or water supply, it addressed one geographic area in which several interdependent decisions were about to be made that would have strategic consequences for later decisions. Plans are likely to be made and likely to be worth making when the first of a set of interdependent decisions is about to be made, especially if these are major decisions, such as an interchange location, and will be hard to reverse later. In this case the key interdependent decisions were all in the Mahomet Corridor and were especially important to these three actors. This scope for this plan makes sense not only because it encompasses these interdependent decisions, but also because each of these actors had already made and was continuing to make other plans of other scopes for other sets of interdependent decisions involving other key actors.

How was the Mahomet Corridor Plan developed? Planners considered land capabilities for agriculture and urban development, feasibility of transportation and sewer infrastructure, current residential patterns, financial implications for the various communities, available regulatory authority, scenarios of infrastructure expansion, and questions of timing and sequence of development. Advisory groups of professionals and citizens participated. Formal decisions, based on the corridor plan, were made by the respective governments. Much of the effort focused on the eventual pattern of land use and on achieving a boundary agreement about which areas should be annexed into which municipality.

None of this is surprising. People have limited attention and they focus on aspects immediately pertinent to the decisions at hand. Processes for accomplishing tasks rely on established routines. The plan presents arguments sufficient for decision makers with authority to make choices and for their constituencies to consent to these choices. Most plans for urban development focus on regulations and on investments in infrastructure and buildings. The annexation agreement was perhaps the most available and immediate action that could be taken now in light of the future actions that had been considered. Strategically, it determined who would have regulatory jurisdiction and who would provide infrastructure. To yield benefits, plans should help make decisions about such current actions that are interdependent with other actions, which may be taken elsewhere, in the future, and by others.

Ideas About Plans

The Mahomet Corridor Plan is in many ways typical of everyday practice. It makes sense in terms of the explanations developed in this book about why and how plans are made. It is not typical, however, of conventional ideas about plans. The planning literature either describes ideal plans and processes that seldom happen and seldom affect decisions, or uses the infeasibility of these ideal plans and processes to argue that plans are never useful in real urban development situations. Citizens tend to think of plans as all-controlling, comprehensive solutions or all-controlling disruptions of individual decision making. Real plans are big and little, support private and public decisions, and affect decisions through information, not directly through authority. Explanations of how plans work are, therefore, tremendously important because they help planners and citizens understand when plans are worth making.

The most persistent image of a plan for urban development is a comprehensive plan—comprehensive spatially by encompassing an entire community or an entire metropolitan area, comprehensive functionally in addressing all aspects of government activity, and comprehensive in time by focusing on a long time period. The Mahomet Corridor Plan focused on one area that was not currently part of any one municipality. A voluntary group hired the planning services, not one jurisdiction alone and not a metropolitan government or formal organization. The plan largely ignored questions of social services, school locations, and relationships to alternative areas of growth available to any of the participating governments. Private developers were simultaneously making other plans for their actions. To explain such observed plans, we cannot rely on ideal reference points of a comprehensive plan or no plans. These reference points do not explain why plans are made but are not comprehensive. To explain what we see, we need a more explicit logic of what plans are, how they work, what they can do in what situations, and how they can be made. Such logic ought to make sense of the Mahomet Corridor Plan as well as plans apparently closer to the comprehensive ideal, such as the Portland 2040 Plan by the metropolitan regional government in Oregon (Metro 2000).

Much of the recent planning literature focuses on processes of interaction, implying that plans are too simple and rigid to be useful in the interactive processes of figuring out what to do amid the complexities of democratic governance and urban development. In the Mahomet Corridor case, however, there was a plan, albeit a "little" plan among many other plans by the same and other parties about the same and related areas, functions, and time horizons. It was a "big" plan, however, relative to the particular set of interdependent decisions of concern because it fulfilled the circumstances for which it was made. We cannot focus only on process to the exclusion of plans because a plan is what relates decisions to other decisions. Interactive processes incorporate plans of scopes that include two decisions by one actor or hundreds of decisions by hundreds of actors and plans that consider actions over which one actor has complete control or over which many actors have only partial control. The "ideal" that interactive processes do not include embedded plans is no more useful for explaining what we observe than is the ideal of a comprehensive plan. Again, we need a more explicit logic that can make sense of all the plans of widely varying scopes that are and should be made in the everyday practice of planning. Explanations of plans ought to make sense of a mayor who "strategizes"—refines plans as decisions are made—so rapidly that plans do not stand still long enough to be captured in fancy documents. These explanations also ought to make sense of the Chicago Plan of 1909, which was published as an elegant book and affected decisions for many years.

When I am asked what I do and respond that I am a planner, people say, "Well, we can certainly use you around here. There is no planning here." Or, "Planning is not working here." I have heard this kind of response in many places including Kathmandu, Nepal, and Seattle, Washington, for both of which there are and have been many plans. Citizens have very high expectations of what plans can accomplish and very vague notions of what a plan is or how it actually works. If they can imagine a better living environment in their locality, there must not have been a plan. If they think that government or private developers ought to have behaved differently, there must not have been a plan. To infer that the lack of planning is the explanation of all problems of human settlements, implies that plans could solve all problems of urban development. Plans, however, can do only certain things and they work imperfectly even in these situations.

Successful human settlements require much more than planning. Some of the outcomes that people often expect of plans are more likely to be achieved by democratic governance or regulation, each of which also can accomplish only certain things and works imperfectly. *In simplest terms, plans provide information about interdependent decisions, governance makes collective choices, and regulations set rights.* Understanding these distinctions will give people reasonable expectations with which to use all three to improve human settlements.

Questions About Plans

What is a plan? A plan identifies a decision that should be made in light of other concurrent or future decisions. Plans are useful if these decisions are (1) interdependent, (2) indivisible, (3) irreversible, and (4) face imperfect foresight. In other words, we can gain by making a plan if (1) the value of the results of a decision now depends on other decisions, (2) the decision cannot be made in infinitesimally small steps, (3) the decision cannot be reversed later without cost, and (4) we lack complete knowledge of the future. This narrow definition identifies what is most fundamental about a plan and is elaborated in chapter 2.

Note that this definition makes no reference to government, the public sector, regulations, or breadth of authority or control. Actors make plans in the private sector, voluntary sector, and public sector as individuals or organizations with partial authority over one decision or complete authority over many decisions. Plans are not inherently about government, collective choice, or centralized control. These other phenomena are part of the complex system within which plans for urban development are made and thus affect what plans accomplish and how they are made.

What is the relationship between a plan and a complex system? Complex systems do not defeat the potential of plans. They enable it. The effects of plans and the situations in which plans can be made depend on the nature of these systems. Two interpretations of "natural" systems—evolution and market economies—are frequently analyzed as contrasts to plans. Complex systems characterized by interdependence, indivisibility, irreversibility, and imperfect foresight create opportunities for plans to improve on outcomes from natural systems. The crucial argument is that when these four conditions are present, the dynamics of change through time defeat the claims that natural and market systems are likely to achieve predictable and good outcomes. The potential for improvement, however, rests on the assumption that intentions are at least partially predictable. Beliefs, attitudes, values, or preferences must be predictable or it makes no sense to consider current decisions in light of future decisions and future outcomes. Making useful plans requires thinking carefully about the dynamic behavior of systems, available actions, predictable intentions, and the potential effects of plans. Chapter 2 considers how plans work in natural systems.

What can plans do? Plans can work as agendas, policies, visions, designs, and strategies. Each of these modes affects systems in different ways and thus fits different specific circumstances. Any one plan may work in all these ways, but distinguishing among them analytically is useful in explaining the circumstances in which plans can work. Strategies are the most fundamental aspect of plans for urban development because strategies directly account for actions, outcomes, intentions, and uncertainty. Strategies address most completely the difficulties created by interdependence, indivisibility, irreversibility, and imperfect foresight. Designs focus primarily on outcomes.

Visions, agendas, and policies are often joint effects of plans that also work as strategies or designs. Visions, agendas, and policies also occur in situations that do not meet the strict definition of plans. That is, visions, agendas, and policies are aspects of how plans work, but they are also phenomena that can exist separately from plans.

Expansion of a sewage treatment plant, for example, is a question of strategy. The expansion decision is interdependent with decisions about locations and capacities of roads. Capacity will be added in a large increment to take advantage of economies of scale in construction and operation. The decision is not reversible once built because the plant is a large physical facility with fixed location and an associated network of pipes. The decision faces imperfect foresight because it must be built long before demand for much of its capacity will be realized. A plan for a treatment plant should thus consider other interdependent actions in order to increase the likelihood that the treatment plant and these other actions will in combination yield desirable outcomes from the perspective of the people making the plan.

Such a plan is most completely interpreted as strategy but also has other aspects. It may have contingent timing rules to construct links in the sewer network just in time to serve realized demand in particular areas. These rules are a policy aspect of the plan. The expected final network can be interpreted as a design aspect of the plan. The capital costs of constructing the plant may appear on a Capital Improvements Program as an agenda aspect of the plan. The capacity chosen for the plant may serve as a vision that affects expectations for rapid growth or slow growth of the community, a vision aspect of the plan. Plans for urban development usually focus on investments in physical capital and on regulations because these types of actions are likely to have the attributes of interdependence, indivisibility, irreversibility, and imperfect foresight. Chapter 3 explains how plans work.

Do plans work? These explanations of how plans work frame criteria for assessing the effectiveness of plans. Did the plan for the Mahomet Corridor have any effect on urban development in the corridor? Did this plan yield a better outcome than would have occurred without the plan? From whose perspective was it better?

In Urbana, Illinois, the sewer collection network was built in 1970 so that it would eventually send wastewater from southeast Urbana to an additional treatment plant to be built east of town. Sewage could be pumped uphill through the same network to the existing plant in the meantime. The additional plant was never built and now probably never will be. This plan, however, was arguably still a success as strategy because it protected future options then believed to be good ones, and it still works with the different expansion pattern that has occurred. If understood as strategy in the face of uncertainty, the internal logic of the plan makes sense even if the most obvious possible outcome did not occur.

Will the Mahomet Corridor plan increase the relative housing and employment opportunities for African Americans or current low-income residents of Champaign? This question may not have been explicitly asked, and was not a primary focus of the planning discussion. Plans should also be assessed on whether they meet criteria of ethical acceptability and moral commitment.

It is more persuasive to evaluate a plan with respect to a particular model of how it could have worked than to ask simply whether good outcomes occurred that might or might not be attributable to a plan. The final section of chapter 3 builds on the ways in which plans can work to frame criteria for judging whether plans do work.

How can plans address uncertainties? Plans face uncertainty about demand or need for housing, commercial, and industrial facilities. These uncertainties derive from uncertainties about population increase, migration, household size, retail and manufacturing technologies, comparative advantage in labor costs, beliefs and attitudes about how the world works, and tastes or preferences. In the Mahomet Corridor Plan, there were uncertainties about who would develop what land when for what purpose under the regulations of what municipality. There were uncertainties about what residential patterns people living in the corridor now or in the future might want. The annexation agreement, which was a regulation based on the plan, reduced uncertainty about annexation and modified other expectations. Much uncertainty remained, however, and both the annexation agreement and other actions must still account for that remaining uncertainty. Plans address uncertainty. They do not eliminate it.

People often think of a plan as choosing one future and trying to implement it. Plans can, however, incorporate uncertainty by including a set (or distribution) of desirable futures, a set of possible outcomes of actions, and a set of possible actions. Forecasts can be developed as distributions of possible outcomes rather than as forecasts of one outcome. The relationships among actions can be organized in sequence and in space so as to consider results from early decisions before making later decisions. A plan then is a contingent path through a sequence of decisions, taking account along the way of uncertainties of many kinds and feedback from early decisions. This explanation also yields a specific criterion for the net benefit of making plans: the expected value of the contingent sequence of decisions that would be made with the plan minus the expected value of the decisions that would be made without the plan. Chapter 4 elaborates strategies, forecasts, and the value of plans as strategy in the face of uncertainties.

Why do voluntary groups, governments, and other organizations make plans? Plans are not inherently about government, but governments do make plans. We need explanations of why governments make plans in particular circumstances. Individuals, firms, voluntary organizations, special purpose public agencies, and general purpose governments take actions and thus face the option of making plans for these actions. They face decisions about whether or not to plan. In some situations, making a plan as an individual (or unitary organization) may not be as efficient or effective, even from the perspective of the individual, as making a plan jointly. Often a plan is most useful to the person who makes it if the information in the plan is shared with others, which makes the plan a collective good. As with other collective goods (such as lighthouses, national defense, or arterial streets), if one person's use of the information in a plan does not reduce its value to others and there is no way to prevent others from using the plan, then special organizational responses are needed to achieve appropriate levels of investment in making the plan. These concepts provide explanations of the institutional forms in which plans are likely to be made. A government may make a plan because the plan is focused on that government's own investments and regulations or because the plan, although focused on decisions under the authority of others, is a collective good. The Mahomet Corridor Plan fits both of these explanations. Chapter 5 explains collective goods, particular circumstances in which plans are likely to be collective goods, and the organizational implications for plan making by governments.

How do regulations differ from and depend on plans? Regulations include zoning, subdivision ordinances, property taxes, impact fees, and any other enforceable assignment or reassignment of rights among individuals, among individuals and governments, or among governments. Regulations affect the scope of permissible actions. Plans, such as the Mahomet Corridor Plan or the Portland 2040 Plan (Metro 2000), provide information about interdependent decisions in relation to expected outcomes, but these plans do not determine directly the scope of permissible actions. Regulations are thus different from plans, so the logic of plans should explain how regulations set the context for making plans and how regulations depend on plans.

The distribution of rights (authority) to make decisions affects what choices are made and whether these choices are likely to lead to desirable and just outcomes. Plans also affect what choices are made, but plans affect choices through information, not through enforcement. Enforcement of regulations relies on social norms, sometimes called social regulation, as well as on government's legitimate monopoly on the use of force. Thus regulations constrain individual actions even if an actor wishes to do something else when faced with a specific instance. Regulations, such as zoning, that are intended to affect the spatial and temporal patterns of urban development are likely to depend on plans. Figuring out what zoning category to apply where depends on a plan, but the zoning regulation, not the plan, changes owner's rights. Regulations can also affect who makes plans and how. Chapter 6 explains the logic of rights and regulations, the implications for who makes plans, and the characteristics needed in plans intended to support specific types of regulations.

What capabilities do humans have to make plans? Human capabilities to make plans, as individuals or in groups, are limited by cognitive capacity and by social structures affecting knowledge and values. People still make plans despite these limitations. The focused scope of the Mahomet Corridor Plan makes sense not only because of the situation in which it was made, but also because of the capabilities of people, both citizens and professionals, to make such plans. Explanations of these limitations provide a framework from which to build justifiable prescriptions for better, but still humanly feasible, ways to make plans. Research in psychology explains many aspects of cognitive capabilities for analyzing situations to make plans. Research in sociology explains the interactions of individual autonomy and social structure. Professional planners have expertise in urban development, use of plans, and techniques for making plans, and they use this expertise to work with and for clients. Chapter 7 considers how cognitive capacity, individual autonomy in relation to social structure, professional expertise, and roles in organizations interact to explain the basis for professional ethics and the use of expertise in making plans.

How do plans differ from and depend on collective choice and participation? Collective choice identifies a common decision for a group of individuals who have different interests and preferences. This function is distinct from what plans do, though plans may affect collective choices and be affected by them. Collective choice mechanisms seek two principles: (1) increased social cognitive capacity—quantity and quality of thinking—through deliberation, and (2) representation of differing beliefs, attitudes, and preferences. Arrow's impossibility theorem argues that no mechanism can be devised to aggregate preferences across more than two choices and still meet reasonable criteria of democratic processes. All sorts of communities, voluntary groups, and government bodies, however, make such collective choices every day. A referendum on a bond issue for a capital project, the election of a city council member, a neighborhood meeting on a project proposal, a council study session on a proposed project, and a local council vote to change zoning are all instances of collective choice.

Several explanations help to understand how the difficulties of collective choice are addressed in practice and how cognitive capacity and representativeness might be increased by intentional efforts to induce participation by persons not usually participating. Collective choices are shaped by interaction among participants, which means they depend on history, not just on immediate circumstances. The city council's study session matters, not just the vote. The mechanisms of collective choice are often modified, as in the consolidation of city and county governments in Lexington, Kentucky, or the creation of the Metro regional government in Portland, Oregon. Induced participation can complement collective choice procedures, but participation *per se* does not resolve the difficulties. Chapter 8 explains how plans differ from collective choice, how plans may interact with processes of collective choice, and what induced participation might accomplish to improve collective choice and plans.

Does the logic of plans explain the plans and plan-making processes that we observe? Local governments, private developers, special districts, neighborhood groups, business groups, and others plan individually and in voluntary groups. They make plans ranging in scope from the 1929 Regional Plan of New York and Its Environs (Johnson 1996), which covered parts of four states, to a subdivision plan for forty acres. If the logic of plans helps to explain when and how observed plans across this range are made, then it can also provide a useful basis to develop improved prescriptions for mak ing plans. Observed plan making can be explained in part as decisions to make plans in circumstances in which plans are likely to be worthwhile, and in part as using available methods that are consistent with cognitive capabilities and collective choice possibilities. Procedural rationality and communicative rationality provide similar standards by which such plan-making behaviors can be interpreted and justified. Diagnostic evaluation of plan making in relation to plan outcomes identifies specific opportunities for improved prescriptions. Chapter 9 explains observed plan making by using concepts from previous chapters.

Under what circumstances should plans be made, by whom, and about what aspects of urban development? How should such plans be made? When compared to observed plan making and to conventional prescriptions, the logic of making plans provides justifications to modify current prescriptions so as to make better plans and use them more effectively. These modified prescriptions suggest the following:

- Recognize opportunities to use plans in the stream of daily activities affecting urban development.
- Create views of plans from the perspectives of decision situations.
- When using plans, recognize opportunities to make plans that will be useful.
- Make plans of efficient geographic, functional, and organizational scopes that fit the specific situation.
- Focus attention on linking consequences to interdependent actions.
- Use formal institutions and induced participation as complementary mechanisms for deliberation and action.

Chapter 10 justifies these prescriptions by building on explanations of how plans work and explanations of observed plan making. These prescriptions will both improve plans and be feasible in practice. They will create reasonable expectations among planners and citizens about what plans can and should accomplish.

Explanation, Prediction, Justification, and Prescription

The underlying premises of this book are that there is a logic of making plans for urban development, that it can be used to explain plans we observe, and that it can be used to justify prescriptions for making plans. This subsection briefly positions these premises among ideas about theory and explanation for readers who might question these premises.

The logic developed here is intended to be a coherent and evolving collection of explanations, not an entirely consistent theory built from central, foundational concepts. It can be useful in dealing with the real world of making plans, even if it is not complete and not generalizable with precision to all situations. Some of it is widely accepted, but even these aspects are seldom articulated. Articulating it here may thus raise disagreements that have been latent and frame opportunities to build better explanations.

Miller (1987, 135) defines theory as explanation: " . . . whatever explains empirical facts (often regularities or patterns) of relatively observational kinds, through the description of less directly observable phenomena." Such explanations are adequate if they are useful in coping with the world, even if they do not support strict deductive results. An explanation makes sense of something at a different level, but explanations are not necessarily unique or mutually exclusive. Either geographic relationships to resources and markets or the creation of social relationships can explain the growth of a city. These two explanations do not contradict each other, but they focus attention on different aspects.

We rely on predictability to cope with the world, often without direct consideration of explanations. When we observe a change in some observable things, explanations—by linking observable things to other observable things—help us to figure out what else might change. Explanations thus enhance predictability of the observable world and predictability of the effects of changes in the observable world. If we want to do things differently in order to do them better, explanations are valuable.

Explanations and justifications are summarized in Table 1-1. The two columns distinguish situations in which plans are or should be made from procedures by which plans are or should be made. The rows distinguish explanations of observed behaviors from justifications of prescribed behaviors.

For example, we would like to explain why we frequently observe plans for downtowns and for new development at the edge of cities but much less often observe plans for existing residential neighborhoods. Why are plans likely to occur in one situation but not the other? Why do we frequently observe planners making population forecasts when making plans, but seldom observe them generating several alternatives except as a means to argue

Table 1-1

Categories of Explanations and Justifications

	Situations in Which Plans Occur	*Behaviors That Yield Plans*
Explanations Predictive	In what situations are what types of plans likely to be made?	What behaviors are likely to occur when people make plans?
Justifications Prescriptive	In what situations should plans of what type be made?	What behaviors should be undertaken to make good plans?

for a particular solution? Answers to these questions would explain why certain events are likely to occur in certain circumstances. A strict interpretation of prediction requires predicting who will do what when. Explanations for plans seldom have such precision. We may not be able to predict which downtown landowner or merchant will suggest making a plan to which peers when, but we can explain why such persons are more likely to suggest making plans and agree to do so than are individual neighborhood residents.

We also want justifications of what a planner should do in a given situation. These justifications are prescriptive. If a state government mandates that local governments make plans of particular scope, then the requirements for these plans should be based on prescriptive justifications of why plans of such scope will be useful to local governments. Prescriptions of how to make plans should be justified by evidence or argument that particular activities that planners can do are likely to result in better plans or to do so more efficiently.

We can consider plan-making behaviors contingent on plan-making situations. Mandelbaum (1979) framed this with different words as settings, processes, and outcomes. Given a particular setting and a particular planning process, what happens? The approach used here does not seek Mandelbaum's standard for a general theory: "The core of a valid general theory of planning would allow an analyst to inspect any list of assertions about the relationship between processes, setting and outcomes and accurately to predict those which will survive empirical tests" (67). In discussing this "covering law" standard of science, Miller (1987, 140) points out that " . . . no science has ever achieved it." My approach here follows Miller in focusing on establishing a coherent collection of explanations of some aspects of making plans—"that certain mechanisms are typically the cause of the most important features of some phenomena" (140).[1]

Summary: Why Plan and How?

Ideas about plans are frequently presented as ideal forms that provide little help in explaining or justifying the wide variety of plans, plan-making situations, and plan-making methods that we observe in everyday experience. People have unrealistic expectations of plans in part because they lack clarity about what plans are and how they work. The logic of making plans for urban development seeks to explain what we see and to justify prescriptions for making plans in particular situations and in particular ways.

2

Plan-Based Action in Natural Systems

What artist, so noble, has often been my thought, as he, who with far-reaching conception of beauty and designing power, sketches the outline, writes the colours, and directs the shadows of a picture so great that Nature shall be employed upon it for generations, before the work he has arranged for her shall realize his intentions.

—Frederick Law Olmsted (1852), *Walks and Talks of an American Farmer in England*

Planning in the complex systems of urban development is like paddling a canoe in moving river water. Your learned canoeing skills are the actions available to you to include in plans, and the river is the system within which you plan. If the water were still, you could point your canoe in the direction you wanted to go and paddle. In moving water, however, you will not end up where you are pointed because the movement of your canoe results from the direction in which you paddle and the direction in which the river is flowing.[1] Planning as river canoeing has five implications.

First, if you know how, you can use the currents to stop, turn, or cross from one side of the river to the other. You can, in other words, move in directions other than the direction the stream is flowing. You can affect the outcomes of urban development by your actions in combination with the complex system within which you act, even though you do not control the system and its apparent intentions are different from yours.

Second, if you wait to plan your course, you will not be where you were. You must always be monitoring (knowing where you are in relation to what you are doing), planning, and acting. Making plans for urban development is something you do constantly, not once.

Third, you must be able to forecast, at least in part, how the river current in combination with your paddling will carry your canoe. Such forecasts must account for variations in river current as you move across or

16

down the stream. You cannot assume that things are constant in space or time. By learning about rivers and how to "read" them, you can forecast the pattern of currents for short stretches ahead in order to plan your maneuvers. If your forecasts are imperfect, you will want contingent actions based on what happens or on what you see later at closer range. The scopes of your plans will depend on the range of your forecasts.

Fourth, you must be able to match available actions with impending problems or opportunities. Moving rapidly downstream toward a rock is a problem, but you cannot simply decide not to hit the rock. That decision is insufficient because there is no such action within your capability. You can only decide how to paddle and position your canoe so that it will move away from the rock. You cannot just decide to have a walkable community. You must choose investments and regulations that will move you toward that opportunity.

Fifth, your available actions are interdependent. Which actions you choose to take now will affect where you end up and thus will affect the results from other actions you may take in the future. If you ferry across the stream to the still water of an eddy on the other side, you can approach the next rapids from a different angle and thus arrive at a different place. Plans become useful when actions cannot be taken in infinitely small steps and cannot be reversed. In turning out of the still water in an eddy into the current to head downstream (an "eddy turn"), you cannot do part of the turn because every position except the beginning (facing upstream and at rest) and end (facing downstream and moving with the current) is unstable. The action is indivisible. If you turn out of an eddy and head downstream, you will not be able to return to that eddy if the stream is flowing fast. The action is irreversible. When actions are interdependent, indivisible, and irreversible it is valuable to think through future actions before taking the first action.

The river is running downhill in a complex way. You cannot move directly upstream unless you are more powerful than the river, and you cannot change the fundamental characteristic that water flows downhill. You can, however, move about in the river with some degree of purpose and intention, which is quite different from just floating along wherever the river takes you. Something between one plan that assumes you are in complete control and no plan at all makes sense for both canoeing a river and planning human settlements.

Error-Controlled, Prediction-Controlled, and Plan-Based Action

A planned pattern of change is typically contrasted with a "natural" pattern of change, where natural means without intentional direction of the overall system. Apparent order can emerge in systems without intentional direction. In order to understand how we can introduce intentional actions within natural systems, we need to understand how natural systems evolve. A fundamental concept is error-control, which underlies evolution, whether in the biological sense or in the economic or social analogues.[2]

A furnace, a room to be heated, and a thermostat make up an error-controlled system. The inside temperature is the variable being controlled, and variation in the outside temperature disturbs this system. The thermostat senses the inside temperature and turns the furnace on or off. The crux of error control is that the thermostat responds to changes in *inside* temperature; it responds *after the fact* to the status of the variable of essential concern. An error-controlled system survives as long as it happens to be able to cope with the range of disturbances by responding *after* the effect on essential variables.

In natural evolution the disturbance consists of all the attributes of the environment of a species. The controller is gene mutation and gene combination within a species. The essential variables (analogous to inside temperature) are the variables such as body temperature that must remain within certain ranges if an individual of the species is to survive. Gene combinations and thus individuals that happen to be able to cope with the pattern of disturbances in their environment survive; individuals that cannot cope do not survive. In this process of natural selection, the survival values are not chosen independently of or external to the total process. The survival values evolve simultaneously with the organisms or processes that tend toward them.

There is no external choice of which individuals should survive or which values of the survival variables should be sought. The controller does not choose responses in order to maintain the individuals. The controller is inherent in the organisms and the response pattern exists only because it tends to maintain itself within the range for its own survival. If the pattern of disturbances in the environment, and therefore the responses necessary to maintain the essential variables within the range for survival, were to change, the error-controller could not choose to change its responses in order to maintain itself. Error-control, and therefore evolution, involves no internal intention. It does not know where it is going. It does get somewhere, however, and *after the fact* it can be explained as behaving as if it were seeking the outcome at which it arrives.

Plans, and the intentions on which they are based, will always be internal to some larger natural system, but can be external to subsystems over which we have some control. We can try to survive by using predictions and plans, but we cannot make our survival, much less our survival in a desirable and just community, the after-the-fact intention of the overall system. Even though evolution can be described afterward as tending toward where it ends up, this outcome has no claim as an inherently desirable intention. On the other hand, we can make predictions and plans about systems, as in canoeing a river or choosing a furnace and setting a thermostat, for which we can set goals at least in part based on our intentions. Three modes are available: goal-directed behavior, prediction-control, and plan-based action.

Goal-directed behavior is analogous to error-control, but with an externally specified goal. After establishing a goal and an appropriate controller, the controller compensates for disturbances whenever it recognizes deviation from the goal. If the goal is to maintain a certain quality of effluent from a treatment plant, then a controller would modify the treatment process if it sensed that quality of the effluent had deviated from the goal. If the goal is a particular land use pattern, such as the higher density, mixed-use, walking neighborhoods espoused by the "New Urbanists," then a controller of land use regulation and monitoring might be implemented. In particular, the zoning ordinance would allow mixed uses. If the land use pattern deviates from the goal, perhaps because density is too low, the regulatory body might modify the zoning ordinance to set minimum rather than maximum densities. Note that in this case, reliance on error-control might not work. Recognizing that the goal pattern of land use is not occurring *after* part of it is built is too late, because it is costly to demolish and rebuild buildings and infrastructure. It is, therefore, unlikely to be changed to achieve the intended pattern.

Prediction-control would be more effective in the land use situation because it would recognize the effect on the essential variable of density before it was too late. Instead of responding to a change in inside temperature, a prediction-controller would predict inside temperature in the future based on outside temperature or, even better, would predict future patterns of outside temperatures. In the effluent quality case, a prediction-controller would monitor *inflow* to the plant and predict needed treatment so that effluent never deviated from the quality goal even sufficiently to be detected by an error-controller. In residential development, realized densities are often lower than allowed by zoning, which provides the basis for a prediction that a zoning ordinance with higher maximum allowable density will not increase the density at which development occurs. Using this prediction, a minimum density zoning ordinance could be enacted before development occurs rather than after initial development deviates from the goal. Without pretending that prediction control can be perfect, it clearly has potential to improve outcomes relative to intentions in situations where actions are irreversible.

Plan-based action is more than goal-directed behavior or prediction control. Goal-directed behavior means only that deviations from the goal will be corrected once recognized. Prediction control means that deviations from the goal will be corrected if predicted based on expected patterns of disturbances and actions. Plan-based action means that an action will be taken based on its relationship to other actions considered prior to the first action. A plan might consider expectations about location, capacity, and timing of expressways, arterials, collector streets, sewage treatment plants, schools, parks, and land use development. Any one of these actions could then be taken so as to be consistent with expectations about the others. A treatment plant can be built of a size and at a location to serve development that will also be served by streets. Prediction is insufficient because these decisions are interdependent. Making a decision about location of an expressway by predicting the location of a treatment plant fails to consider whether the treatment plant should be located elsewhere so that the combined effect of the treatment plant and expressway is improved. A plan identifies a set of interdependent actions that work in combination.

Using an example from anthropology, Suchman (1987, 187–189) makes a similar distinction between plan-based action and goal-directed behavior. A navigator in the European tradition figures out a route as a sequence of compass bearings and distances at each bearing, as an interdependent set of actions that work in combination. Once the planned course is executed, the ship arrives at its destination. Error-controlled corrections are used to stay on each bearing along the planned route. Micronesian navigators apparently use stars, currents, and other evidence to keep track only of deviations from heading toward their final destination. They do not plan a route, but correct their direction so as to be heading toward their destination.

Error-controlled action may be too late. Prediction-controlled action improves lead time by treating one decision as depending on a prior decision. Plan-based action can address interdependence, when each of two decisions depends on the other. There are always many levels of control going on simultaneously. When we try to control one level by inserting our intentions, there is always error-control going on at higher levels and at lower levels. There may also be other prediction-control and plan-based action at other levels.

Equilibrium, Prediction, and Optimal Outcomes

Economists and environmentalists often argue that planned actions disrupt the behavior of a system that would naturally arrive at a predictable, stable, and desirable equilibrium if just left alone. It is important to understand the basis for such claims and the circumstances in which the logic behind these claims breaks down, circumstances in which plans can be useful.

Systems are often analyzed in terms of equilibrium, which is a state that a system remains in once it arrives there. Many analyses of economic and ecological systems focus on conditions under which an equilibrium exists, is unique, and has desirable attributes. The concept of equilibrium is pertinent to prediction, to evaluating outcomes, and to considering the opportunities to improve outcomes by making plans. If, for a given system, one and only one equilibrium exists, then the best prediction of the state of the system is that it will be in that equilibrium state. It is, therefore, also pertinent to evaluate the attributes of that equilibrium to decide whether we want to let that equilibrium occur or act within the system to achieve a different outcome. In the section on page 23, we will consider the question of whether a system is likely to reach equilibrium from a given starting point.

Alchian (1950, 220) uses the analogue of evolution to explain the familiar arguments about the optimum-seeking, equilibrium model of microeconomics: "The economic counterparts of genetic heredity, mutations, and natural selection are imitation, innovation, and positive profits." In a market system, the system outcomes we observe consist of the firms that survived. If there is competition among many firms, then the firms that survive will be those that, by whatever means, realized profits. Microeconomic theory identifies a set of conditions in which this model has a unique equilibrium in which no individual has reason to change actions and in which resources cannot be reallocated to increase the value of outputs.[3] If many firms and production events occur so that all (or at least many) possible production choices are tried, then the surviving firms will be the firms that are operating optimally in the limited sense of producing the most valuable output given available resources. The firms that survive at equilibrium are the ones that happen to be operating at optimal production levels, even if each production choice was made arbitrarily. This optimal outcome depends on an initial distribution of wealth among actors and is optimal only with respect to allocation of resources among production processes, not with respect to any external notions of justice or fairness. Thus, from a larger external perspective, this equilibrium is not necessarily a desirable outcome, regardless of whether it occurs "naturally."

Changes in the setting in which firms operate will change the characteristics that the surviving firms have, but not because any particular firm is able to change its characteristics intentionally. The downtown retailers of fifty years ago were replaced by new firms using new retail technologies in malls and later big box retail strips. That is, few if any firms were able to transform themselves intentionally to survive in new conditions. Rather, firms that happened to identify new technologies were the new survivors. Microsoft replaced IBM; IBM did not become Microsoft. Predictions based on equilibrium predict the attributes of survivors, not the behaviors by which firms make decisions.

In a very stable environment, it would be wise to imitate survivors. In a changing environment, however, it would be wiser to generate variety so that firms (or organisms) will occur that can survive new circumstances. In a changing environment, careful imitators of "best practice" may be less likely to survive than risk takers with luck. Which risk taker will survive is difficult to predict, but a system with a variety of risk takers is more likely to result in at least some survivors than is a cadre of imitators.[4] For example, efficient, compact metropolitan areas with good earthquake policies but located on coastlines must still be complemented by inland cities if we are to survive global warming with rises in sea level.

The complex systems we deal with have evolved a domain of stability based on surviving a range of shocks through their history. The systems we observe are precisely those that have survived these shocks. If we work entirely within the range of this history of shocks, we can expect the systems to absorb our interventions. Resilience is thus a function of the range of disturbances that a system has survived in the past. A system that has seldom been disturbed may have little resilience. We are in an evolved system with a very long physical and biological history and a long enough social history to have created significant resilience to change within the domain of past disturbances. This resilience is an opportunity and a problem. It provides a sufficiently stable system that we can risk intentional changes without destroying the entire system. It also, however, resists changes we may wish to make, such as resolving ethnic conflicts that are destroying human settlements physically and as communities. The challenges are to avoid creating a disturbance beyond the domain of the system as a whole, while creating changes sufficient to achieve changes in subsystems. Plans may be useful in order to change the "natural" equilibrium outcome.

Dynamic Adjustment

Focusing on equilibrium analysis ignores the dynamics of adjustment from an initial state to an equilibrium state. To make sense of plans, we must consider these dynamics. A system can be described as moving from state to state through transformations or actions, which change one state to another. A sequence of such states and actions is a path. If actions creating urban development could be reversed without cost, then a large number of locators could try all sorts of locations. An error-controller could respond by reporting net benefits to each locator, and locators could keep moving until no one had reason to move because no one could identify a location better than the current location. This costless adjustment process is the underlying assumption of equilibrium analysis. Urban location decisions are not, however, reversible. Once a physical or social structure is built, it cannot be moved or recreated in some other form or place without significant cost. Where the first retail store locates affects the entire ensuing pattern of development.[5] Thus, even if the equilibrium outcome of a market system were deemed desirable, it would not be likely to occur when actions are irreversible.

As Ohls and Pines (1975) explain, gaps in suburban development left by "leapfrog" developments may result from recognition of irreversibility. It may be appropriate to leave a parcel of land vacant and build low-density development on a parcel of the same size more distant from employment, shopping, and infrastructure. Later, high-density development, which generates more trips per unit of land, can be built on the parcel that is closer to jobs, shopping, and infrastructure. In the long run such a pattern will be more efficient. A development sequence that built low density on the closer parcel initially would not yield the same outcome because it would not be worth the cost of knocking down low-density development once built in order to make it higher density later.

Equilibrium models have been used to predict the pattern of residential location relative to transportation costs given a transportation network. Such models must assume either that individuals keep changing residential location until equilibrium is reached or that individuals can choose, on their first try, locations that will be in equilibrium. Neither assumption is plausible. Each action in the adjustment process is costly and not reversible without additional cost. This is true in particular of construction of roads and buildings. It also costs time and money to rent an apartment or purchase a house: time to search for the right one, legal fees, and taxes. It costs money and time to move. Once moves are made, whether in error, or as individual adjustments, they will not be changed without additional costs.

These transaction costs of making changes are not accounted for in the equilibrium approach because, for urban development, many things change much too fast to claim that there is sufficient adjustment time to overcome these costs and make repeated trials at locations or densities. When retail technology changes the locations of stores, residential locations do not quickly adjust to be in equilibrium with the new locations. If we attempt to create "new urbanist" walking communities, we cannot simply build new high-density retail and expect residential densities to adjust quickly. The transaction costs will prevent moves that would otherwise lead to the predicted equilibrium because the predicted gains will not be sufficient to compensate the reversal costs of previous actions.[6] Individuals could not choose equilibrium locations on their first choice unless they computed the equilibrium before acting, that is, unless they made a plan.[7]

The analytical response to this problem of dynamic adjustment is indicative planning. The original exemplar of indicative planning is French industrial planning as described and interpreted by Cohen (1977). In the French model, a government agency solved for the equilibrium values of production in each industry and made this information available as a plan for production. "The motor of indicative planning is a benign circle: the more industry follows the plan, the more accurate the plan's information will be; the more accurate the plan's information, the more reason industry will have to follow the plan" (10).

This concept can be extended to consider choice among equilibriums and the use of equilibrium prices rather than equilibrium quantities as indicators or signals. In this version, indicative planning requires that we solve for the set of equilibrium prices for the equilibrium we wish to achieve. In the land use case this implies finding an optimal land use pattern and a set of changes in prices through taxes or fees sufficient to bring it about (Hopkins 1974). In simplest terms, indicative planning predicts and chooses an equilibrium, computes the implied prices (signals) at equilibrium, and establishes those prices in the market. By responding in their first decisions to these equilibrium prices, the equilibrium can then be achieved by firms acting individually because no iteration toward equilibrium is required. This target is both predicted and chosen. Intention becomes prediction. If it were only predicted, it would not be followed because it would not be accepted as desirable. If it were only desirable, it would not be followed because it would not be accepted as the equilibrium that would occur and thus the prices that would prevail.[8]

Even if we focus only on efficient allocation of resources in the limited sense of microeconomic analysis, urban development systems do not have the necessary characteristics to fit the traditional equilibrium analysis. In addition, we may, as in the river, wish to achieve a state other than an equilibrium toward which a system is moving or has arrived "naturally." Whether to achieve economic efficiency or other criteria we choose, plans can be useful in overcoming the problems of costly dynamic adjustment.

Interdependence, Indivisibility, Irreversibility, and Imperfect Foresight

Interdependence, Indivisibility, and Irreversibility of decisions in the face of Imperfect foresight—the "Four I's"—are the four characteristics that defeat the process of costless, rapid adjustment of decisions to equilibrium on which the arguments of neoclassical economics are based. Thus in these circumstances markets fail for reasons more fundamental than the usual focus

Table 2-1
The Four I's

	Interdependence	Indivisibility	Irreversibility	Imperfect Foresight
Definition	Result of action A depends on action B.	Size of increment of action affects value of action.	No action available to return to previous state without cost.	More than one future is possible.
Examples	Value of land (or road) depends on road access (availability of land).	Road linking two locations must be complete and of width sufficient for vehicles.	Road cannot be relocated or resized without cost.	Jobs could increase at various rates and at various locations.
Implications	Actions are not separable.	Continuous marginal adjustment is not efficient or not possible.	History and dynamics matter.	Uncertainty cannot be eliminated.
Responses	Consider effects of combinations of actions.	Consider the sizes of changes.	Consider interdependent actions before taking action.	Consider uncertainty of actions, outcomes, and values.

on externalities and collective goods, which are considered in chapter 5.[9] As summarized in Table 2-1, the Four I's define the circumstances in which plans can improve outcomes. They are the key explanatory predictors of circumstance in which plans are likely to be made and the key justifications of prescriptions of why they will be worth making.[10]

A decision is a commitment to action (or inaction) and is made by some individual or entity with the capability to act. The alternatives may include indecisiveness, inaction, or other actions, but a decision implies at least two choices. Actions may be created rather than given. A planner might devise a new regulatory device or downtown development proposal and thus create the option for local council members to vote for it. In nonroutine situations, actions imply decisions to take particular actions. In routine situations, actions may imply only habits, conventions, or rules.

Interdependence means that the value of the outcome of one action depends on another action and vice versa. The benefit from building a treatment plant of a given size in a given location at a given time depends on whether roads are built, employment opportunities are created, demand for housing occurs, schools are built, and many other actions are taken. It also depends on the locations and timing of these actions. The treatment plant is of little use unless demand emerges when and where it can be served. In turn, the benefits of these other actions depend on the decision about the treatment plant, because they cannot occur at the same intensity, locations, or times without a treatment plant to serve them.

Independence, dependence, and interdependence of actions can be distinguished using simple games in which there are two landowners, A and B. Each owns a parcel of land on which either residential or retail structures can be built. The benefits for each of these options, or payoffs as they are usually called in game theory, are specified in the game tables that follow. You can think of them as dollars, but they could be any measure of utility such that you prefer a larger number to a smaller one. For each pair of decisions, the first number gives the payoff for player A, and the second the payoff for player B.

In Game 2-1 each owner has a choice between two actions and the resulting individual payoffs do not vary with the action taken by the other owner. Thus A receives a payoff of 12 for residential whether B chooses residential or retail. B receives 13 for retail whether A chooses residential or retail. The decisions are independent.

Game 2-1
Independence Game

		Player B	
		Residential	*Retail*
Player A	Residential	12, *8*	12, *13*
	Retail	9, *8*	9, *13*

Game 2-2

Dependence game

		Player B	
		Residential	*Retail*
Player A	Residential	1, *8*	10, *13*
	Retail	17, *8*	9, *13*

In Game 2-2, the dependence game, A's payoffs depend on B's choice, but B's payoffs are independent of A's choice. A can benefit from knowing what B will do. If A knew B's payoffs, A would predict that B would build retail regardless of what A did. B, however, can gain nothing by predicting what A will do. Dependence is asymmetrical and therefore results may be affected by the order in which decisions are made. A might be able to wait to see what B does.

In Game 2-3, the interdependence game, A would be better off choosing retail if B chooses residential, but A would be better off choosing residential if B chooses retail. Similarly, B would be better off choosing retail if A chooses residential, but B would be better off choosing residential if A chooses retail. The decisions are interdependent because each decision depends on the other.

Indivisibility means that we cannot take arbitrarily small increments of action. A road is useful only if we build all of it to connect two locations. We must build a width of at least one lane. Indivisibility is closely related to economies of scale. If we build a very small sewage treatment plant, the cost per unit of treatment capacity will be much higher than if we build a large treatment plant. Indivisibility and economies of scale matter because they prevent us from adding increments of capacity just in time as we need them.

Game 2-3

Interdependence game

		Player B	
		Residential	*Retail*
Player A	Residential	11, *8*	10, *12*
	Retail	17, *8*	9, *5*

We must predict capacity for some period of time related to the size of increments that are feasible to build or to the size of increments that are efficient to build. We thus can gain from a plan when increments of capacity are indivisible or when increments of capacity are much less costly as the size of the increment increases.

Irreversibility means that we cannot take an action, then undo it or replace it with another action without incurring significant costs. We cannot build an interceptor sewer, then increase its capacity tomorrow by a small increment. We cannot build it one place, then move it somewhere else. We cannot build a major new office building and build a light-rail transit station three blocks away, then move the office building next to the transit station.

Imperfect foresight means that we do not know the future values of variables pertinent to our decision making. We do not know whether or when the population and employment will increase to absorb the capacity of a sewage treatment plant or an expressway. We do not know whether attitudes and preferences for residential neighborhood types will change. Imperfect foresight means that some expectations can be identified but uncertainty remains.

Streams of Opportunities for Action

Decisions are made within and by organizations such as planning agencies, local public utilities, land development firms, and municipal governments. Organizations are highly structured and complex systems, but a great deal of ambiguity about actions remains. That organizations have formal structure, histories of internal and external interaction, and established routines creates partial predictability of actions so that plans can be useful (see e.g., Alexander 1995). It is the remaining ambiguities of structure and predictability that complicate the use of plans. Plans must confront unstructured or partially structured decision processes. There are many explanations of organizations and organizational behavior,[11] but the "garbage can" model of organizations provides a useful framework for present purposes. In this model " . . . an organization is a collection of choices looking for problems, issues and feelings looking for decision situations in which they might be aired, solutions looking for issues to which they might be the answer, and decision-makers looking for work" (Cohen et al. 1972, 2).[12] The analogy of things floating in water makes more sense for present purposes than the analogy of things thrown into a garbage can. The garbage can model is therefore reinterpreted here as the "stream of opportunities" model. Imagine intermingling patterns of the following relatively independent phenomena floating in a stream.

- Decision situations are choices about actions we have the capacity, authority, and opportunity to take, such as signing forms to hire an employee or expend funds, voting to approve a zoning change, recommending an element of a plan for adoption by a city council.
- Issues are things we care about, such as homelessness, racial prejudice, traffic congestion, failing sewers, budget deficits, or polluted lakes.
- Solutions are things we know how to do, such as organize homeless shelters, enact concurrency requirements for infrastructure, use affirmative action procedures in hiring, build highways, build treatment plants, or charge fees for water based on quantity used.
- Decision makers are the people with authority, capacity, and opportunity to take actions, such as mayor, council member, or planning director, but they have limited attention and energy to focus on decisions, issues, and solutions.

These four types of things are floating around in a relatively unstructured way and the chance meeting of these things may lead to decisions and actions.

We cannot decide or act on issues directly. We cannot decide there will be no homeless. Regardless of the importance of the issue, we can only decide to do things within our capacities to act. In canoeing, we cannot simply decide not to hit a rock. We can only decide which direction to point the canoe and how to manipulate our paddle so as to achieve this. Some connection must be found linking issues to available decisions or decisions will be made as they arise without regard to issues. If racial prejudice is an issue related to hiring, then affirmative action procedures remind us, when we face a hiring decision, to consider whether racial issues are inappropriately affecting our decision. The procedures remind us to link a decision that comes across our desk to an issue that may be floating around but not immediately in the vicinity of the hiring decision. We can frame policies related to issues in terms of decisions that may arise. Set a policy: If a devel-

oper agrees to pay for the added costs of infrastructure, extend the sewer network now, even if the planned extension is five years in the future. The issues of concurrency and budget deficit are thus linked to available actions that come across the desk. A capital improvements program is intended to keep issues in mind in a succession of yearly budget decisions. Effective action recognizes opportunities to use available decisions, especially mundane, everyday decisions, to address important issues.

Solutions are floating around "looking for issues to which they might be the answer" and also looking for decisions through which they might be enacted. Robert Moses, working in New York City, was famous for having a stock of projects designed and ready to go whenever an opportunity for funding (a decision) arose or a political issue arose to which the project might provide a solution (Caro 1974). Neotraditional development (the New Urbanism) is claimed to be a solution to problems of transportation congestion, separation of residential uses from retail services and employment, consumption of land that could be used for resource or recreation purposes, and lack of personal interaction among community residents. Solution mongers advocate these solutions and look for decision arenas in which they might be enacted and issue forums in which they can be given prominence and credibility. Prominent solutions and prominent issues, those more frequently discussed in available forums, those more immediately displayed in decision situations, are more likely to be attended to and to be enacted.

Decision makers have limited attention. They cannot focus on everything, much less everything at once. They cannot focus on many decisions, many issues, and many solutions. Decision makers are looking for things to do within their limited budget of attention. They allocate some of this attention to forums in which issues are raised, modified, and elaborated and thus become more or less prominent. They allocate some of this attention to learning of solutions that might be relevant to decisions and issues they face. They allocate some of this attention to making decisions. Plans figure out relationships among sets of interdependent decisions and relate these decisions to issues and solutions. Plans thus increase the likelihood that available decisions will address issues using good solutions. Plans make sense even in the ambiguities of organizational decision making and decision making in complex systems.

Summary: Plan-Based Action in Natural Systems

Systems evolve and will be observed in some state. Natural evolution can be described after the fact as tending toward where it has arrived, but there is no inherent value or preference for the apparent intention of this "natural" outcome. The apparent intention of evolution—ecological, social, or economic—should not be relied on as a justification of the existing order. Such equilibrium outcomes present both opportunities to maintain stability and challenges to achieve new outcomes in place of existing, undesirable ones. Actions should be designed either to yield outcomes within the domain of stability or intentionally to exceed it, depending on whether the system's current equilibrium is desirable or undesirable.

Plans consider interdependence among actions. When these actions are also indivisible, irreversible, and face imperfect foresight, the costless, incremental adjustments assumed in market processes fail to achieve efficient outcomes, even with respect to the narrow efficiency standards of neoclassical economics. Similarly, the Four I's further undermine the argument that the naturally evolved world is in an inherently good situation. The sequence of actions must be considered and chosen. These conditions create opportunities to gain better outcomes by considering actions in relation to each other before acting, opportunities to gain by making plans.

A stream of opportunities model, built on the garbage can model of Cohen et al. (1972), provides one way to think about plans in complex systems: A plan-making situation is a collection of interdependent, indivisible, and irreversible decisions looking for issues; a collection of issues looking for interdependent decision situations in which they might be pertinent; a collection of solutions looking for issues to which they might be an answer; and a collection of planners looking for work. The stream of opportunities model makes clear that plans must work without requiring complete predictability or control over a system.

3

How Plans Work

In the United States city planning is essentially a process of vision and survey, push and pull, barter and sell, education and exhortation, diplomacy and expediency, courts and juries.
—Walter D. Moody (1919), *What of the City?*

The plan here given is a program of improvements calculated to cover a period of many years. The order in which improvements are made, and when, is not so important as that each shall be so done as to fit into its place in the general plan.
—Harland Bartholomew (1924), *The City Plan of Memphis, Tennessee*

The free and easy meeting of problems as they arise will no longer suffice, and more than ever officials are looking for a solution of current problems in terms of the predictable future.
—Robert A. Walker (1950), *The Planning Function in Urban Government*

It is the intent of the Legislature that public facilities and services needed to support development shall be available concurrent with the impacts of such development.
—Florida Statutes 163.3177(10)h, adopted in 1985

How do plans work? Through what mechanisms or causal processes do plans affect actions? How can we explain why a particular plan is likely to have particular effects? As Moody, Bartholomew, Walker, and the Florida statutes quoted above demonstrate, plans can work in more than one way and planners have, for a hundred years, explained how they expected plans to work. These explanations do not provide precise predictions of what will happen in specific situations, but they do make sense of what we observe and enable us to talk about what we should do. This chapter considers how plans work and thus what plans are and how we can assess their success. The bulk of the book elaborates these concepts and explains plans in relation-

ship to other aspects of urban development. Chapters 7, 8, and 9 consider how plans are made; in chapter 10, these explanations are used to suggest ways to make better plans.

Agendas, Policies, Visions, Designs, and Strategies

Table 3-1 summarizes five different ways in which plans work: agendas, policies, visions, designs, and strategies.[1] The definitions stipulated here and throughout the book are necessary to avoid the ambiguity of many meanings of "plan." For each distinct meaning, I have used a word having a dominant connotation close to the narrower definition, even though the word may also be used to refer to other concepts. These words also have wider and richer meanings in related fields, such as the use of the term "policy" in policy analysis. To paraphrase Wildavsky (1973), if a word can mean everything, it can only mean nothing.

Explanations of how plans work identify relationships between the attributes of plans and the effects that plans have. They thus identify what plans can achieve. Any one plan can work in one or several ways, which means that these are not categories for classification of plans but different mechanisms through which plans affect the world. The cases noted as examples in Table 3-1 are discussed throughout the book.

An agenda is a list of things to do. An agenda works by recording a list to remind us what to do, or to share publicly a commitment to do these things. Agendas work when there are too many actions to remember or when there is benefit in gaining trust among people affected or legitimating actors as accountable. Publishing or publicly advocating an agenda serves both as a memory device and a commitment. We write down an agenda for a meeting so we will remember to discuss the intended issues. At the same time it is a commitment to others to discuss these issues. An agenda also implies repeated efforts to accomplish something. Agendas may merely list independent actions that only come together because someone chooses to focus on them at the same, or nearly the same, time. Once created, a Capital Improvements Program (CIP) or budget may function as an agenda. It keeps a record of a list too long to remember and known to be within the budget constraint set by projected revenues. Citizens who know that an item is on or not on the Capital Improvements Program list find some credibility in the assumption that it will or will not be built within a particular time. In

this explanation, each citizen or each city council member is not concerned about any relationships among the projects or any interdependence among the decisions. Deciding on the CIP, however, is a focus of conflict among projects for different departments and different political wards and different interest groups as well as a competition for available budget. The process of creating a CIP is thus working in some way other than as an agenda.

Agendas differ from objectives. Agendas identify issues or actions; objectives identify valued attributes of outcomes. We can check off everything on our list of things to do, but still not accomplish the objectives that led to the list of things to do. We could create a list of measurable objectives but still have no ideas about what actions to take to achieve them. All explanations of plans must contend with the relationships of actions to outcomes and outcomes to objectives.

The items in the agenda of a meeting have in common the timing of decisions at the same meeting and perhaps a common decision-maker's authority, but the choice for one item need have no relation to the choice for another. Agendas are of interest to planners because they are a tool that focuses the attention of a constituency, whether an individual, a legislature, a group, an electorate, or the public at large. Setting agendas and pursuing agendas are thus ways of affecting the decisions that will be made. Agendas keep our attention focused on important actions or issues rather than merely on what "comes across our desk" at the initiative of others. An agenda is one way to focus the attention of decision makers on some decisions rather than others.

A policy is an if-then rule. A policy works by automating repeat decisions to save time or by ensuring that the same action is taken in the same circumstances, which yields fairness or predictability. Policies fit situations in which there are many repeat decisions and decisions are costly to make, consistency is viewed as fair, or predictability of repeat decisions is beneficial. For example, if the developer will pay for the cost of the sewer extension, then extend the sewer. This policy would save the costs of making this decision in each case, treat all developers alike, and make development actions predictable. Knowing the policies of other decision makers provides evidence for forecasting their decisions. Policies are distinct from regulations in that regulations change legally or administratively enforceable rights whereas policies identify standard responses for repeated instances of the same situation. If the policy is to grant tax incentives to new industrial

Table 3-1
How Plans Work

Aspect	Agenda	Policy	Vision	Design	Strategy
Definition	List of things to do; actions, not outcomes	If-then rules for actions	Image of what could be, an outcome	Target, describes fully worked out outcome	Contingent actions (path in decision tree)
Examples	List of capital improvement projects	If developer pays for roads, then permit development	Social equality, picture of beautiful city	Building plan or city master plan	Road projects built depend on how much land development occurs when and where
Works by	Reminding; if publicly shared, then commitment to act	Automating repeat decisions to save time; taking same action in same circumstances to be fair	Motivating people to take actions they believe will give the imagined result	Showing fully worked out results of interdependent actions	Determining which actions to take when and where depending on situation when actions are taken

Works if	Many actions to remember and need trust among people affected	Repeated decisions should be efficiently made, consistent, and predictable	Can raise aspirations or motivate effort	Highly interdependent actions, little uncertainty about actions, and few actors involved	Interdependent actions by many actors over long time in relation to uncertain events
Measures of Effectiveness	Are actions on list taken?	Is rule applied without constant reconsideration, or is rule applied consistently?	Are beliefs changed as evidenced by beliefs elicited directly or revealed in actions?	Is design constructed or achieved?	Is contingent interdependence sustained in actions, and is information used in timely fashion?
Cases	Chicago Plan of 1909	Chicago Plan of 1967, Cleveland Policy Report of 1974, Lexington, Kentucky	Chicago Plan of 1909, Portland 2040, Washington, D.C. 2000	Chicago Plan of 1909	Lexington, Kentucky 1958, Integrated Action Plans, Nepal

firms, then when a new industrial firm proposes to locate in the community, tax incentives should be granted. The policy simplifies decision making by deciding once on a decision rule to apply to all situations of the same class (Kerr 1976). Policies work in three ways: saving decision costs, ensuring consistency (fairness), and increasing predictability.

A vision is an image of what could be. Visions compel action. Visions work by changing beliefs about how the world works (beliefs about the relationships between actions and outcomes), beliefs about intersubjective norms (peer group attitudes about good behaviors), or beliefs about the likelihood of success (raising aspirations or motivating effort).[2] A vision could be interpreted as a normative forecast: a desired future that can work if people can be persuaded that it can and will come true. Visions, however, focus first on the outcome and then on the possibility of actions to attain this outcome. Henry David Thoreau expressed it this way in the concluding chapter of *Walden:* "If you have built castles in the air, your work need not be lost; that is where they should be. Now put the foundations under them." Visions are useful in situations in which they can change beliefs and thereby change investment actions, regulations, or activity patterns of residents. Visions are distinct from target designs, which are focused on a feasible solution to a complex problem of interdependencies. Visions work by their effect on beliefs, not by their feasibility of construction.

A vision can help overcome resilience in a system. Resilience dampens feedback that would give immediate responses to actions we might take. Lack of feedback makes intentional action both difficult and risky. If you are trying to change the attitudes of one ethnic group about another ethnic group, resilience is a hindrance. Even interventions that might change attitudes eventually with sufficient time or effort might not yield visible results in time to keep the effort going forward. The effort will then be stopped even though it might have succeeded eventually. A vision can help to motivate continued effort.

Guttenberg (1993) describes a "goal plan" approximately equivalent to this idea of vision: "The image is credible, it bears some relation to existing opportunities in the region, but apart from its ability to persuade, to move people by its attractiveness, it includes no explicit measures for ensuring that these opportunities will be realized" (190). "The purpose of a goal plan is more to state a desired objective persuasively than to plot a course of action for the intervening years" (193).

Graphic and verbal descriptions of future situations—social utopias or beautiful cities—have been developed for centuries, and "visioning" is a currently popular tool in urban planning. Visions can reframe problems by describing the present and its relationship to possible changes in a different way. Visions also describe what the world will look like after proposed changes occur. The literature on strategic planning for corporations and Bryson's (1995; Bryson and Crosby 1992) extension of this literature from hierarchical organizations to "shared power worlds" use visions in all of these ways.

The Chicago Plan of 1909 is a familiar example of plan as vision. It included both graphic renderings of a physical vision and verbal descriptions of the characteristics of a great city.

> In creating the ideal arrangement, every one who lives here is better accommodated in his business and his social activities. In bringing about better freight and passenger facilities, every merchant and manufacturer is helped. In establishing a complete park and parkway system, the life of the wage-earner and of his family is made healthier and pleasanter; while the greater attractiveness thus produced keeps at home the people of means and taste, and acts as a magnet to draw those who seek to live amid pleasing surroundings. The very beauty that attracts him who has money makes pleasant the life of those among whom he lives, while anchoring him and his wealth to the city. The prosperity aimed at is for all Chicago. (Burnham and Bennet 1909, 8)

The Portland 2040 Plan also uses images of the implied future to sell its less palatable actions (Metro 2000). Planning for small towns often focuses on "visioning," a collaborative effort by a large portion of the town's citizens to follow a process fairly similar to the corporate strategic planning process (Howe et al. 1997). The Atlanta 2020 Project used a visioning approach (Helling 1998).

A design is a fully worked out outcome. Designs work by determining a fully worked out outcome from interdependent actions and providing this outcome as information before any action is taken. Designs fit situations in which there are highly interdependent actions, actions are easily inferred from information about the outcome, and there is little uncertainty about implementation of actions. We usually think of design as a process in which many ideas are tested and modified, but entirely in some simulated environment before any action is taken in the real world. Harris (1967) identifies design decisions as reversible at zero cost. All the decisions involved in design of a single building are tested as hypotheses in combination through diagrams and calculations to see how they fit together before any action is taken to construct the building. Designs usually focus on patterns of capital facilities rather than on the human activity patterns that will occur given these facilities. Measures of success should, however, assess these human activity patterns.

Design works by figuring out a result for many interdependent actions before acting. It thus avoids the problems of interdependence, indivisibility, and irreversibility through a presumption of perfect foresight. There is no iterative adjustment; the result is determined first so that each action can immediately fit the solution. Bacon (1974, 260–262) illustrates how the design concept breaks down over time in urban design but still results in somewhat coherent physical forms. A complete and coherent design for a section of a city is proposed. Some elements of the coherent design get implemented, but other elements do not because of citizen complaints, budget constraints, changes in government, or power relations. Then, situations change and new designs are proposed that in part relate to the elements of the previous design. Some of the elements of the new design are implemented. The realized urban form results from this sequence of dependent designs, none of which is implemented in its entirety.

As projects become more complex and more easily decomposed into actions that can be carried out separately (e.g., more than one building, phased buildings to be constructed with long periods between each phase), they take on the character of a sequence of design projects linked by strategies about related decisions. Although any architect designing buildings will point out that in many cases the design may be modified during construction and that the cost of design changes is not zero, these costs are small and these modifications are minor relative to the whole design. In larger urban development situations, actions taken at different times are each of similar magnitude, such as building an interceptor sewer now and an expressway later. Modifying the expressway capacity or service area before it is built to complement a sewer system designed to absorb twenty-five years of growth is a different level of relationship from modifying details as a building is constructed.

A design approach solves problems *before* acting on any decision, whereas a strategy approach decides what action to take now cognizant of related future actions. We do not need to make all related decisions simultaneously, but we can consider potential future decisions before making a decision now. Note that the target creating of design is also different from agenda setting. An agenda is a list of things to do; a target is something to shoot at. A target might prompt an agenda. A strategy might be devised to achieve a target.

A strategy is a set of decisions that forms a contingent path through a decision tree. Strategies work by determining what action should be taken now contingent on related future actions. Strategies fit situations in which there are many interdependent actions under the authority of many actors and occurring over a long time in relation to an uncertain environment. In sequential decision making, at the time action is taken on a current decision, the future decisions have been thought through for each outcome from that current decision. Saying that we plan to do something means that we will take certain actions under certain conditions when the time comes. Design and strategy represent the continuum sometimes described between synoptic or blueprint plans and incremental, decision-centered planning (e.g., Faludi 1987). The crucial difference is the degree to which all decisions should or can be taken at once or only sequentially.

Strategy is arguably the most inclusive and thus fundamental notion of plans because it is the most explicit about the relationships among interdependent actions, their consequences, intentions, uncertainty, and outcomes. Strategies address most completely the problems of interdependence, indivisibility, irreversibility, and imperfect foresight. In contrast, designs focus primarily on outcomes. Visions, agendas, and policies are often joint effects of plans that also work as strategies or designs. Visions, policies, and agendas, as explained earlier, can also address situations that do no meet the strict criteria of interdependence, indivisibility, irreversibility, and imperfect foresight.

Plans address spatial phenomena, which is a direct result of interdependence among decisions in space. On the other hand, policy analysts tend to ignore spatial phenomena and focus on the impacts of individual programs or policies, not on plans for related actions. Analysis for a single decision or for repeat decisions of the same type may benefit from forecasts of impacts, but when interdependent actions can be taken sequentially, the relationships between decisions and forecasts become more complex. Plans working as strategies depend on functional, spatial, and temporal relationships among decisions themselves and their impacts. Policies are distinct from strategies, because policies apply to repeated decision situations of the same kind whereas strategies coordinate different but related decisions. Strategies may yield policies as statements of decision rules, such as "Allow development if the developer pays for cost of sewer extensions." This policy might implement a strategy of providing sewer infrastructure over time concurrent with development. Plans may be hierarchically related. For example, under California planning legislation, area plans (or specific plans) are subject to policies and strategies set out in general plans (Olshansky 1996). The Chicago plan of 1966 (City of Chicago Department of Development and Planning 1966) set policies for area plans that were developed for each neighborhood.

In contrast to plans, regulations set the rights of a decision maker by identifying what decisions are permitted and by setting the range of discretion of choices and criteria in making these decisions. Regulations are enforced by the state through its monopoly on the use of force. For example, zoning restricts the range of uses, building height, and land coverage that may be undertaken on a particular parcel. A subdivision ordinance restricts the patterns by which land can be divided into building lots. Regulations may be created by private groups under the force of contracts, which are in turn enforced by the state. Thus a homeowners' association may impose design regulations for its members. Regulations affect decisions by restricting the set of choices, whereas plans affect decisions by providing information.

In contrast to regulations, none of the ways in which plans work is inherently binding on actors. Plans that work as strategies set forth contingent decisions that affect choices made now, but there is no current or future change in the range of alternatives from which the decision maker is permitted to choose. The effect on current decisions is only through the decision maker's own assessment of related decisions. Regulations define the set of future alternatives from which a decision maker may choose, which can help to determine which decision is best for action now. Regulations are discussed further in chapter 6.

Plans also work as a focus of deliberation—discussion, argument, conflict, and resolution. Such work occurs both in the creation of plans and in their use to guide action. These aspects of how plans work are considered in chapters 7 through 9, which focus on making and using plans.

Investments and Regulations

Investments in physical infrastructure or facilities and regulations are widely recognized as the two major components of urban development plans (see e.g., Alexander 1992a, 98ff; Neuman 1998). As in political interpretations, these different types of actions imply different tasks for plans. Investments, whether by public agencies or private firms, change the capital stock of infrastructure or buildings. Regulations change rights, the range of discretion in making decisions. Plans often include recommendations for enabling legislation from a higher level of government to allow a lower level of government to take certain kinds of actions. Enabling legislation is thus analogous to regulation but is among levels of government rather than between governments and individuals. That we observe this pervasive focus of plans, whether made for governments or private firms or individuals, suggests that we should be able to explain why plans are made for investments in physical facilities and regulations rather than for other types of actions.

The simple explanation is that infrastructure investments, whether by public, private, or joint actors, are interdependent with other investments. They are partially indivisible and subject to significant economies of scale; they are durable—long lasting—and costly to reverse once action is taken; they are subject to imperfect foresight with respect to demand, technology, and related actions. When iterative adjustment does not work, plans that work as designs or strategies can yield improved outcomes because such plans consider other actions before taking an action now. Plans can yield such improvements not only from the perspective of a government, but also from the perspective of a private firm or individual.

Investments in physical facilities mediate between geographic space and people's behaviors. Thus two kinds of decisions matter: the decisions to invest in infrastructure and the decisions to use the resulting infrastructure in particular ways. Indicators of quality of life depend on activities of populations, including their interactions with each other; the physical facilities in which they live and work, including the networks that connect these facilities; and the geographic locations in which these activities and facilities occur. Thus an indicator of vehicle miles traveled per person per day depends on where people who work downtown live and over what type of network they travel, which depends in turn on the geographic character of the

site of the city. The important point is that investments occur in fixed locations and they create the physical context within which locational choice
and daily behaviors occur. Whether investments are in buildings—housing,
schools, treatment plants—or networks—roads, sewers, light-rail transit—
they are fixed in place and cannot be moved without great cost. They are
built with specific capacities, which cannot be changed without additional
investment. Increments of capacity are subject to significant economies of
scale. It is less costly per unit of treatment, for example, to build a larger
rather than a smaller sewage treatment plant. Although a treatment plant
may take ten years to site, design, and build, it will still be expected to serve
expected demand for a fifty-year life. Thus forecasts of demand for sixty
years may be pertinent and must be precise enough to be useful. If demand
occurs more slowly or at different densities than forecasted, however, contingent pipe sizes and construction timing should be available as strategy. It
is very expensive to replace pipes to increase their capacity, however, so robust strategies for the major pipes in the network may be appropriate.

People choose to live or work in facilities that exist at particular locations
because someone invested in the facility at that location. People choose
transportation mode and route over a network of streets and transit based
on investments made to link locations by roads or transit routes. The outcome of the investment is realized only when the location choice and travel
choice behaviors occur. We must therefore estimate these behaviors for
given investments rather than trying to estimate the effects of investments
directly.

This logic of plans for investments also applies to capital investments
by the private sector. Anas et al. (1998) give the example of the creation of
new nodes in a multinucleated city. In many cases, no one developer has sufficient capital or land to build an entire new center alone. If several developers try to locate new subcenters when only one or two can be sustained,
however, then some subcenters will fail. The capital invested will be lost and
the underutilized land will displace other uses because of the high cost of
conversion. Even the successfully established center will be slower in developing than necessary because some development and tenants will have
to move from other failed centers. The private developers have much to
gain from figuring out ahead of time which new center will succeed and
building there initially. Public infrastructure providers and house buyers
would also be affected by the uncertainty of location of new centers.

Regulations have a structure similar to investments with two kinds of decisions: decisions to regulate and decisions to act given the regulations. A decision to zone a municipality by land use type and density is a decision to regulate. A decision to build a house in one of these zones is an action given the regulation. Usually the decision to regulate will be collective and the decision to act individual. In order to use regulations, decisions must be made about where to impose what regulations. These decisions are analogous to investments in that they face interdependence, indivisibility, irreversibility, and imperfect foresight. To implement a zoning regulation, we must consider a sufficiently large area to figure out a pattern of land uses that will reduce negative effects of adjacency of different uses and provide access to services. The area to be zoned must be considered in finite increments; it is indivisible. As with investments, regulations cannot, therefore, work by iterative adjustment. If a regulation is to reduce external effects of adjacent land uses, it will be effective only if it is imposed before the conflicting land uses invest in locating next to each other. If a regulation is to match density with infrastructure capacity, it can only be effective before investments are made.

Investments and regulations are logical elements of plans that work as designs or strategies because they are likely to benefit from such plans. Social programs or other actions that are not interdependent, indivisible, irreversible, and subject to imperfect foresight are much less likely to benefit from such plans. For example, state-funded health care would affect quality of life and is worth careful analysis. A housing voucher program may be a valuable public program. Such programs may be on an agenda, may be implemented through policies, or be expressed as visions, but they are not likely to be the focus of a design or a strategy because they do not have the attributes of capital investments or spatially expressed regulations of interdependent actions.

This observation does not mean that such programs are unimportant; it means that instruments different from plans working as designs or strategies are likely to be more useful in achieving the intended outcomes. This observation also does not mean that equity goals or social purposes should not be criteria by which investments or regulations are judged. Regardless of the criterion of success, investments once made are costly to change. It is no more possible to iterate toward a social equity goal than toward an economic efficiency goal if the actions involved are irreversible investments.

Investments and regulations are likely to benefit from plans as designs or strategies because of the characteristics of these types of actions not because of characteristics of particular criteria for evaluating them. A full range of criteria is likely to be and should be considered.

Determining Whether Plans Work

Do plans work? These explanations of how plans can work—as agendas, policies, visions, designs, and strategies—provide a means by which to assess whether plans do work. These explanations indicate what we can expect to observe if plans are working and how we can explain relationships among these observations. We can observe

- plan-making behaviors—the things planners and their collaborators do when they make plans,
- plans—information available at particular times to particular people,
- people using plans while making decisions,
- investments and regulations that may have been affected by plans, and
- outcomes in terms of activity patterns resulting from these investments and regulations.

All of these observable phenomena provide opportunities for assessment. We will consider evaluation of plan-making behaviors in chapter 9. Here we focus on plans and whether they work, not on how they are made.

There are four broad criteria for assessing whether plans work:

- Effect: Did the plan have any effect on decision making, actions, or outcomes? For example, if it was intended to work as an agenda, how many of the listed actions were taken?
- Net benefit: Was the plan worth making and to whom? For example, if it was intended to work as strategy, were the gains in efficiency of infrastructure provision over time sufficient to compensate the costs of making the plan?
- Internal validity (or quality): Did the plan fulfill the logic of how it was intended to work? For example, if it was intended to work as strategy, did it address interdependence, indivisibility, irreversibility, and imperfect foresight in appropriate ways?

- External validity (or quality): Did the outcomes intended or implied in the plan meet external criteria, such as claims for a just society? For example, if it was intended to work as a vision, did the vision include equity? Ethical acceptability is a crucial component of external validity.

Several authors have developed such typologies, none of which I follow completely, but some of which share common elements with this typology. Talen (1996) provides a thorough review of this literature and makes a strong case for the importance of assessing plans on the basis of whether they achieve objectives. Alexander and Faludi (1989) discuss the range of possibilities, including conformity of the actions to the plan, rationality of planning process, quality of the plan solution assessed before or after it has affected decisions, and whether the plan is utilized in the decision-making process. Others (e.g., Berke and French 1994; Dalton and Burby 1994) consider whether plans that meet standards in the literature or in state legislative mandates are more likely to result in a greater number of implementation tools being in place. More recently, Mastop and Faludi (1997) argue for a "performance" approach, which requires looking at how a plan affects decisions and how these decisions in turn affect outcomes. This causal chain links the plan to outcomes, which is consistent with my argument that we need explanations of how plans work.[3] Connerly and Muller (1993) identify frequency of consultation of the plan by decision makers as a measure of plan quality, which highlights the necessary causal link but does not explain what the expected effects of use should be. Baer (1997) provides a checklist for assessing plans based primarily on the plan as document and the reported procedures by which it was made.

Some of the typologies focus more on what to assess and others on how to assess it. As most of these authors point out, it is very difficult to assess the effects of plans on outcomes and thus on measures of goal achievement. In urban development processes, it is almost impossible to say what would have happened without the plan and compare this to what did happen with the plan. Or, conversely, it is impossible to say what would have been different if there had been a plan. Calkins (1979) developed one of the most complete descriptions of the monitoring of plan accomplishment with respect to time and space. His key concepts are to recognize both underlying trends independent of the effects of a plan and trends caused by the plan.

Note that all of these assessment approaches are distinct from the question of evaluating a particular action in a plan, such as estimating the net benefits of a highway project or choosing between a transit-oriented or auto-oriented development pattern. That is, none of the above types of assessments addresses evaluating alternative plans in the process of choosing the content of a plan. Rather, they ask: Did the plan work?

Did the plan have any effect on decision making, actions, or outcomes? Plans work by affecting actions, indirectly if not directly. Whether the actions taken yield intended outcomes is a distinct but important question. Good plans must not merely be more likely to affect actions. They must also be more likely to include actions that will yield intended outcomes. Does Chicago "look like" the Chicago Plan? Were the aspirations achieved based on some set of indicators? Does Cleveland "look like" the Cleveland Policy Report in the sense that indicators show an increase in choices for people who are least well off? Do the new towns of Reston, Virginia, or Milton Keynes in England look like the plans for them? To use this basis, we not only need to be able to measure outcomes pertinent to the plan, but also to provide an explanation of how the plan caused these outcomes. One difficulty is uncertainty in the relationship of actions to outcomes. Even if planned actions are taken, the intended outcomes may not occur. Even good choices in locating land uses relative to flooding or other natural hazards may yield larger losses over a given period than before the plan because of a particularly large flood or a cluster of hazard events. A plan that is based on the belief that people will use transit if they live in a transit-friendly environment may be used in decisions and affect actions but still not gain the outcomes that the plan sought because the belief about how the world works was wrong.

Talen (1996) argues strongly for the value of assessing plans directly in terms of the resulting activity patterns rather than in terms of actions taken. Rather than focus on the investment or regulation actions, she focused on whether the intent of the plan was achieved, in particular whether the equity distribution sought by a plan for city parks was achieved (Talen and Anselin 1998). If the objective of the plan is to provide parks for neighborhoods or types of households that are currently underserved, then a measure of whether the relative level of service for such neighborhoods and households improved is more pertinent than whether parks were built in the specific locations and sizes shown in the plan. This distinction returns us to explanations of how plans work. Whether the objective of equitable distribution of parks was achieved or not, the question of what effect a plan had on this remains to be shown. On the other hand, if the parks were built where the plan recommended and the plan recommended these locations in order to achieve equitable distribution, then just showing that the plan caused parks to be located in these places is also insufficient.

If the spatial diagram or map in the plan was meant merely to persuade constituencies of the possibility of action with respect to goals, then the specific locations of parks would not matter. The locations would be in the plan as an illusion of precision to achieve persuasion. If, on the other hand, the explanation of how the plan is intended to work is as a set of fully worked out interdependent actions, then the particular locations of parks may be related to transit stops, dwelling unit densities, diagonal pedestrian access routes, and traffic calming street patterns. In this case it matters a great deal whether parks were built in particular places in conjunction with other actions. In this latter situation the assessment of equitable distribution with respect to demographic characteristics is insufficient. The substantive logic of the relationships among actions in the plan matters, and the logic of how the plan might affect actions matters.

The 1929 Regional Plan of New York and Its Environs was several years in the making, involved many planners, and took a forty-year perspective. Johnson (1996) takes advantage of the resulting visibility of the planning process and the opportunity to track actions and outcomes to develop a thorough assessment of the effects of the plan. His analysis includes consideration of potential effects of the plan working as vision, agenda, policy, design, and strategy, though not based on the strict definitions and explanations presented here. He points out the difficulties of assessing whether a plan worked as an agenda.

> It is difficult to separate forecasts of events that would have occurred, plan or no plan, from events whose occurrence is attributable to the Plan. And what of long-standing proposals which predated the Plan and were simply incorporated into it? To what extent can the fact of their being part of the Plan be credited with their realization? Each specific project or proposal needs to be analyzed as an individual case study if definitive judgements are to be made about the causal relationships of plan and reality. (244)

Johnson also identifies difficulties in assessing the effects as policy or perhaps as vision.

For example, should decentralization be encouraged or discouraged? Or, should highways be emphasized over transit? General policy reveals itself in the making of specific decisions, but it is itself subject to modification and influence by plans, among other factors. But the extent to which plans as paradigms influence general policy is usually difficult to ascertain. The plan, if it embodies accepted public policy, can reinforce that policy, but the strength of that reinforcement can only be a matter of speculation. Where the plan breaks new ground or attempts to alter accepted policy assumptions, it may be a simpler task to estimate impact by reference to points at which policy changes. (244)

Johnson compares forecasts in the plan, such as population, to historical outcomes to interpret contingent strategies, though the plan itself did not identify such contingent strategies. He also reports which major projects were accomplished and which were not and computes percentages of open space projects completed by subregion, but as he argues, causal explanations linking these outcomes to the plan are difficult to construct.

Even a case study as detailed and thoroughly observed over several years as the traffic reduction scheme for Aalborg Denmark (Flyvbjerg 1998), however, still faces some of these difficulties. Flyvbjerg's interpretation centered on the power of certain actors to oppose parts of the plan on which he focuses his narrative. He interprets the inability to implement all of the interdependent elements of this scheme because of powerful opposition as a plan failing in the face of power. The proposed scheme in the plan he analyzes, however, contradicted the logic of interdependent actions of major capital investments made just before the plan was adopted. The plan's failure might be interpreted as the success of a previous plan that withstood the attempt to change it. Incomplete implementation of one plan is not generalizable as evidence that plans do not work.

Each of the ways in which plans work implies an explanation of how a plan affects the world and thus an assessment based on that particular explanation. The measure of effectiveness for an agenda is whether the tasks were accomplished. We may also be able to observe whether actors or citizens, to sustain the implied commitment to the list, referred to the agenda as a reminder. Such observations would be evidence that the actions occurred because of the plan and because it served as an external memory device.

For policies, there are distinct measures of success for its distinct purposes. For decision efficiency, the measure of effect is whether decisions were made by reference to the policy rather than by considering the next decision situation from scratch. Reference by decision makers to the policy may be observable. Or, the policy may become habit and therefore not be directly observable, even though conformance with policy can still be observed. For decision fairness or consistency, the measure of effectiveness is whether the policy was applied accurately in similar situations. This can be determined by assessing a sample of situations in which the policy should have been applied.

Observing beliefs of the plan's target audience before and after the plan and asking whether beliefs changed can assess the vision mechanism. Beliefs might be elicited directly or inferred or revealed in actions. To determine whether these changes in beliefs also changed actions as intended would require observations of actions. Without observation of changes in beliefs or inference of such changes, however, we could not tell whether a plan was working as a vision.

For designs, the measure of success is whether the design is constructed or achieved. This measure of conformance has been used in several plan effectiveness assessments (e.g., Alterman and Hill 1978). It is generally not linked to a particular mechanism of how plans work, but rather a general notion of linking the plan directly to the outcome. Note that because the design mechanism is directly associated with the outcome, there is no intervening measure. The presumption is that we can recognize the outcome as resulting from the design because the design is sufficiently distinct that the outcome would not otherwise have occurred by chance. If design is not the mechanism by which a plan is expected to work, however, then conformance alone is not a sufficient measure of effect.

For strategies, the measure of success is whether the contingent strategy was pursued. Use of the strategy may or may not result in the most likely outcome being achieved. So for this explanation, the conformance measure is not directly pertinent. The logic of assessing the effect of strategies is developed in more detail in chapter 4.

Finally, it is important to distinguish between lack of plans and lack of action. In Kathmandu, Nepal, people lament the lack of planning, but there are actually many plans. There is a lack of action, in part because of severe budget constraints, and a lack of certain types of land development regulations. It is the lack of investments and regulations that people often mean when they say there is a lack of planning. These plans may have identified actions that were logically linked to good outcomes, but they are not good plans because they failed to consider whether any actor could take these actions. Or, if the plans are explained as visions, then they may be working, though slowly, by changing people's beliefs about how an urban settlement works and what other people believe is worth doing or feasible to do.

We can determine whether a plan worked by linking three observable phenomena:

- Was the plan used? Or, a plan is good because persons use it in choosing actions.
- Were the actions taken? Or, a plan is good because the actions implied by the plan were taken.
- Were the outcomes achieved? Or, a plan is good because the outcomes sought by the plan were achieved.

The combination of these three types of observations can yield a persuasive argument that a plan affected decision making, actions, and outcomes in turn. They can test an explanation of how plans work and thus provide generalizable implications for other similar circumstances. Whether the outcomes were and still are valued and ethical is a question of external validity discussed below.

Was the plan worth making and to whom? Even if a plan is shown to have effects on decision making, actions, or outcomes, it may not be worth the cost of making the plan. There is so little empirical evidence of the effects of plans, that it seems unnecessary to consider whether the effects compensate the costs. The question must be acknowledged, however, and effects should be identified in ways that might allow comparison to costs. Measuring the costs of making plans is conceptually straightforward. Measuring the benefits from the effects of plans, which might be negative, is a minefield of difficulties.

Helling (1998) reports a cost-effectiveness study of the Atlanta 2020 collaborative visioning project. She assumes that the vision, the result of the process, and the process of creating the vision should somehow affect actions, which is consistent with explanations presented here. She concludes that the plan was relatively ineffective at anything other than increasing the interaction among participants, which might eventually have indirect effects on actions. She also estimates the costs for creating the vision at $4.4 million. These costs were carefully calculated as opportunity costs of resources used, including the opportunity cost of the time contributed by the twelve hundred participants. With no identifiable direct effects on actions, was the plan worth this cost? If it is intended to work as a vision, it might have changed beliefs, but not yet affected actions. Changes in beliefs are difficult to measure at best. In either case, costs matter. We can at least ask whether the benefits are plausibly greater than $4.4 million.

To value the effects of a plan requires considering all the ways in which the plan might work, distinguishing effects of the plan from what would have happened anyway, and estimating the value of these benefits. Uncertainty confounds these aspects further, as discussed in chapter 4. Clearly the value of the benefits is different across individuals and groups and raises all the problems of assessing changes in social welfare if we take a collective perspective. Even from the perspective of a particular institution, such as a sanitary district planning for sewers, the estimate of benefits is problematic. In practice, the most practical way to ask whether a plan was worth making is to estimate the costs of making it and then ask whether it is in rough terms plausible that the benefits could justify these costs. That is, it is unnecessary to estimate benefits any more precisely than whether they are greater or less than the costs. Thus Helling's example is an excellent model for addressing this question not just for the vision aspect of plans but for all aspects.

Was the plan internally consistent with the logic of how plans work? Internal validity depends on attributes of the plan itself. The internal validity of a plan can be determined by looking only at the plan. As with any decision in the face of uncertainty, the question is whether a good plan was made given the information available when it was made, not whether the outcomes that resulted were good outcomes. The typical approach is to ask whether a plan contains a certain set of components, such as transportation and land use, or has a particular set of attributes, such as being organized for reference by decision makers. A more careful interpretation would ask whether a plan fulfills at least one of the logics of how plans work. For the strategy aspect of a plan: Are the actions linked together in contingent strategies that meet the logic of decision analysis? Or for the design aspect: Are the elements combined into a designed target configuration that works, in which the interdependent elements should function as intended?

Kent (1964, 91) identified the attributes of good plans:

Subject-Matter Characteristics

The General Plan—

  (1) Should Focus on Physical Development
  (2) Should be Long-Range
  (3) Should be Comprehensive
  (4) Should be General, and Should Remain General
  (5) Should Clearly Relate Major Physical-Design Proposals to the
       Basic Policies of the Plan

Characteristics Relating to Governmental Procedures

The General Plan—

  (6) Should Be in a Form Suitable for Public Debate
  (7) Should Be Identified as the City Council's Plan
  (8) Should Be Available and Understandable to the Public
  (9) Should Be Designed to Capitalize on Its Educational Potential
  (10) Should Be Amendable

These are characteristics of a plan, not of the process by which it was created or of the effects it had on the world. They are internal validity criteria.
Some of these criteria can be derived from explanations of how plans work
and thus argued to measure internal validity in this stronger sense. The
Four I's argue that plans should focus on physical development. A plan for
physical development is sufficiently difficult and sufficiently independent
from other municipal functions that it makes sense to have a plan that focuses on physical development only. Long range is probably too narrow an
interpretation, but the concern with time horizons is pertinent because it
recognizes that a set of interdependent actions may occur over time. The
focus, however, should arguably be on multiple time horizons pertinent to
particular sets of interdependent decisions. Comprehensive for Kent implies comprehensive across physical elements, comprehensive in scope of
effects considered, and comprehensive in covering the entire municipality.
Kent argues that it should be general in focusing on major policies and
major physical design proposals rather than details. These claims are consistent with focusing on those projects that, because of the Four I's, are likely
to benefit from plans. Characteristics 6 through 10 increase the likelihood
the plan will be used in making decisions, and thus link these internal validity criteria to the explanations of how plans affect actions and outcomes.

Plans funded by the federal government under section 701 of the Housing Act of 1954 (Feiss 1985) and state-mandated local plans in several states
must include particular elements, presumably because of a belief that good
plans must have such elements. California, for example, requires land use,
circulation, housing, conservation, open space, noise, and safety (Olshansky 1996). These requirements address both scope of decisions and scope
of effects to be considered. Why states should mandate certain characteristics of plans raises a whole range of issues beyond the internal validity of
plans. Such mandates demonstrate, however, that decisions about how to
plan are made in part on the attributes of plans themselves, not on the way
they are made or on the effects they have. Thus internal validity is an important category of criteria.

*Did the plan seek outcomes that are ethically appropriate through means that
are ethically appropriate?* A plan that seeks to achieve equity for the least well
off is a better plan than one that seeks to increase the efficiency of urban development in a way that the efficiency gains accrue only to the most well
off. Without elaborating ethical claims here, it is clear that a plan can affect
decision making, actions, and outcomes, yield benefits sufficient to compensate its costs, be internally consistent in its logic, but still be a bad plan
because of the goals it pursues or the means it employs. External validity
calls a plan to the standards of ethics.

Keating and Krumholz (1991) assessed the effects of downtown plans by
comparing six plans based in large part on whether they tended to accomplish what those who initiated and supported them intended to accomplish.
Did the plans affect outcomes? They applied criteria from Sedway and
Cooke (1983) who argued that plans for downtown development are worth
making if there is support of major property owners and tenants, support
and cooperation from all departments in city government, a citizens advisory committee, and a citywide plan within which the downtown plan can
be set. These criteria are predictive of whether a plan is likely to yield benefits to those who fund it that are sufficient to compensate its costs. Keating and Krumholz found that the six plans they studied all fit the Sedway
and Cooke criteria. They were plans of a type that we expect to occur because they were initiated by landowners, business leaders, and local government, all of whom can benefit from downtown development. These actors have incentives to produce these types of plans that are focused on
decisions they can make and benefit from. None of the plans, however, dealt

in a significant way with equity, which was predictable given who initiated them. The plans failed an external validity test on a prescriptive criterion of equity.

If we can explain situations in which plans are likely to be made and likely to work based on the first three broad criteria—effect, net benefit, and internal validity—then we can prescribe situations in which planners who measure success as plans affecting actions, and at costs that are compensated, should make plans. Such plans and planning are likely, however, to achieve what is easy and normal, not to accomplish unusual changes such as improvements in social equity. All four criteria—including external validity—are thus pertinent to evaluations of plans.

Summary: Plans Work in Particular Situations

Plans can work in more than one way. Given explanations of how plans work—explanations that link observable phenomena—it is possible to assess to what extent plans work in particular situations with respect to their effects, their net benefits, their internal validity, and their external validity. These explanations can also be used to predict that plans that meet these evaluation criteria will, in general, work in these ways in appropriate situations. They thus provide a basis for predicting what plans will be worth making.

Plans for urban development often include agendas and policies as means of framing the actions implied by the plan. The vision, design, and strategy aspects of a plan are most pertinent, however, to figuring out the substantive logic of a plan for urban development and thus precede these agendas and policies. The fundamental reason for this precedence is that visions, designs, and strategies address interdependence among actions while agendas and policies do not. The strategy aspects of plans must also face uncertainty and thus forecasting, which leads us to an interpretation of plans through decision analysis in chapter 4.

4

Strategy, Uncertainty, and Forecasts

Still we might argue that hope and vision are rational in the probabilistic context since they encourage people to work harder, to make greater commitments, to mobilize social and natural resources in previously unimagined ways, and to enlarge the range of action beyond what was ever taken as reasonable. . . . And so to be hopeful will actually change the probabilities and payoffs.

—Martin Krieger (1991), "Contingency in Planning: Statistics, Fortune, and History"

The most fundamental aspect of making plans for urban development is making choices about interdependent decisions—decisions for which the choice made in one decision depends on the choice made in the other decisions. Choosing what courses to take in college illustrates the generic form of such planning situations. In this case, there are eight decision stages if you complete school in eight semesters. Before each semester you must decide what courses to take, given contingent decisions on what courses you will choose to take in succeeding semesters. You must also fit the courses for the imminent semester into a feasible weekly schedule. You take prerequisites so that you can take other courses later. You make sure that the combination of courses you choose will earn the degree and major you are seeking. The outcomes from registering for these courses, however, are uncertain. You may not pass all the courses. You may discover that you like a subject more, or less, than you realized. Thus, you should consider the implications of changes in your preferences as the result of taking particular courses from particular teachers. Certain courses may no longer be offered by the time you get to them. You should consider robust decisions when available, choosing courses that make sense for several majors so that you can change majors. If you planned to be an engineer, but later decide to be an historian, you must know when and how to revise your plan. You want to focus on learning, not on planning to learn, so you must, implicitly at least, decide how much effort (and worry) to put into planning your courses. The sequence of related decisions, the uncertain outcomes, the changing preferences, and the externally specified but possibly changing requirements for obtaining a degree make this typical of situations in which the strategy aspect of plans will be useful.

Interdependent Actions, Plans, and Expected Values

Decision analysis provides a coherent framework in which to consider the relationships among actions, outcomes, uncertainty, and forecasts. It ties planning situations to a well-developed literature about such problems. Its usefulness in explaining how plans work should not be confused, however, with the use of decision analysis as a problem-solving tool for a specific problem, which is the way it is usually presented (e.g., Stokey and Zeckhauser 1978; Kirkwood 1997). By your own experience, you know that you have never structured the curriculum-planning problem as a decision tree explicitly, much less calculated expected values arithmetically. The usual tools for curriculum plans include a set of eight lists of courses, one list for each semester. A form on which to check the requirements that have been met, and thus highlight those that have not, is also useful. This list also helps check that prerequisites are being fulfilled so that you will be able to take future courses. Often students (or their advisers) identify contingent course options for future semesters to confirm that various options are kept open. For example, in semester four you will take either an engineering course or a history course depending on your grade in freshman English (or math).

In urban development, investments and regulations do not yield an immediate and unique outcome. If choosing an action does not determine a unique outcome, then we need a concept of the expected value of an action. If preferences among current actions depend on future actions, then we may gain by forecasting future context, decisions situations, and preferences before making current decisions. If preferences change, then we should consider the possible effects of our actions on our preferences, that is, their formative effects. These questions are explained conceptually in this chapter by describing planning situations as decision trees.

Imagine that you are faced with the problem of choosing a number of dwelling units for an area of new development and a capacity of sewers and arterial streets to serve the area. For the moment, set aside the questions

Table 4-1

Infrastructure and Housing Illustration

	Low Density		High Density	
	Revenue	Cost	Revenue	Cost
Infrastructure	20	15	15	5
Housing	70	40	50	30

of whether these two decisions—housing and infrastructure—are under the authority of one decision maker or two, or can be made simultaneously or not. Focus instead on how to analyze what difference it would make to plan. What is the gain from considering both decisions before acting on one of them?

The decision trees in Figures 4-1, 4-2, and 4-3 describe this problem in three different ways using the hypothetical data in Table 4-1. For simplicity, the cost of land is ignored. The numbers are in thousands of dollars, but they are hypothetical numbers to illustrate an idea, not empirical numbers to make an empirical claim about a particular result.

Figure 4-1 organizes the infrastructure decision with two alternatives. The tree consists of decision nodes (shown as squares) and branches, with

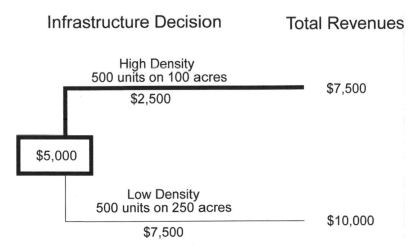

Infrastructure Decision   Total Revenues

High Density
500 units on 100 acres
$2,500 $7,500

$5,000

Low Density
500 units on 250 acres
$7,500 $10,000

Figure 4-1

Decision about infrastructure independently

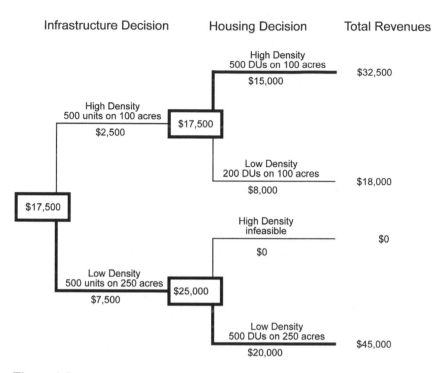

Figure 4-2
Decisions about infrastructure and housing considered together

each branch representing an alternative with a cost or value for that alternative. Working backward from the right, the total revenue resulting from each branch is shown at the end of the branch. Using data in Table 4-1, total revenue for 500 units of high density at $15 per unit is $7,500. The cost for this branch is $500 \times \$5 = \$2,500$, which is shown below the branch. The value of choosing this branch is revenues minus costs or $5,000, which is shown in the decision box because this value is greater than the $2,500 that would result if the lower branch were chosen. In this case you should choose high-density infrastructure as shown by the bolded lines. You could construct an analogous node and branches for considering the housing decision alone, in which case you would choose low-density housing.

If you were to consider both decisions together, as shown in Figure 4-2, you should choose low-density infrastructure, which is different from the decision you should have made if you considered only infrastructure. The revenues and costs for infrastructure are treated separately because the costs are incurred for an expected number of units, but revenues are received for a realized number of units at the infrastructure revenue rate for the density of housing actually built. If you build low-density housing after constructing high-density infrastructure, you can build only 200 units instead of 500 units because you can fit only 200 low-density units onto the 100 acres that have infrastructure services. In this case, infrastructure revenue is $20 per unit because it is serving low-density housing and is multiplied by 200 because you can only collect revenues from units served. High-density housing cannot be built if infrastructure was built for low density, because the pipes serving given locations do not have sufficient capacity. In this case there are no revenues. Therefore, the revenue for the top branch is $500 \times \$15 + 500 \times \$50 = \$32{,}500$, for the second is $200 \times \$20 + 200 \times \$70 = \$18{,}000$, and so on. Given these revenues, you can work backwards from right to left by subtracting cost incurred for each branch to find its value at each decision node. As shown by bold lines, in this case you should choose to build low-density housing.

To contrast making the infrastructure decision without a plan to making the infrastructure decision with a plan, consider two interpretations of not having a plan. First, you might treat the decisions sequentially because you might be unaware of the housing decision, or you might be aware of it but ignore its relation to the infrastructure decision. Then, given the infrastructure decision, you would make a housing decision. Second, you might treat the housing decision as uncertain and, with no knowledge, assume all choices for housing are equally likely. Note that for the moment these decisions are all under the authority of one decision maker who must still face the task of considering more than one decision at a time.

By the first interpretation, being unaware of or choosing to ignore the decision on housing, you make the infrastructure decision with respect to its own payoffs, thus choosing high-density capacity infrastructure as in Figure 4-1. Given high-capacity infrastructure, you would then choose high-density housing as shown in Figure 4-2. The net revenue would be $17,500, shown in the decision node for high-density housing, minus the $2,500 cost of high-density infrastructure, resulting in a net value of $15,000. Note that this result is not as good as you achieved by considering both decisions together, which yields $17,500, as shown in Figure 4-2.

By the second interpretation, shown in Figure 4-3, the housing decision is represented as a chance event (an oval in the figure). The likelihood of

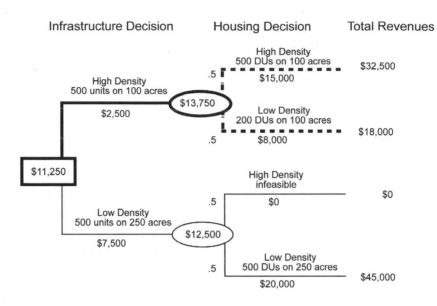

Figure 4-3
Decisions about infrastructure and housing treating housing as uncertain

each outcome from a chance event is represented as a decimal fraction from 0.0 to 1.0. The list of outcomes is taken to be exhaustive, so the likelihoods of outcomes from any one action must sum to one. The difficulty of exhausting all possible outcomes can be overcome conceptually by having one outcome branch represent "unknown" outcomes. If the outcome of a decision is uncertain, then the value of that decision should be an integration across the possible outcomes. The standard approach is to compute an expected value. In a discrete formulation, expected value is defined as the sum across outcomes of the likelihood of each outcome multiplied by the value of that outcome.[1]

Expected value calculations are shown in Figure 4-3. This tree differs from Figure 4-2 only in that two decision nodes have been replaced by two chance nodes and their probabilities. Each of the two outcomes is equally likely and thus has a probability of 0.5 because all outcomes together have a probability of 1.0. The expected value for the upper chance node is 0.5 × ($32,500 – $15,000) + .5 × ($18,000 – $8,000), which equals $13,750. Similarly, the expected value for the lower chance node is 0.5 × ($0 – 0) + 0.5 ×

($45,000 – $20,000), which equals $12,500. The expected value minus the lost of high-density infrastructure is greater, so you should choose to build high-density infrastructure if you have no information about the likelihoods of housing density. Assigning equal likelihood to each outcome is the standard assumption for no information.

After computing what the plan would be, we can compute estimates of the value of a plan under each of the two interpretations (Figures 4-1 and 4-3) of what it means not to have a plan. In this illustration, the difference between the value from making both decisions together and the value from making the best housing decision given the best infrastructure decision is $17,500 minus $15,000, which equals $2,500. This comparison can be made in Figure 4-2 by comparing the combined choice to the choice of housing given high-capacity infrastructure, which is the choice that would have been made considering infrastructure alone. By the second interpretation, the difference between making both decisions together and making the first decision while treating options for the second decision as equally likely is $17,500 minus $11,250 equals $6,750. Plans are in general less valuable if you assume that the second decision will be chosen contingent on the first rather than assuming that the choices for the second decision are equally likely. Thus the benefits of a plan depend on what you would have done without it.

Note that these estimates of the value of a plan can be computed only after the plan is made. They can tell us whether the plan was worth making. To estimate the value of making a plan before making it requires some distribution of possible plans (possible combinations of choices of actions) and their expected values. From this distribution, the expected benefit of making a plan could be compared to the choice that would be made without making a plan. If you can gain a higher payoff by considering both decisions together, you should be willing to pay up to the difference in these payoffs to someone (a planner) who can help you do so. The cost of making and using the plan must be less than the gain it yields.

This logic is useful in thinking through what the benefits of making a plan might be but not in calculating benefits numerically. For example, if there is some possibility that an area at the edge of a city might be acquired by the county as a regional park, but, if not, might be developed at urban densities of residential, then a provider of sewers might judge that the potential of ignoring this other decision would have a large effect on whether a sewer investment would yield revenues. A plan that carefully considered the probabilities of such acquisition and possibilities for flexible or robust sewer extension strategies might be worth making. On the other hand, if a currently unsewered area is already served by an interstate highway and is clearly suitable for urban development, there may be no reason to invest in making plans because they are unlikely to affect the value of outcomes of investments in sewers. In simple terms, the benefits of plans increase with increasing differences in the values of potential outcomes based on inter-dependence, irreversibility, and indivisibility of actions.

Sequential Decisions and Uncertainty

Developers must consider whether to acquire a parcel of land and how many units to build each year. The payoff from this sequence of land use decisions depends on the realized demand each year. An infrastructure provider must decide whether (1) to begin building a big sewage treatment plant now, then when to build each of several sewer interceptors that will feed that plant, or (2) to build a small plant now and then another small plant later. The outcomes from these decisions will depend on the realized demand for these services and when the facilities become available. The de-mand might be realized before infrastructure of sufficient capacity is com-pleted, as is currently often the case with highway capacity at new urban centers around major metropolitan areas. In each of these cases there is a sequence of related decisions with uncertain outcomes.

Uncertainty arises in several ways. Friend and Jessop (1969) have iden-tified three: uncertainty with respect to the environment, uncertainty with respect to related decisions, and uncertainty with respect to values. There is also uncertainty with respect to available actions or alternatives.

Uncertainty with respect to the environment refers to events that can-not be known with certainty and are not under the direct control of other decision makers. Uncertainty about future interest rates is uncertainty about the environment, because the average rates do not directly result from par-ticular decisions of particular decision makers. The interest rate set by a par-ticular bank or for a particular program might, however, be treated as un-certainty about a related decision.

Uncertainty about related decisions may refer to other decisions faced by the same decision maker or decisions over which other decision makers have authority. Uncertainty about other decisions of the same decision maker can be framed as in Figure 4-3. Uncertainty about decisions of others must acknowledge that they also are considering uncertainty, as discussed in chapter 5. The combination of uncertainties about the environment and uncertainties about related actions yields uncertainty about consequences of actions.

Uncertainty with respect to values refers to incomplete knowledge of preferences among different outcomes. This uncertainty arises because the decision maker represents others and does not know their preferences or an appropriate aggregation of their preferences. Or, a decision maker's own preferences may change over time in uncertain ways.

Uncertainty with respect to alternatives refers to incomplete knowledge of possible alternative actions. Ideas for action are created and the process of considering and manipulating ideas also affects values. Thus uncertainties about values and alternatives are confounded in the processes of making plans. Neither alternatives nor preferences can be taken as given.

Expressing these conditions of knowledge as uncertainties is useful for conceptual purposes, but if pursued too literally leads to difficulties. March (1978) labels situations in which there is insufficient information to structure a situation in a decision analytic framework as "decision making under ambiguity." The purpose here is to think about how plans work, not how to estimate uncertainties and compute expected values.

Decisions about land development and infrastructure provision require commitment in advance of demand because of the lead time between decision and availability of the intended service. Once the commitment is made, the funds are spent and there are generally no alternative uses for developed land or for infrastructure for which no demand is realized. The private developer that decides to initiate a major development and the municipality that decides to install infrastructure face similar problems. The developer's investment in land and site improvements must be committed in increments of various sizes over time, but in advance of the sale of units. The sale of units determines the revenues that can pay off loans or yield returns. The municipality must also invest, usually in facilities with longer lead times to complete construction and larger increments of efficient size than those the private developer invests in. For example, sewer interceptors serving a major sector of the city are larger increments of efficient investment than the developer's concern with sewerage laterals serving one street. The munici-

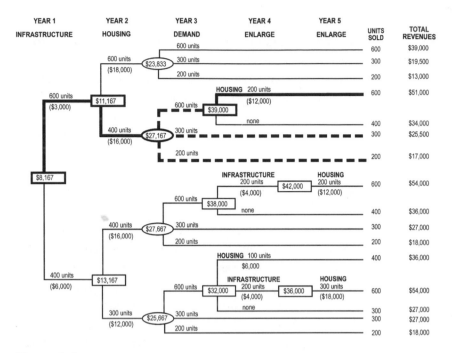

Figure 4-4
Land and infrastructure development under uncertainty

pality must borrow money and earn revenues from taxes or fees to repay the loans. Each thus faces a sequence of related decisions with commitments before realization of revenues and uncertain outcomes. These similarities in decision situation create opportunities for developers of land uses (often private firms) and developers of infrastructure (usually public entities) to share risks in costs and revenues and to make joint efforts to reduce risks through plans, regulations, or collective action. The implications of such shared interests are elaborated in chapter 5.

Figure 4-4 describes a hypothetical land development problem from the perspective of a public or private developer. The major point of this example can be seen graphically: In some situations it makes sense to make some investments (infrastructure in year 1 and housing in year 2), observe the situation at a later time (realized demand in year 3), then decide what to do based on that information (enlarge in year 4 or year 5). The crux is that what you choose to do in the first year depends on your forecasts of potential future outcomes and the contingent decisions you would make. Your

Table 4-2

Data for Land Development Illustration

	300–599 units	*600 units or more*	*Added units*
Infrastructure			
Revenue	20/unit	15/unit	20/unit
Cost	15/unit	5/unit	20/unit
Housing			
Revenue	70/unit	50/unit	70/unit
Cost	40/unit	30/unit	60/unit

strategy should consider the related decisions before making the first decision.

To explain this illustration numerically, in year 1 the developer faces a decision about infrastructure capacity: Should it build infrastructure sufficient for 600 dwelling units or 400 dwelling units? The lead time from infrastructure decision to infrastructure availability is two years, so infrastructure will be available at the beginning of year 3. In year 2, a decision must be made about the number of housing units to build, with a lead time of one year, implying they will be available at the same time as the infrastructure. If infrastructure for 600 was built in year 1, then either 600 or 400 dwelling units can be built. If infrastructure for 400 was built, then either 400 or 300 dwelling units can be built.

Given the costs and revenues in Table 4-2, the tree in Figure 4-4 is constructed with three equally likely outcomes of demand for each housing decision.[2] The realized demand for housing units at the beginning of year 3 is uncertain, represented here as a discrete, equal likelihood of 1/3 that demand will be 600, 300, or 200. The uncertainty might represent variation as a function of immigration, incomes, household formation, tax changes, and any number of other factors.[3] In this example the realized demand does not distinguish between changes in the number of units sold and changes in the price of each unit. As demand is realized, the additional housing can be built in year 4 if infrastructure capacity is available. Or, infrastructure can be expanded in year 4 and additional housing one year later. In this numerical illustration, the plan should be to build infrastructure for 600 units, then build 400 housing units. If demand for 600 units is realized, then build 200 more housing units in year 4.[4]

A strategy in the face of sequential decisions and uncertain outcomes is a path through the tree contingent on realized outcomes at the chance nodes. A strategy helps to determine what action to take now in light of related decisions, some of which may occur later after realization of some uncertain outcomes. If all demand were known, then this could be treated as a design problem: All infrastructure and housing could be determined through an iterative process before anything was built. If built in sequence, however, it is a strategy problem. Decisions should be made for those parts of the development to be built now with contingent decisions for other parts of the development.

Sequential Decisions and Irreversibility

Urban development actions occur in sequence, not simultaneously. The high costs of demolition necessary to change physical investments are an important reason that plans for urban development are often worth making. The following examples explain why plans as strategies may hold some land vacant for future development.

A development firm owns two large parcels that front on two miles along a major arterial at the edge of a community that is growing at a moderate rate. It proposes to construct single-family housing on the parcel farthest from the edge of the city. It contends that this is logical because there is demand for this housing during the next five years, but no demand during that period for higher-density housing. After five years, or whenever demand justifies it, the firm will build higher-density housing and some commercial on the parcel that is nearer to the city. Ohls and Pines (1975) presented this problem in the framework of land economics. The higher density generates more trips and other infrastructure flows per acre than low density. Thus the infrastructure cost is less if the high density is closer than the low density to the primary destination of infrastructure flows. The problem is whether the eventual benefits of having higher-density development built closer to major destinations and sources of infrastructure, when it does get built later, outweigh the added travel and infrastructure costs in the meantime for single-family housing built at a greater distance. There is also the possibility of building single-family housing in close now, then later converting it or razing it and replacing it with higher-density housing and rebuilding lower-density housing farther out. Unless the time lag until high density is built is long, however, the costs of demolition and reconstruction will almost certainly be prohibitive.

Bahl (1963) calculated differential costs for such a case in Lexington, Kentucky. Cost estimates suggested an annual differential cost in 1963 dollars of $580,000 (or $590,000 if certain capital costs are annualized) for a two-mile "leapfrog" over vacant land of new low-density development. Forty-four percent of this was private commuting cost. Fifty-eight percent of the cost was borne by leapfrog subdivision residents, and the remainder was borne by other residents of the metropolitan area.[5] Costs of this order of magnitude suggest that the length of the time interval that land remains vacant will be crucial in deciding whether leapfrog development is beneficial.

It may be appropriate to skip over parcels of land in the development process, and there is a conceptual frame with which to think about this question and the factors that should lead to a particular decision. The decision to be made now by the public sector regulator is whether low density should be permitted on the far parcel. The plan as strategy is that higher-density housing will then go on the nearer parcel. A regulator or planner considering rezoning, annexation, or provision of infrastructure for such a project should think about it in decision analytic terms, as should the developer. The higher-density development will generate more trips per acre and greater demands per acre on infrastructure such as sewerage. In the long run it is preferable to have the higher density closer in. How much does it save to have higher density in the near parcel than lower density? How much added cost is there for placing the low density in the outer parcel? What is the likelihood that demand for high density will appear in any given year? What would it cost to convert low density to high density when demand appeared? What is the likelihood that demand would lead to development of the inner parcel as low density after all? Decision analysis provides a conceptual framework for these general types of planning situations. For specific instances of decision making, drawing a decision tree is often useful in thinking clearly about a situation even without generating numbers and carrying out calculations.

Ohls and Pines (1975) interpret three conditions that lead to the situation in which land should be held vacant for future, higher-density development. The discount rate has a lower limit and an upper limit. If it is too high, the future benefits of having a more efficient pattern in the end cannot outweigh the increased infrastructure costs while closer parcels are vacant. If it is too low, the savings in construction costs based on density will not compensate for infrastructure costs given that construction costs in the final pattern will always be the same (because in their example there are always one high- and two low-density parcels), but infrastructure costs will depend on the spatial pattern. Also, the additional cost of high density must be sufficiently greater than infrastructure costs to justify construction of low density on more distant parcels with higher infrastructure costs. This simple illustration assumes that the pattern remains fixed after completion, but the basic logic applies to consideration of continuing patterns of development. Ohls and Pines (1975) develop a similar logic for reserving land for commercial development.

The downtown of Reston, Virginia, is an example of such a landholding situation. When development was initiated in the early 1960s, land was set aside for a downtown center, knowing that there was insufficient demand then for the intensity of development envisioned. Development of this town center began in the late 1980s with high-density buildings in a traditional downtown layout of buildings at front lot lines and a gridded street pattern. The reservation of the location made this kind of development possible. In contrast, Columbia, Maryland, another new town begun in the 1960s, built its downtown from the beginning at suburban density and in a suburban form. It is inconceivable that Columbia's downtown would now be rebuilt at the density of Reston's downtown.

Forecasts in Decision Situations

Forecasts are statements about outcomes that may occur at some future time. Decisions taken now depend on information available now, planned future decisions, and the forecasts of probabilities on which the plans about future decisions depend. The value of a forecast, analogous to the value of a plan, is the improvement in the value of the decision we would make with it compared to the decision we would make without it. Lave (1963) and Sonka et al. (1986) estimated the benefits of weather forecasting in relation to planning strategies of agricultural production, both within a given year and over several years, but no such studies have dealt with forecasts for urban development. Forecasts have several characteristics that affect their value as information: lead time until the forecasted event, forecast horizon, spatial resolution; and temporal resolution (Mjelde et al. 1988).

Lead time gives the weather forecast in the morning, before a decision is made on taking an umbrella in case of rain in the remainder of the day. Lead time for farmers may require annual forecasts in order to decide what crops to plant. Lead time for infrastructure providers must be sufficient to forecast demand far enough in advance that infrastructure can be designed, approved, and constructed by the time demand for it is realized. In a forecast of future preferences, lead time allows a prediction in time for a decision to save a wilderness area now that will be valued by persons not yet born. You must predict what their preferences will be to assess its future value. The benefit of a forecast depends in part on whether the lead time fits the decision situation.

Forecast horizon is the length of time for which the forecasted information is provided. We might get daily weather forecasts for the next week. The day is thus the temporal resolution and the week is the horizon, which means we get seven daily forecasts. For urban planning, spatially and temporally disaggregated forecasts are important. We want to know when and where school capacity and sewer capacity will be needed by forecasting population with sufficient outcome specificity to choose among school sites and sizes and interceptor sites and sizes. In general, the more disaggregated a forecast, the harder it is to make. It is easier to forecast the population of a state than of one municipality in that state. It is easier to forecast growth of a metropolitan area than of a particular district.

The problem diagrammed in Figure 4-4 could be expanded to consider forecasting. The decision tree would, however, become so complex that it is easier to explain it than to draw it. You ought to consider not only investment in infrastructure and housing, but also investment in forecasting. If you do not forecast, the expected values of the decisions to build high or low infrastructure are the same as in Figure 4-4, which are based on equal likelihoods of three levels of realized demand. The equal likelihoods imply no information. A forecast should change these likelihoods, but you will not know what these forecasted likelihoods will be until *after* you have made the forecast. If you decide to forecast, then, implicitly, you assume a distribution of possible outcomes from forecasting. Each possible outcome is equally likely and consists of a set of probabilities for each of the outcomes in the original problem. *After* you have forecasted, you will learn new probabilities on the population outcomes and can make decisions contingent on these new probabilities. With these new probabilities, new expected values must be computed.[6]

You could also consider the possibility of then forecasting the demand for housing before deciding in year 2 how much housing to build. Forecasts made closer in time to the decision are likely to be more accurate, just as forecasts of rain on the morning when you decide to carry an umbrella are likely to be more accurate than forecasts a week ahead of time. The decisions about a sequence of forecasts imply a contingent path through a tree, a strategy for forecasts. Computing numerical values will almost never be practical, but recognizing the possibilities of forecasting again later is still worthwhile.

Forecasts of population are ubiquitous in plans, but the forecasts typically presented in conventional plans are of little direct use for choosing strategies. Population forecasts are usually produced without reference to any particular decision situation. They are seldom presented in terms of probabilities of different population outcomes. In most decision situations it is not future population that we wish to know, but some derivative of population such as demand for housing or infrastructure. Quite aside from the question of how to conduct a specific forecast of population (see e.g., Isserman 1984), the situations described in this chapter make clear that forecasts ought to be pertinent to the decision situation at hand. The issues of lead time, specificity, and accuracy are pertinent to this fitting of forecasts to decision situations. In addition, we should be aware of self-fulfilling forecasts and the difficulty of forecasting surprising changes in existing trends or patterns.

Forecasts that are *not* pertinent to decisions may be more acceptable to decision makers.

> Occasionally, population projections fit in directly with decisions on the size of future service facilities such as schools, airports, or sanitation systems. But, in general, population projections do not correspond to particular alternatives to the extent that acceptance of a specific projection narrows the range of reasonable alternatives. The fact that population projections are usually far removed from the point of decision means that they are less threatening to policy-makers guarding their own policy preferences.
>
> . . . The multiple-series format of the Census Bureau projections can flatter the forecast-user by allowing him to choose the particular projections series that best fits his own expectations. (Ascher 1978, 31)

Ascher (46) further argues that the middle projection of Census Bureau forecasts is the one usually used because it is symmetrically bracketed by alternative projections. This is another instance of the Bernoulli principle: If you have no information, assume that outcomes are equally likely. The average outcome or its most obvious pretender, the middle projection in the set, is an obvious choice. Regardless of the projection chosen, these population projections are largely irrelevant to decision situations because relevant forecasts should be contingent on the alternative actions taken and sensitive enough to distinguish among them. Census Bureau population forecasts meet neither of these criteria. Further, a decision should consider not merely some most likely outcome, but a sufficient number of possible outcomes to take into consideration preference across the risks of uncertain outcomes.[7] Forecasting should fit strategic thinking about an action. The ubiquitous population forecast, finely tuned but abstracted from any decision situations, is unlikely to contribute to improved decisions.

In some forecasts it is important to keep in mind the distinction between forecasting demand, in the strict economic sense of a curve relating quantity purchased to price, and forecasting the realized market clearing quantity. If demand is easily adjustable in short time periods but supply is not, as in the case of housing after World War II, then the amount supplied will set the market clearing quantity regardless of any predicted quantity based on a demand curve and a fixed price. Thus a low forecast of housing demand will result in fewer units supplied and higher prices in the short run. These forecasts also affect the aggregate behavior in that each individual supplier must make some assumption about the behavior of other suppliers.

A normative forecast (e.g., Ascher 1978, 212) combines intention with prediction. As Louis Kahn would phrase it, a plan "wants to be" a prediction. That is, if I believe a plan will be implemented, then the best prediction is to predict the outcome from the plan (Harris 1960). If I do not believe that the best prediction is the outcome, or better yet the distribution of expected outcomes, of the plan, then the plan is not fully developed because it does not account for what I think will happen.

Traditional comprehensive plans, such as the many 701 plans made in the 1950s, 1960s, and 1970s, begin, both procedurally and as documents, with an aggregate population forecast. These forecasts were almost never normative, as evidenced by their use as a starting point in figuring out what to do and in arguing for the plan. If the assumption is that the plan affects only the internal arrangement of the city and not its comparative advantage with respect to other cities or to rural areas, then assuming an exogenous population distribution might make sense. Implicitly, such plans assumed that the size of the city was not at issue. The garden city idea of the early 1900s and the growth control initiatives of the 1970s argue that city size matters. Thus normative forecasts of population are central to plans with such goals. If the focus is on controlling growth rate, as in Petaluma, California, then normative forecasts of growth rate are pertinent.

Robust, Flexible, Portfolio, and Just-in-Time Strategies

To oversimplify, consider providing classrooms for classes of uncertain sizes. A robust strategy might build large classrooms because they would work for many sizes of classes. A flexible strategy would provide easily movable walls so room sizes could change. A portfolio strategy would provide classrooms in a mix of sizes so that when one size would not work, another would. A just-in-time strategy would deliver mobile classrooms to sites a few days before classes begin. These concepts are pragmatic ways to cope with uncertainty without direct use of decision analysis to calculate strategies. It is the decision analytic framework, however, that highlights the reasons why these strategies work in certain types of situations.

Robustness is the range of outcomes over which a particular decision is still the preferred decision. One way to make robust decisions work is to aggregate geographically. A large, regional sewage treatment plant for all the expected growth of a region is a robust decision because it does not matter where the growth occurs. Robust decisions must balance advantages and disadvantages. A regional plant requires more piping and larger interceptors. Is it worth the trade-off? That depends on the particular pattern, the relative lead time to construct treatment plants versus sewer interceptors, and the economies of scale associated with plant size.

Robustness may also refer to data error or forecasting accuracy. Decisions that would hold for wide variations in the likelihood of rain are robust to the accuracy of the likelihoods. Decisions that would hold for wide variations in costs or benefits are robust with respect to these data. Robustness is the sensitivity of a decision to differences in uncertainty of outcomes or ranges of error in any other data of the problem.

Robust decisions are useful because attitudes toward risk aversion are hard to elicit from decision makers and data are estimates with some degree of error. If expected utilities could be elicited accurately, incorporating risk aversion, then robustness of decisions with respect to outcomes or data error would not matter. Robust decisions also bring costs, however, because building a larger classroom to hold possibly larger classes wastes money if smaller classes occur, even though it would be less costly than having to build bigger classrooms later if larger classes occurred. A large classroom is also a less comfortable environment in which to hold small classes.

Flexibility is the range of different decisions that can be made without significant difference in expected value. A more flexible plan or sequence of contingent decisions is one in which more options are available at each ensuing stage. Sequential plans are more flexible than target plans—that is, designs—because subsequent decisions can be made in light of uncertain outcomes from preceding decisions. Thus, with uncertain outcomes it is better to make sequential plans when possible because some of the outcomes will be known before some of the decisions must be taken. Robustness implies that decisions can stay the same and make little difference in the overall value of the sequence of outcomes. Flexibility implies that decisions can change and make little difference in the overall value of the sequence of outcomes. Using portable classrooms is a more flexible strategy than permanent classrooms, because they can be moved to alternative locations or sold to another school district. Providing sewage treatment with septic tanks is a flexible strategy because the treatment facility can be put wherever the development occurs and whenever it occurs in increments equal in capacity to a single dwelling unit.

Portfolio strategies can also be used to address uncertainty. If one action will come out well if interest rates rise, but poorly if they fall, then complement that action with a "hedge" action that will come out well if interest rates fall. Choose a combination of actions, one of which will do well in one circumstance, the other of which will do well in another (e.g., Raiffa 1968, 97). Developing a downtown shopping area and a suburban mall may be near-perfect hedges; if one does not work, the other will. If we cannot predict which type of shopping shoppers will prefer, we might build a portfolio that includes both. A transportation strategy that provides for walking, mass transit, and automobiles would be a portfolio strategy with respect to uncertain events in the price of energy or changes in technology or lifestyle. Diversity connotes a slightly different idea than a portfolio strategy. A portfolio of actions is something in which all actions occur but their outcomes complement each other. Diversity increases the pool of options from which survivors can be selected as environments change. Only some of the options are, however, chosen by the selection process.

Plans as Investments: Scope, Horizon, Revision, and Learning

Plans are themselves investments (Hopkins 1981), investments that incorporate interdependent elements, are indivisible, are irreversible once acted on, and involve imperfect foresight. Thus the analysis of whether to make a plan is an investment problem that is in many ways analogous to the analysis of any other investment. Decision analysis helps frame pertinent questions. What scope of related decisions should the plan address? What time horizon should the plan consider? When should the plan be revised? How does the potential for learning about the system affect choice of time horizon and revision interval?

The scope of consideration should be based on interdependence and the potential for decomposition. A plan should consider the decisions that are sufficiently interdependent to affect choices for each decision, which in turn affect expected payoffs sufficiently to compensate for the effort of considering more decisions. We cannot calculate this expected net benefit of the scope of a plan because it becomes an infinite regress: How much effort should we expend considering how many decisions we should consider? Calculation would be impossible in any case because there is no way to obtain useful data. We can, however, ask what the presumed relationships creating interdependence are and whether feasible reductions in uncertainty are likely to yield big differences in payoffs given remaining uncertainties. Plans for transit and plans for sewers are interdependent at the level of gross land use densities and expected timing of development. Specific collector sewers and collector streets can be sized at the time of land development because the lead times to build them are the same, about one year, as for the construction of buildings. We do not, therefore, need to work out collector sewers and collector streets in a plan of metropolitan scope. In contrast, the location and sizing of a sewage treatment plant and the location and capacity of expressways and transit lines belong in the scope of a metropolitan plan for directions of growth that may hold for fifty to a hundred years because these decisions are interdependent, indivisible, and irreversible. The logic of scope again emphasizes that there will be and should be many plans with different scopes and time horizons.

Intriligator and Sheshinski (1986) formalized the problem of choosing a time horizon and an interval between plan revisions as an inventory control or capacity expansion problem. The time horizon is analogous to the order quantity or the increment in facility capacity. The revision interval is analogous to the order interval or the time between expansions. For example, typical capital improvement programs have a three-year time horizon and a one-year revision interval. Three years of budgeted expenditures and projects are considered at a time, and the plan (the capital improvements program) is revised each year. In addition to choices of time horizon and revision interval, there are choices about the actual investments or regulations being planned.

Intriligator and Sheshinski assume that expected values of decisions, and thus impacts of decisions, can be calculated for infinite forecast horizons so that only the horizon for which decisions are considered is pertinent. Such infinite forecasts are impossible in practice. In addition to Intriligator and Sheshinski's definition of the plan horizon as the time period for which decisions are determined, we should also define an impact forecast horizon, which may be longer, though not infinite. For example, the 1929 Regional Plan of New York and Its Environs used forecasts for a forty-year period as a frame for its development. It focused, however, on actions that would occur in a much shorter time frame of about ten years (Johnson 1996). The wedges and corridors concept of the Washington 2000 Plan is based on an impact forecast horizon that is indeterminate, though not infinite, but addresses actions in a shorter period.

The plan horizon, impact forecast horizon, and plan revision interval depend on a particular scope of actions considered in a plan. Comprehensive plans with twenty-year horizons may be a bad compromise for different elements that should have different horizons. The choice of plan horizon depends on economies of scale or indivisibilities in the actions being planned and on levels of uncertainty about demand (Knaap et al. 1998). The plan horizon also depends on the costs of planning because the costs of planning increase with the length of the horizon.

We might revise a plan with a fifty-year-plan horizon after ten years because of new information about likely densities and locations of development and realized outcomes in the timing of development. Such revisions can be time driven or event driven, just as in standard inventory or capacity expansion models (Freidenfelds 1981; Sipper and Bulfin 1997). Time-driven revision means the plan is revised after some number of years regardless of the state of the system. Event-driven revision means the plan is revised if some condition occurs. For example, the plan would be revised when and only when the sewer capacity available is sufficient to supply only five years of growth in demand. Event-triggered planning is, in general, more efficient than time-triggered planning if the cost of monitoring to recognize trigger events is low compared to the net benefits of revising the plan. The revision interval depends on the costs of planning and the rate of learning relative to uncertainty.

Learning may occur with any of the four types of uncertainty identified earlier: uncertainty with respect to the environment, with respect to values, with respect to related decisions, and with respect to available alternatives for any one decision. If you learn that new regulations make you liable for environmental hazards on your property, then it is appropriate to consider revising your plan in light of new information about the environment. You may realize that you mind carrying the risk of financial losses more than you thought, either because you misjudged your preferences or because your preferences have actually changed now that your wealth has decreased. You should consider revising your plan in light of new values. If you learn that a new development company has entered the local market, then you should consider revising your plan in light of new related decisions. If you learn that through new technology you can build housing units less expensively, then you should consider revising your plan in light of new alternatives.

In particular, revising plans should be considered in light of the availability of new forecasts. A properly formulated plan intended to work as strategic action—a contingent path through a decision tree with uncertain outcomes—should *not* be revised just because the most probable or most desirable of the uncertain outcomes did not occur. Such plans already account for such situations and set the contingent decisions in advance. If, however, the information on which the plan is based changes, then the plan should be revised. A high rate of learning implies a high rate of change in the available information and thus a high frequency of revision.

If learning is high, then forecasting is less valuable because the likelihood decreases that the forecasts of the environment, preferences, other decisions, and available alternatives will still be correct when future contingent decisions are made. The effect is equivalent to the question of accuracy of forecasts. Whether the forecast is inaccurate—that is, incorrectly predicts outcomes—because of limitations in forecasting or because the phenomena being forecasted changes (learning), the effect is the same. If learning is very high, different outcomes approach equal probabilities of occurring. The expected value with forecasting thus approaches the expected value without forecasting because the best we can do is assume equal probabilities for each outcome. Investing in forecasts may lose value because we cannot expect to improve on assuming equal probabilities, but investment in plans may still be valuable because choosing among actions still matters. Different actions will, in general, still have different expected values even if the probabilities among possible future states must be assumed to be equal.

In cases of high uncertainty or high rates of learning, monitoring previous outcomes relative to current decisions becomes more valuable because knowledge is changing so rapidly that it is valuable to keep learning, but not to keep forecasting. Monitoring is, in a sense, the inverse of planning. Rather than relating future decisions to forecasted outcomes from current decisions, monitoring relates current decisions to recorded outcomes from previous decisions. Monitoring is also the basis of forecasting. If phenomena, or knowledge of them, are changing slowly, then forecasting is worthwhile because forecasting must be based on experience of the system being forecasted.

In cases of high rates of learning, intentionally formative strategies become more valuable. If the effects of intentionally formative strategies on beliefs and attitudes are at least partially predictable, they increase the probabilities of some outcomes relative to others and thus move away from forecasts of equal probabilities for each possible outcome. We can reduce uncertainty about future values and beliefs by "teaching the vision."

We return to descriptions of plan scope and horizons in chapter 9 in discussing how plans are made based both on the logic presented here and on the logic of human problem solving considered in chapter 7. Not surprisingly, and despite the traditional comprehensive ideal, we usually observe many plans of different geographic and functional scopes with different plan horizons and different revision intervals.

Summary: Strategies, Uncertainty, and the Value of Plans

The value of identifying a plan as strategy is the difference in expected value between the decision that would have been made considering only the immediate decision, and the expected value of the decision that would be made considering a set of interdependent decisions. The net benefits of a plan must take into account the costs of making and using the plan. Interdependent, indivisible, irreversible decisions for which specific, accurate, and timely forecasts can be made and for which rates of learning are low are likely to benefit from plans. The lack of estimates of net benefits of plans is a major gap in research about planning, but these general characteristics of situations in which plans are likely to work give qualitative guidance on how much to plan and when.

Sequential decisions with uncertain outcomes, forecasts, contingent decisions, and the benefits of plans explain how plans can incorporate uncertainty. Stokey and Zeckhauser (1978, 213) suggest that using decision analysis makes a time frame explicit, increases the likelihood of considering the potential of gathering information, and " . . . emphasizes flexibility in contrast to the construction of an immutable master plan." These benefits can be achieved by careful conceptual structuring of decision situations without actually doing any numerical calculations.

5

Plans by and for Voluntary Groups and Governments

Uncertainty about the future is a major factor like land, population and finance to be taken into account when planning. The essential purpose of a plan for a complex activity such as Docklands, where many different people and agencies are involved and where anything one does depends upon others, is to reduce the uncertainty about what other people are going to do and ensure as far as possible that individual actions and decisions combine to achieve the intended objective. The plan will not do this if it is so general that 100 different people can interpret everything it says in 100 different ways. Neither will it do this if it is based on the illusion that all future influences are known, for events will expose the illusion and the plan will lack credibility.
—*Docklands Strategic Plan* (1982), quoted in Marris

The major task of this chapter is to work out and illustrate the implications of many decision makers making decisions about whether to plan and whether to forecast. Why would individuals voluntarily form a group to plan? Why would they ask a government to plan for their own individual actions or the government's actions? Why would residents of a neighborhood choose to participate in a planning effort? Individuals, voluntary groups, and coercive groups such as governments decide to take actions and, therefore, may also decide to make plans. Groups may decide to plan for individual actions. One group may decide to plan for the actions of another group. The decisions to act are distinct from the decisions to plan, but are subject to the same difficulties of individual action and aggregate outcomes.

Situations in Which Plans Are Likely to Be Made

An individual, or unified organization, is likely to make a plan with respect to its own actions if it believes that the cost of making plans is compensated by the gains from considering additional actions before taking immediate action. This abstract explanation is unlikely to be sufficient to fully explain all observed planning behavior, but it is useful to work out the implications of this explanation. Additional explanations, such as social norms in favor of plans, are considered in chapters 7 and 8. Developers plan the size, character, and timing of developments, usually phased to maintain flexibility with respect to timing of demand and changing tastes. Public utilities develop plans for the expansion of services. Retailers plan the locations of stores, considering potential locations for a second and third supermarket before building their first in a new market. Such plans make sense and can be explained in this way. In some cases, the planning process may be sufficiently engaging that some people make plans because it is an exciting activity in its own right without requiring that it have sufficient instrumental value toward improved decisions to justify their participation. Or making plans may be "in fashion."

When individuals plan for urban development, they immediately confront uncertainty about what others will do, which might create incentives to plan together in some way. A story of redevelopment in downtown Urbana, Illinois, illustrates some of the possibilities.[1] In the late 1950s, downtown Urbana's role as a retail center was declining rapidly. The changing situation caused concern in the local business community and the city. Representatives of the private sector investigated alternative approaches to improve the situation. Their efforts eventually resulted in a cooperative project between the city and a private developer to build a covered downtown shopping mall.

Three people were key figures during the initial phase: an attorney, a merchant, and the manager of a downtown hotel. Public officials were also interested in finding a way to revitalize downtown Urbana. In the fall of 1959 a joint committee was formed with representatives of the Urbana City Council, the Urbana Association of Commerce, and the Urbana Economic Development Committee. A subcommittee, which included the three initiators, undertook the major planning effort. The three were important members not only because of their initiative, but also because of their pro-

fessional and social stature and connections. The private sector representatives dominated the planning process during the first phase of the development process. Two of the initiators approached one of the national retail chains with a proposal to expand its existing store in downtown Urbana.
The management of the store showed no interest. Indeed, they indicated
that their own plan was to relocate outside of Urbana. *In this planning activity, a voluntary private group attempted to create alternatives by obtaining information, by considering possibilities, and by obtaining information about the
planned actions of others.*

The realization of the impending loss of the downtown's major anchor
store increased the urgency of the committee's efforts. The subcommittee
subsequently met with the president of Carson Pirie Scott, a Chicago-based
chain of department stores. He was unwilling to commit to the construction of a store in downtown, unless it was part of a larger retail development
with off-street parking. His company paid for a consumer survey to determine the market potential of downtown Urbana. The information obtained
through the survey convinced him that Urbana was a promising retail market. *An individual firm produced information to reduce uncertainty about the environment and about the values of others.*

The involvement of Carson Pirie Scott changed the scope of the project envisioned by the committee. The project now focused on a large-scale
retail development entailing several blocks and requiring the closing of
some streets to through traffic. It was clear that the private sector could not
succeed without the participation of the public sector. Although the public
sector was represented on the joint committee, up to this point it had played
no part and it was not informed about the results of the planning activities
carried on by the subcommittee. Only a few people were aware of the negotiations between members of the subcommittee and Carson Pirie Scott.
Even the mayor of Urbana was unaware of the project until 1961. *These
planning activities were undertaken secretly in the private sector.*[2]

The public sector became an active participant after the project had already progressed quite far. About 80 percent of the land parcels were already secured. The city's power of eminent domain was needed only to conclude the acquisition phase. *The city became involved in the planning only when
its own action, eminent domain, became a necessary element of the project.*

The city's bargaining position was weak. Urbana was about to lose a
major department store after a period of general decline of retail activities

in the downtown. There were no attractive alternatives to accepting the plans presented by the private sector. The involvement of the city in the final stages of the acquisition process led to an overlapping of the acquisition and the approval phase. The city's participation in securing the land constituted a de facto approval of the project. *The role played by the city reduced the uncertainty of whether formal approval could be obtained.*

The shopping mall was completed in 1964. As time went on, other retail development, in particular the opening of a big suburban shopping mall, resulted in renewed difficulties for downtown Urbana. The downtown Urbana shopping mall was not as profitable as anticipated. The difficulties were due in part to the inferior performance of the Urbana-Lincoln Hotel, an old hotel that had been incorporated into the shopping mall. The hotel had been an elegant structure, but like other buildings in the downtown area, it had started to deteriorate. In 1975, the city cited the hotel for building and fire code violations. Its owner, Carson Pirie Scott, put the building up for sale. In 1976, Busey Bank, a large local bank, started negotiations to purchase the building. The bank was expanding and needed additional space to accommodate its growth. Eventually, Busey Bank signed an option to purchase the hotel subject to its obtaining certain concessions from the city. In particular, the bank wanted to buy some city-owned property on lots adjacent to the hotel. *The bank expended considerable money in evaluating this alternative. An option to purchase was used to maintain the alternative while attempting to reduce uncertainty about the actions of the city, which was not yet a party to this planning.*

At about the same time, the city hired a consultant to investigate possible alternatives to revitalize the downtown district; retail sales tax revenues were a major concern. In April 1976 the consultant's recommendations were made public: The shopping mall should expand, the city-owned real estate would be needed for expansion, and an additional street should be closed, cutting off visibility for the proposed bank location. After evaluating these recommendations, tacitly adopted by the city, the bank removed its bid to purchase the hotel and expanded its facilities elsewhere in the downtown. *The city hired a consultant to plan for the possible expansion of a privately owned shopping mall, in part because the city receives sales tax revenues and in part because the city held key land parcels. The information resulting from this planning led to the city's decision to hold on to some of its land parcels in order to preserve its options to act in the future.*

These events in downtown Urbana illustrate ways in which many actors plan, both individually and collectively and in the private and public sectors. Actors invest in planning to reduce uncertainty about available alternatives, values, the environment, and actions of others. They tend to focus on information pertinent to their own immediate actions, though some of this information is jointly valuable to others. The information resulting from planning and the fact that planning is occurring may be kept secret. Information may not be shared even though others know that planning is occurring, or information may be shared as planning occurs. Plans are worth making when there are interdependent decisions, indivisible actions, irreversible actions, and imperfect foresight. Such plans are not, however, straightforwardly comprehensive; there may not be any formal document. The scope and horizon of plans tend to fit the needs of decisions. It is clearly important to understand how the many individuals who are planning might interact.

The Chicago Plan of 1909 was created by a voluntary group of leading businessmen, was claimed to benefit all individuals in Chicago, and was turned over to the local government for implementation. The content of the agenda is what would be expected in a plan provided by private funding from business leaders. The interests most completely and directly addressed are those of the small, leadership core of a large public coalition, which was expanded through one of the most elaborate public education campaigns ever launched for a plan. The immediate agenda of the commercial group was claimed to be in the interest of the larger public because the votes of residents were needed to pass bond issues required to carry out the plan.

The plan evolved from the activities of the group involved in designing and carrying out the Chicago World's Fair of 1893. Two businessmen's clubs initiated the effort and later merged into the Commercial Club of Chicago. These businessmen saw the plan as similar to managing their businesses, and thus as something they knew how to do, even if it was being done in part for the benefit of the city.

Cost estimates seem to conflict, but Moody (1919, 359) indicates that the Commercial Club subscribed $85,000 "for the original work on the Plan. This sum was for the actual creation of a technical plan and for the publication of the club's magnificent Plan report." Burnham donated his own time. The mayor appointed a commission of 328 leading citizens with

Charles H. Wacker as chair and an executive committee of 27 to study the plan and inform citizens about its content (Walker 1950, 235).

Walter Moody was hired as a "hustler" to promote the plan. He developed a pamphlet distributed throughout the city to property owners and those paying greater than $25 a month rent. He authored *Wacker's Manual of the Plan of Chicago* (Moody 1912), which became part of the eighth-grade curriculum in city schools. Moody advocated strongly in his book *What of the City?* that promotion of a plan was essential. In contrast to the $85,000 subscribed to develop the plan, the Commercial Club provided within the first ten years of implementation another $218,000 to promote the plan and the city provided another $100,000 for technical work of the commission (Moody 1919, 359). They spent more to promote the plan than to create it, which reinforces the interpretation of the plan as a businessmen's agenda for public improvements. These were improvements they had neither the resources nor the authority to accomplish, but the city had both bonding power and eminent domain.

In both the Urbana and Chicago cases, voluntary groups formed to initiate plans, but these groups turned to governments because government powers were needed to implement the plans. These instances of plan creation, advocacy, and implementation can be interpreted in terms of the powers and abilities of voluntary groups and coercive governments to provide collective goods.

Collective Goods and Collective Action

A lighthouse is a collective good. It signals danger at the same cost regardless of how many ships are looking at it. Therefore, consumption of its services is "nonrival." If it is available for one ship to see, it is available for all ships to see. Therefore exclusion from its services is "infeasible." Goods or services for which consumption is nonrival and for which exclusion is infeasible are called collective or public goods.[3] Another frequently used example of a collective good is national defense, which emphasizes the point that a collective good is always collective to some particular group.

Many interesting instances of collective goods involve some rivalry and the potential for exclusion at very high cost. Highways are nonrival below peak capacity but become rival due to congestion as traffic increases. Such instances are called collective goods with congestion. Users can be excluded

Game 5-1

Collective good

		Investor Two	
		Join	Don't Join
Investor One	Join	2.5, 2.5	–5, 10
	Don't join	10, –5	0, 0

from highways by toll gates at least for long trips or unusual connections such as bridges. Such instances are called "toll goods." On grazing lands in the western United States, it is difficult to enforce exclusion because these lands are too extensive to fence or patrol, but the use is clearly rival because there is a limited carrying capacity. If too many animals graze, the available grass is used up faster than it can regenerate itself. Such instances are called "common pool" resources.

The basic dilemma is that no one has an incentive to pay the costs to provide an appropriate quantity of a collective good because once provided, everyone else can use it without paying any of the costs. The "prisoner's dilemma" game, so called because of the story traditionally used in describing it, frames the collective good problem.[4] Assume the collective good is a highway from a suburb to the city. There are two investors who are investing in land development in the suburb. Each can choose to join, in building the highway jointly or not to join, as shown in Game 5-1.

If both investors join together and each pays half of the 15-unit cost of the highway from which each benefits 10 units, then each has a net benefit of 2.5. If either investor chooses not to build, then the cost for the solo builder is 15 and the benefit for the individual is 10 for a net benefit of –5. The other investor cannot, however, be excluded from benefiting, so the other investor has a net benefit of 10. If neither investor builds the highway, there are no benefits or costs so that each has net benefits of zero. This configuration of net benefits constitutes a prisoner's dilemma game. Each investor should choose not to build because, regardless of what the other does, the return from not building is greater. The outcome of 0,0 that thus results is, however, less desirable than the outcome of 2.5, 2.5 that could result if both invested in the highway.

If there were only two persons and communication were possible, they might find a way to commit to participate and thus arrive at 2.5, 2.5. The logic of collective goods, however, is most telling for large numbers when the problem of providing persuasive commitment is difficult at best. Even if this were a many person game in which the cost were, say, 1,000 units and the benefits to each individual were 1, the individual logic of behavior would be the same. Each individual would choose not to build. But for any group larger than 1,000, with the costs equally shared, the benefits to each individual would be greater if the facility were built.

Even if an individual knows what other individuals claim they will do, it is advantageous to defect from participation in providing the collective good. The problem is not one of information or of coordination in the sense of shared information. It is instead a problem of commitment, which can be solved by (1) individuals being able to signal a credible commitment, (2) forming voluntary groups, or (3) forming coercive groups such as governments. Repeated interaction among participants and the ability to detect and punish or exclude a defector are fundamental to all three solutions. First, we focus on signals of individual commitment, based primarily on *Passions within Reason* by Robert Frank (1988). Then we consider group formation.

If I know that you cannot look me straight in the eye and lie, or that you cannot lie without blushing, then your inability to lie without blushing is a commitment mechanism. In any specific instance, you will wish that you could lie without blushing, but you will benefit from this inability by saving resources that would otherwise be necessary to persuade me that you are telling the truth. In cases in which monitoring of your behavior is not feasible, you might be prevented from participating if you lacked this inability to hide a lie. Emotions such as anger and guilt serve these functions. Even though my culture may teach me to repress anger as unproductive, an expectation of my temper may preclude it being needed. As Frank (1988) points out, many transgressions, such as petty theft or harassment, would be rational for a perpetrator who believed that the victim would respond rationally. It would not be worth the victim's time to carry through with retaliation or other modes of deterrence or prevention. But if I am believed to be irrational about dealing with minor harassment, it is less likely to occur in my jurisdiction. Similarly, feelings of guilt serve to monitor my own commitments. Emotions that you cannot control are valuable resources for commitment.

Empirical observation (Rapaport and Chammah 1965) and decision rule simulations (Axelrod 1981) suggest that the best strategy in playing the prisoner's dilemma repeatedly against the same opponent is to cooperate. If your opponent does not cooperate, then on the next turn and only for one turn, retaliate by defecting. This approach leads to stable cooperative outcomes, at least if the players believe that repetitions of the game will continue indefinitely. This strategy is one explanation of the benefits of small groups. They increase the likelihood of repeated interactions with individually identifiable players against whom selective retaliation can occur in similar, if not identical, repetitions of the collective good situation.

The more elaborate form of repeated interaction is the confirmation of emotional traits of commitment. These traits must be identified with particular individuals. The commitment explanation thus works even when defection cannot be detected and the retaliation strategy cannot be implemented. Confidence in loyalty is enhanced by shared experience. If persons move frequently from place to place, then the likelihood of developing cohesive groups decreases. This disadvantage of mobility counters the benefits of mobility in adjusting to new conditions such as new locations of jobs as the economy restructures. A mobile society may gain by eliminating adjustment lags, but it will also need to allocate resources to solve commitment problems that were previously solved by repeated interaction in cohesive groups (Frank 1988). Fukuyama (1995) argues that societies vary in the amount of trust of other persons, especially unrelated persons, and thus vary in their "spontaneous sociability," their ability to form voluntary groups, especially large ones. The emotions and related traits that solve commitment problems are part of the capital of a society.

The commitment logic also sets the basis for the formation of groups that will successfully provide collective goods. The classic argument is in *The Logic of Collective Action* (Olson 1965). Group size and the pattern of relative benefit among group members are crucial predictors of whether groups will form to provide collective goods.

In very small groups, interpersonal commitment may be sufficient. Repeated interaction with an identifiable individual or a few such individuals combines the effects of emotional commitment and the potential to use retaliation. Each individual will know other individuals well enough to judge whether each will fulfill the commitment to an agreement. In the smallest groups, one individual may gain sufficiently from the collective good to justify providing it, even if others did not participate. Even if no one individual can justify providing it alone, each individual provides such a large fraction of the total cost that all other members would immediately recognize and have reason to react to the withdrawal of any one member.

Groups may also form by a logic equivalent to oligopoly. Individuals are more likely to come together if the net benefits differ among individuals. If one individual benefits greatly, though not sufficiently to provide the good alone, and this fact is observable by others in the group, then that individual is an identifiable leader. In neighborhood groups that form voluntarily to fight proposals such as highways and landfills, the leaders are usually those most immediately affected because they are closest to the intrusion. Given the recognition that an obvious leader is identifiable, others will be persuaded that a group can form. The group will face organizational costs to bring its concerns to bear and these will be less if the group is smaller, if individual leadership roles in the group are self-evident, and if the individuals have some prior social affinity (Olson 1965). A group of downtown business people will readily form around the leadership of the largest retail operator or the largest landowner, especially if these people are members of the same clubs, churches, or other social groups. Membership in other social groups can also be used to impose social status benefits on those who participate, and to retaliate against those who do not.

For large groups, in which the contribution to the collective good by any one individual is so small that it will not be noticeable to others, the above mechanisms are unlikely to be sufficient to provide collective goods. Selective incentives or coercion will be needed. Selective incentives provide some benefit from which nonparticipants can be excluded, thus a benefit distinct from the collective good. The ubiquitous insurance policies, travel programs, and publications associated with large voluntary groups serve this function. I can be persuaded to join a professional organization that lobbies for the interests of the planning profession (a collective good) in part by receiving a magazine as an individual benefit (a private or individual good).

Governments are coercive groups that claim a monopoly on the legitimate use of force. Once formed, membership is enforced through formal punishments of fines or imprisonment. As Olson (1965, 13) points out, ". . . despite the force of patriotism, the appeal of the national ideology, the bond of a common culture, and the indispensability of the system of law and order, no major state in modern history has been able to support itself through voluntary dues or contributions." People may choose to become members of coercive groups to obtain collective goods that would otherwise not be provided. The degree to which individuals choose, or would choose, to be members of coercive groups is a major question of the philosophy of social justice and of the practical questions of legitimacy of national governments. Empirically, taxes require coercion in some form. Selective incentives, social affinity, repeated interaction, and emotions reduce the costs of direct enforcement but have never been sufficient alone. Regulations are enforceable, however, only if the coercive group can be sustained.

The concept of collective goods is confounded with the logic of plans in several ways. Plans, in general, cannot resolve the problem of collective goods. Of the five ways in which plans work, only vision or agenda aspects might affect trust or attitudes in a way that would create commitment. Plans used in these ways, are usually used by one group to persuade others of a point of view, not as a mechanism for achieving mutual commitment to provision of a collective good. The logic of regulation and collective action is thus distinct from the logic of plans. The distinction is subtle but important. This analytical distinction does not mean that the repeated interaction that may occur as plans are developed does not or cannot also play a role in increasing trust and thus commitment to providing collective goods. This role of repeated interaction or deliberation is true, however, of any kind of decision activity and thus does not help to understand plans as plans.

This distinction does not mean that plans cannot address regulations among the interdependent decisions for which the plan is made. It is the regulation, not the plan, that resolves the difficulty of providing collective goods. A regulation may require landowners to pay fees to a drainage district to cover the costs of maintaining drainage ditches, which are a collective good to landowners of the drained area. The size of these fees, alternative drainage networks, and patterns of impervious surface that affect the quantity of runoff might all be considered as interdependent decisions in a plan. It is still the regulation requiring payment of fees, not the plan, that resolves the collective good. These analytical distinctions are useful because they are precise about what plans can do as plans.

Asymmetric Information and Signaling

If I am trying to sell you a house, I have the opportunity to know aspects of its quality that you do not. In this transaction, information available to the two parties is asymmetric. You can observe obvious characteristics, but to learn more you must expend resources for a detailed inspection, including perhaps an inspection of local ordinances, capital improvement programs, tax proposals, and neighborhood lore. You consider what information is implied in the actions of others and whether observable prices present useful information. Information is a central element in how plans work, so alternative sources of such information must be considered.

Akerloff (1970) described the "market for lemons" using the example of used cars, but it applies to used housing as well. If I am the seller and know that my house has no hidden flaws (is a "peach"), I would be better off if I could convince you, the buyer, of that distinction. If I know my house has hidden flaws (is a "lemon"), I am better off if you do not find out. Because it is costly for you to discover hidden flaws, the price for both the high-quality and the low-quality house will tend to be the same. One reason to sell a house is to get rid of a lemon—say a house in an area with infrastructure problems so that the backyard floods and the sanitary sewers back up. Other reasons might be to obtain a larger house or to move out of town. The buyer cannot distinguish the lemon from the peach, so the buyer will pay the average price for a house of a given type in a market with some "peaches" and some "lemons."

The buyer or seller might choose to pay for a "signal," additional information to distinguish good houses from bad. A house owner who knows that the house has no flaws may hire a credible, independent inspector to say so. The buyer has no reason to believe the seller directly, because the seller has little to lose by lying. This seller is unlikely to sell another house in this market. The inspector, however, would not be able to get future inspection jobs if reports were not validated by the ensuing experience of buyers. If, however, sellers of "peaches" hire inspectors, then this behavior itself will signal that other houses are "lemons." Buyers will infer that any house that does not come with an inspection certificate must be flawed or the owner would have had it inspected. Owners of slightly flawed houses will then have an incentive to hire inspectors so as to distinguish themselves from the "real" lemons. This phenomenon is familiar in the offering of guarantees to distinguish product quality. If the product is not good, the seller cannot afford to back up the guarantee. A product without a guarantee is a signal of low quality.

If such information becomes available, then the sale prices of houses will be differentiated on account of differences in quality. The prices themselves will thus provide at least part of the necessary information. This phenomenon returns us to the problem of collective goods. If, when some buyers or sellers pay for information, this results in pricing changes that signal this information to others, the information takes on characteristics of a collective good. The information each buyer wants is the same. A buyer who pays for the information gains by getting the more accurate price relative to actual quality of the house, but in doing so the price will be observable by others. If there is an area with an infrastructure deficit, will the prices differentiate it from other areas of the city? The sellers will not want to distinguish themselves because they hold hidden flaws. Buyers will, however, underinvest in information because they will act as if others had obtained information on which they can free-ride by relying only on price. If these claims are fulfilled, prices will not differentiate areas with infrastructure problems from areas with good infrastructure.

Signaling interacts not only with prices but also with regulations. Frank (1988, 107) cites the example of regulations that prevent employers from asking questions about marital status when interviewing job applicants. If candidates know that the employer prefers unmarried candidates, then those who are not married will gain by voluntarily identifying themselves as unmarried. The employer can thus infer that anyone who does not freely volunteer such information is married. The employer need ask no questions and thus follows the regulation, but the regulation is rendered ineffective. This is an example of "counterregulatory behavior." A correct prediction of the effect of a regulation must consider the behavioral responses it will induce and the effect of these responses on outcomes (Hopkins 1984a).

If the forecast of growth is useful to many municipalities, private developers, banks, home buyers, school districts, and so on, which ones will have an incentive to participate in providing a forecast? They may be able to observe the actions of others and infer forecasts from these actions. It thus becomes crucial to know whether others have forecasted, but observing their actions may be sufficient to infer the forecast. For these reasons, plans and forecasts in such situations are likely to be collective goods.

Plans as Collective Goods

Plans, or normative forecasts, are sometimes collective goods. Consider the following situation. A private sector firm or a public sector agency is con-

Game 5-2
Informed and uninformed decisions

		Player Two	
		Join	*Don't Join*
Player One	Join	8, *8*	6, *10*
	Don't join	10, *6*	7, 7

sidering the construction of a subdivision or the infrastructure to support one. The decision to initiate such a project depends on an expectation about demand for such housing, and this demand must be forecasted to occur over several years in order to build the major pieces of infrastructure and initiate a large subdivision.

If one developer decides to make a plan, then that developer will obtain new probabilities for various levels of demand. If there are many developers, the result of this decision to plan will benefit many other developers. It will be difficult to keep the results of the plan secret because in order to benefit from the plan, the developer who paid for it must decide what action to take, which other developers could then observe. If a developer is known to have planned, then other developers can benefit by imitating that developer's actions. In this case the plan is a collective good. Use of the plan is nonrival because other developers can use the same information simultaneously, or nearly so. Exclusion is infeasible if it is known that a plan was made because its content can be inferred from observable actions.

This situation can be represented as shown in Game 5-2. The payoff is 10 from the development decision that would be made if the player is informed of the plan results and is 7 if the player is not. The cost of making the plan is 4, and the results can be obtained either by paying for it or by observing what another developer does. If both players pay, they split the cost. The dominant strategy is then not to join in paying for the plan. If there were many such developers, then no group would be likely to form to make a plan without coercion or external inducements as discussed above. These ideas are analyzed further using game theory in Hopkins (1981). If there were only a few developers with different gains from the plan, such as different-sized developments or differences in locations, then the leader-follower behavior of oligopoly might occur, with the largest developer lead-

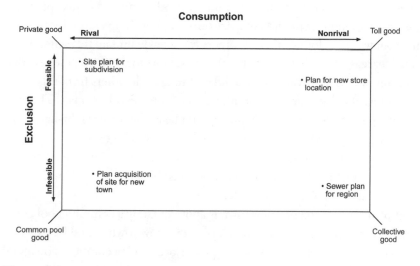

Figure 5-1
Attributes of plans as collective goods

ing the formation of a voluntary group. The large developer gains almost enough to make it worth making a plan on its own, so it has the incentive to put the effort in to collecting small amounts from others to fully compensate the cost of making the plan. Other developers recognize the obvious leader and are willing to follow.

The implication is that in many situations, because of these collective good characteristics, the level of investment in making plans will be lower than it should be. In general, therefore, plans would be underprovided without collective action responses of the kind described above. Different plan-making and forecasting situations are, however, likely to fall in different places with respect to the two dimensions of collective goods: rival consumption to nonrival (or joint) consumption and feasible exclusion to infeasible exclusion as illustrated in Figure 5-1.[5]

A site plan for a single subdivision is a private good because its content yields little or no useful information to other developers. To be useful for one subdivision, it must be specific to that land area, which means consumption is rival and others can be excluded from benefiting from it.

A plan for locating a store is partly nonrival in consumption and infeasible to exclude others from its benefit. For most types of stores, there is an agglomeration economy in locating near other stores because of multi-purpose shopping trips and comparison shopping. If one store locator figures out where to locate and acts, others can quickly imitate this action without decreasing the benefit to the first locator, which means that consumption is nonrival. It is also difficult to exclude others from this benefit because the first store locator must act and thus reveal the plan. This case is not a pure collective good (which would be at the lower right-hand corner of the diagram) because the first locator might buy excess land and sell it to later locators at its now greater value and thus recoup at least part of the cost of making the plan. Consumption is thus in part rival and, by this means, exclusion becomes feasible.

A plan for location of a new town is approximately a common pool good. In contrast, a plan for the internal layout of a new town would be a private good equivalent to a subdivision site plan. Location is a common pool good because ability to acquire all parcels at reasonable cost without holdouts requires acquisition in secrecy. Consumption is thus rival, because if anyone else learns of the plan, its benefits to its creator are greatly reduced. Exclusion is, however, difficult because of the large number of acquisition transactions, which are difficult to hide and from which others could infer enough to raise their asking price. Acquisition of land for Columbia, Maryland, managed to overcome this problem by acquiring land under different names through different agents, but it is the exception that proves the rule. Other attempts to create new towns on many land parcels have involved government powers of regulation and eminent domain.

An area plan, or specific plan as it is called in California, can be a toll good in which consumption is nonrival but exclusion is feasible. The content of the plan is specific to a particular area, and thus exclusion is feasible if there are only a few developers, each dealing with a large portion of the area being planned. In this case, a government that requires such plans can charge each developer for a share of the cost, which frequently happens in California (Olshansky 1996).

Finally, a major infrastructure plan for a metropolitan area is a collective good because its content must be shared among many developers, infrastructure providers, and municipalities over a long period of time in order to be useful to anyone who would pay to make such a plan. The plan contents are thus nonrival in consumption and exclusion is infeasible. It is still not likely to be a perfect collective good because those who participate in paying for it are more likely to be able to influence its content to their own advantage. Others will still have to follow the plan once conceived because it will determine to a large extent where infrastructure occurs and thus what land is developable. Land speculators are likely to have incentives to participate in such plans.

The benefits of plans for infrastructure can be elaborated by considering the plans of sewers (Knaap et al. 1998). One possibility is that the plan is devised considering land use patterns and sewer network layout and capacity. The strategy of information in the plan might then be used only by the sewer provider, which would monitor its own investments and land development and build increments to the network following a contingent path implied by the plan. In this first case the land developers would simply respond to the construction of sewers and not actually use the information in the plans directly in making their own decisions. This case would make sense if the lead time required for land development was short relative to the lead time for sewer construction. There is then no advantage in knowing where sewers will be located because the developer can wait for the announcement of the construction of the sewers. Clearly, a speculator buying land can gain with this asymmetric information about the value of land, information that the seller does not have. Thus speculators might use the information in plans, but developers would not. Speculators and developers may sometimes be the same people, but the roles are distinct. A speculator does not need to make a commitment to the use or pattern of development, but a developer does. A developer thus needs more specific information than a speculator, but may benefit from more specific information with a shorter lead time than a speculator. In this case we should expect new information in plans to affect speculation and thus land sales transactions, but not development actions such as subdivision or building permits. That is, if a plan is changed or becomes public, we should expect speculators, not developers, to use it.

A second possibility is that additional benefits can be gained from the plan developed by the sewer provider if developers use information in the plan. These benefits would occur if the developer could be more accurate in choices or more efficient in timing by using information about expected timing and capacity of sewers before sewer construction occurred. If the lead time for land development were longer than the construction time for sewers, then there would be some concurrency gains because sewer capacity would be used more quickly. Also, if the lead time for development were long, this might preclude mismatches in the construction of land use density and the construction of sewer capacity. If developers are committed to uses and densities before sewers are built, but are not watching the expected capacity, then either the developer or the sewer provider will have to pay the costs of increasing the capacity or the costs of excess capacity without expected revenues to cover its operations. These two aspects of losses can be summarized as short-run concurrency and long-run congruence of capacity. Note that plans and lead times affect both situations because of the durability and irreversibility of both the sewers and the land development.

In this second case we would expect developers to consult sewer plans and we should expect new information in sewer plans, if it was about relatively short time horizons of, say, five years, to affect developer decisions evidenced by subdivision approvals or equivalent indicators for multifamily or commercial projects. The sewer provider has an incentive to share the plan because that would increase the likelihood of concurrency and more precise matching of capacity. The question here is whether the lead times and interdependence of actions involved in planning for sewers are so different from the lead times and interdependence of relationships to land development that a dependence relation is sufficient. In the dependence case, the sewer provider gains by predicting the land use demand, but the developer need not predict sewer capacity. If the lead times for sewers and land development are similar, however, the relationship will be interdependent and both can gain by predicting the other.

Despite high-resolution data, we have had difficulty demonstrating that land developers were reacting to information in plans for the westside light-rail in Portland, Oregon (Knaap et al. 1996). Looking at the evolution of the plans over the preceding twenty-five years, the general corridor remained fairly predictable but the precise alignment and the station locations changed as plans were revised and refined. It may be that the information in the plan was not sufficiently precise, or credible, to be useful to developers. The interdependence logic of the light-rail plan—what it connects and what kind of land uses and densities occur near stations—was sustained over the twenty-five years. Further evidence that developers would not simply respond to information in the plan is that immediately upon committing to station locations, overlay zones were imposed to regulate land uses and densities in the station locations. Speculators had a game to play and take risks in. Developers apparently could not take advantage of any lead time in constructing the station land uses because there was not sufficient certainty to risk investment. The losses would be the lead time to get uses constructed, and since the light-rail itself took almost four years to build once stations were committed, land development could respond easily with this lead time. The other possible loss would be land use patterns created before the station locations were committed that would have been built differently if the station locations had been considered. These uses may eventually change to different uses or higher densities, but there will be a time lag until the costs of conversion can be absorbed after the current capital has depreciated. This is another instance of the Ohls and Pines development timing problem.

Initial observations of lag times of residential construction after sewer construction in the southwest portion of the Portland metropolitan region appear to be long enough—five to ten years—that the land developers would not have gained from using the plan directly (Hanley 1999). Developers could react to construction of sewers as construction occurred. For construction of sewers, the contingent logic of the sewer plan was followed. There were major changes because the changes in federal funding programs in the early 1970s, just after the 1969 plan was completed, encouraged fewer, larger, regional treatment plants. Thus, in this case the plan was apparently of use to the sewer provider but not to developers. The plan may have been of use to speculators.

Voluntary Groups and Government Inducements to Make Plans

This section describes situations and cases of plan making that can be explained in terms of collective goods. These are not necessarily uniquely valid explanations, but they provide useful insight and suggest reasonable expectations for similar situations. They thus help to understand and to inform prescriptive recommendations for organizing decision making about when to make plans.

Much of the planning for land development has been and continues to be the work of private individuals or corporations or of voluntary groups, including voluntary groups that include both private and government members. This pattern of planning is not at all unusual, as suggested by the

Chicago Plan of 1909 and two additional examples presented here: development in DuPage County, Illinois, in the 1970s, and forecasting efforts of the Northeastern Illinois Planning Commission.

O'Mara (1973) describes the roles of various different local governments and development corporations in the planning of major new development focused on four thousand acres near Aurora and Naperville, Illinois, about forty miles west of Chicago. The parcel was purchased in secrecy in 1966 by Urban Investment and Development Corporation (UIDC) for a community, Fox Valley East, to be built over twenty years. When city officials learned of the project in about 1970, it raised many issues of planning by whom and for whom. Two cities, Aurora and Naperville, became competitors for the tax base potential of a major retail project. Availability of professional staff, discussions among planners working for different governments and private developers, an Aurora Area Technical Liaison Group led by UIDC as an oligopolistic group to provide common planning services to the local governments and developers, and differences in trust placed in staff by different political leaders all affected the outcomes.

In its Annual Report for 1990, the Northeastern Illinois Planning Commission (1990) provides a cogent description of the nature of its population forecasting efforts, how these are of value to its constituencies, and how they affect its ability to raise voluntary contributions. The Commission is a voluntary group of local governments and private individuals, and it provides various planning services. Forecast accuracy is, perhaps, distinct from forecast usefulness, but the forecasts are clearly seen as being collective goods in which sufficient resources will be invested to achieve appropriate quality if voluntary contributions are increased. The offer to tailor forecasts to needs of individual members can be explained as selective incentives for individual members to encourage contributions to a collective good.

The fundamental problem of collective goods is that individuals acting alone are unlikely to provide as much of the collective good as they would want if they could enforce participation to share in providing it. This does not mean that the group formed to decide how much of the collective good to provide must produce the collective good. Once the amount to be provided has been determined, the group can contract with a private firm to provide the agreed-on amount of the good. This applies to the provision of a plan as a collective good and, in particular, to the provision of plans by local governments. A voluntary group or a local government need not produce its own plan.

A small community may demand planning activities too infrequently to have specialists employed full-time. In such circumstances it makes sense to have a consultant "on retainer," meaning that you pay only for the amount of service you need. You work with the same person so you can build up a working relationship, but that person also works elsewhere, therefore taking advantage of specialization to develop and maintain a high level of skill and up-to-date knowledge. A large city is likely to employ planners for those activities that become regular and repeated, but may still hire specialized consultants for irregular tasks. In a medium-sized city, a downtown plan or solid waste plan might be contracted out to a consultant because these activities are not conducted frequently enough to justify maintaining in-house expertise. Subdivision review, zoning review, and rezoning proposals might, however, be maintained in-house because these activities are conducted frequently. In a larger city, all these items might be in-house.

An alternative to hiring consultants for small communities is to form a regional planning commission, but not primarily to plan for the region as a region. Instead, its primary purpose is to achieve economies of scale in producing planning services for a group of communities. The regional agency could justify hiring specialists in transportation planning, neighborhood planning, infrastructure, and land use, which none of the individual municipalities could justify alone. Regional agencies are subject to alternative explanations. Is the task of the regional agency to plan for a unitary region? Or, is the task to plan as a collective good for the member municipalities? Or, is it to produce plans for municipalities in order to gain economies of scale and specialization? All three may apply.

In the United States, local governments make most of the public-sector decisions about whether to make plans. They make these decisions based in part on their own perceptions of the benefits and costs of making plans, but these benefits and costs are significantly affected by federal and state incentives and regulations.

At various times the federal government in the United States and the national government in England decided that local governments were not of their own initiative making sufficient plans. They enacted incentives or requirements to plan in order to receive central government benefits such as funding for infrastructure. These incentives also resulted in prescriptions of what constituted good plans sufficient to meet the requirements of these acts. This approach could, and many argue did, result in a mismatch between the requirements for plans and the usefulness of plans to local governments.

> Experience in England since the passage of the 1947 Town and Country Planning Act, and in the United States since 1949 when Congress imposed the requirements of a general physical-development plan as a condition for federal financial aid for city planning, provides convincing evidence that we are once again in the midst of a period when higher levels of government will attempt to specify, for their own purposes, what they consider to be the essential uses and characteristics of the general plan and the contents of the official general-plan document. . . . Because the contents and characteristics of the urban general plan are now actually being defined by federal regulations, everything possible should be done—for the sake of the state and federal programs as well as for the success of local programs—to encourage municipal governments to do their own thinking and make their own decisions on general-plan questions, and to do so, always, on the basis of their own technical and political needs. (Kent 1964, 130–131)

Kent notes that a special booklet was published in Cambridge, England, to explain their plan in a way that was locally useful but possible only outside statutory guidelines "because the official plan document adopted by the Council, which had to comply with national regulations, was simply not useful locally" (131).

From approximately 1949 to 1981, the federal government required local governments to produce plans as a condition of receiving funding under various programs for urban development and transportation. From 1954, federal funding was also available to create these plans. Referred to as "701 plans" because they were required by Section 701 of the Housing Act of 1954, these plans were produced by municipal staff or by consultants with standardized content and format to meet the guidelines. The primary logic and local government motivation was to meet the requirement for a plan in order to qualify for federal funding. Feiss (1985) notes that most larger cities had adequate planning programs and plans without the federal intervention. Although there was a drop in planning employment with the end of

701, local government planning was by then well established and, in general, continues based on other motivations.

Several states also require local governments to plan. California has the longest record of such requirements, but Florida, Oregon, and more recently Washington have more stringent requirements and oversight of the substance of local plans. California specifies what elements must be covered; Oregon specifies what goals must be sought. Oregon and Washington require metropolitan areas or cities to establish growth boundaries. One interpretation of the effect of the growth boundary in Portland, Oregon, is that it serves as a regulation of municipalities by the Metro regional government. Metro has no power to zone, which might be a more appropriate tool to achieve some of its objectives, but it does control the growth boundary. The growth boundary in turn affects the municipalities and counties, which do have the power to zone. The growth boundary can thus be interpreted not as a direct regulation of developers but as a regulation of local governments by regional government because the regulation affects the content of local government plans. Florida requires communities to establish and implement concurrency requirements for adequate infrastructure before permitting development.[6]

Federal funds have also induced other more specialized plan making. The model cities program in the 1960s and the competition for designation as Empowerment Zones in the 1990s induced particular types of neighborhood planning and community organizing. Transportation planning has been subsidized by federal funds, most recently through the Intermodal Surface Transportation Efficiency Act and its extensions.

Governments induce planning by the private sector for public sector interests. A recent planning process for light-rail in Taipei, Taiwan, illustrates an example. Private investors were invited to bid for a "Build, Operate, and Transfer" project to build a light-rail system, operate it for fifteen or twenty years, then transfer it to the government. The basic requirement is that the system must connect the international airport with the downtown. Within this constraint, the route and station locations are open to alternative strategies developed by bidders. Thus the bidders have an incentive to plan an effective system that they can manage and operate efficiently. It is also clear that a winning bid must require less government financing, which will be achieved in part through real estate development by the bidder in conjunction with rail stations. Thus the process creates incentives to devise inter-dependent land use and transportation actions because the potential gains accrue to the bidder. Thus the bidders have incentives to plan, and to plan for relationships among infrastructure and land use even though the infra-structure will be funded in large part by government and will require gov-ernment participation to obtain right-of-way. This case is reminiscent of streetcar development in the United States in the late nineteenth century (Warner 1978) or of the Shaker Rapid Transit from downtown Cleveland, Ohio, to Shaker Heights in the 1920s (Garvin 1996, 330–331), though in these cases there was not a prior expectation of transfer of the transit lines to government.

Summary: Who Has Incentives to Plan and for Whom?

Individual plans occur when individual actors invest to plan for their own decisions, as when a developer plans where, when, and what to develop in a subdivision. Public sector plans occur when government agencies plan for their own actions, as when a state highway department plans which high-ways to build where, when, and with what capacity. Plans by voluntary groups occur when several actors jointly invest in plans, as when a com-mercial club hires a downtown development consultant or a group of de-velopers hires a transportation planning consultant to consider transporta-tion among developments. Regulations or incentives for plans occur when an enforceable requirement is applied, as when communities are required to develop plans before being eligible for government grants or when fi-nancing for plans by localities is provided as a merit good by the federal or state government.

All of these circumstances occur frequently. Making plans for urban de-velopment is not inherently a public sector or a group activity. It does focus on relationships among decisions, but it does not require or necessarily in-volve all the decision makers who have authority over those related deci-sions. Providing plans in these different modes leads to different types of plans and different distributions of planning costs. These ideas explain who has incentives to plan and for whom, and thus suggest situations in which plans are likely to occur.

The concept of collective goods helps to explain these situations. The need to address collective goods is often used to justify planning as a general idea and thus implicitly to justify plans (see e.g., Moore 1978), but plans seldom serve this role directly. The fundamental notion of a collective good is that *even with perfect information but lacking mechanisms for commitment*, individuals will not act to provide the appropriate amount of the collective good. Plans add information but do not change the rights to make decisions. Regulations, on the other hand, change the decision situation by limiting options or reframing the question organizationally to deal with collective goods or collective good externalities. Plans are a response not to the market failure of collective goods or to the political problem of collective choice but to the more fundamental problems of interdependence, indivisibility, irreversibility, and imperfect foresight.

6

Rights, Regulations, and Plans

The western painter, Charles Russell, has portrayed a dramatic interaction between cowboy and Indian during a mid-1800s trail drive through Indian territory [shown in frontispiece in original]. The cowboys are bringing cattle from the western ranches to the rail heads for shipment to the population centers of the East. The Indian is seen signaling to the trail boss as other Indians are cutting from the herd a cow that will be taken back to the tribe for food. But what is going on in the minds of the participants? Is it theft? A prize of battle? Or is it a gift or act of charity? Does the cow represent the payment of a tax to a sovereign with the Indian as tax collector? Or has a trade been consummated where the Indian has agreed to allow passage and use of his land in return for a negotiated rental payment?

The physical movement alone tells us nothing about the intangible relationships between the parties or about the thoughts of the participants. Yet these relationships and perceptions have something to do with tangible consequences. They may effect [sic] the production of the beef, grazing practices, and of course, the relative distribution of wealth.

—A. Allan Schmid (1978), *Property, Power and Public Choice*

In Snowmass, Colorado, developers, local residents, and vacation-home owners had different rights with which to affect development and hire planning services (Hopkins and Schaeffer 1983). A small group of new permanent residents led a drive to incorporate the community so that a local government would have powers to plan and regulate land development. The developer, who was the major landowner, and the vacation-home owners, who had no right to vote locally, used other strategies of group formation to achieve their objectives. The newly incorporated town, the private developer, and the ski company that provided the major attraction and economic base for the town shared the cost of a plan. A local government, which is a coercive group, thus played a particular role as a member of a voluntary group organized to undertake planning. The differences in rights in this case were crucial. Only permanent residents had rights to vote in a local municipality. Seasonal residents, the developer, and the ski company did not. Thus, regulations were determined, directly at least, only by permanent residents. The ski company leased land from the federal government for the ski slopes. The developer had acquired most of the land in the valley, but had sold lots to residents and others. The mix of rights in land and rights to vote affected both the making of plans and the enactment of local regulations. Private planning, voluntary groups forming to plan, and local governments newly incorporated in order to take land use actions also characterized a similar situation in Sanibel Island, Florida (Babcock and Siemon 1985; Johnson 1989).

Plans for urban development set out contingent, interdependent actions that will yield desirable patterns of development. These actions include regulations, such as zoning, subdivision regulations, and official maps. Urban planners are involved in land use regulation, but it is important to distinguish between plans and regulations. This chapter considers systems of rights related to land, how these rights affect who plans what, how regulations change these rights, and how plans provide the basis for such regulations. In general, regulations are enacted by a collective choice mechanism as discussed in chapter 8.

Regulations modify or establish some dimension of rights and are usually thought of as defining rights granted by social norms, formal constitutions, or laws, though any distinction is at best fuzzy. Regulations may thus formalize social norms into explicit rights or make changes in rights. The logic that might explain the creation of a constitution is similar to the logic that would explain the choice to regulate (see e.g., Ostrom et al. 1994). Clarification of rights occurs through interpretation of legal precedent, legislation, and administrative regulations. This chapter focuses on regulations as changes in rights within a given cultural and constitutional frame. Intentional efforts to change cultural norms are considered further in chapter 7. Such efforts may be substitutable for changes in rights because norms also affect behavior and condition the behavior in response to regulations.

Rights to Decide

The cow being cut from the herd makes clear the multiple possible interpretations of even one apparent acknowledgment of rights.[1] It is quite possible that two parties to a transaction understand the meaning of the rights exchanged in fundamentally different ways, as was demonstrated again and again by transactions among Native American and Europeans. (See e.g., Cronon 1983; Satz 1991.) People operate in societies in which the society has granted rights formally or informally to make certain decisions. The distribution of rights among decision makers affects the efficiency of the allocation of resources and the fairness of the distribution of returns from resources. Systems of rights also affect motivation, power relationships, and social status. Choices among systems of rights should, therefore, depend on reasons of efficient or fair outcomes and on reasons of inherently preferable social structures. Many different distributions of rights among individuals and collectives are possible and these differences affect who decides through time, in particular across generations, and over space.

Rights, as modified by regulations, specify the decisions that each decision maker is permitted to make, the range of options that may be considered, and the considerations that may be taken into account. A homeowner may have the right to sell a residence, but may not have the right to consider the race of the buyer as a criterion in choosing to whom to sell. Whether *de jure* rights (rights established in law) are or can be enforced, given social norms and the feasibility and costs of policing, must also be considered in predicting behavior in response to rights.

Regulations might be characterized as if-then rules with enforcement. In contrast to policies, which are also if-then rules, regulations imply enforcement. Individual decision makers may have incentives to break a regulation in each instance in which it becomes binding, even if they acknowledge the legitimacy of the regulation in general. Speed limits on highways are one obvious example. Policies can only remind us to do things we are willing to do in individual instances. Regulations require us to do things we might not want to do when a specific instance arises.

A plan can take rights as given and enforced and devise strategies within these constraints. Alternatively, a plan can include actions to change regulations. For example, a plan might include a size and location of an expressway and a change in a zoning ordinance so as to yield densities of development that would be consistent with the planned capacity of the expressway. In this case there is a plan for regulations, but the plan itself does not create or enforce the regulation. The regulation is an ordinance enacted by government under its police powers (its monopoly on the legal use of force) to change the rights of its residents. At a different level, the Declaration of Independence might be interpreted as a plan and the U.S. Constitution and subsequent laws as regulations. The first declared a vision and an underlying strategy. The latter created enforceable rules.

The most fundamental notions of rights, in Western philosophy at least, adhere to people, albeit historically only to particular types of people, as individuals or groups. Rights are recognition by others of an individual's or a group's authority to make particular decisions. Rights can be characterized by the following attributes:

- Authority: Over what decisions and with what scope of discretion is authority granted?
- Origin: By whom was it granted or legitimated and by what logic?
- Enforcement: By whom is it enforced or sustained?
- Exclusivity: To whom is it granted and from whom is it thereby excluded?
- Transferability: To whom may it be transferred, in what form, and through what means?
- Spatial extent: Over what area(s) is the authority acknowledged?
- Temporal extent: Over what time is the authority acknowledged?

Authority of a right. We generally talk about a bundle of rights associated with a particular parcel of land and a particular person or persons as property rights in land. Actions related to rights almost always address a particular bundle of rights, but it is important to recognize the elements. "Owning" a piece of land, as if there were an inherent absolute concept of complete authority, is at best a distortion. Neither a "homeowner" nor a renter has complete authority over a parcel of land, only a set of distinct authorities related to a parcel of land.

A landowner in the United States has the authority to do many things with a piece of property. Discretion over what can be done is limited, however, by a wide range of federal, state, and local laws on crimes against persons, nuisance, mineral rights, water rights, taxation, zoning, subdivision regulations, building codes, health regulations, and contract obligations.

Authority over a particular decision almost never gives complete discretion. Regulations may restrict which alternatives may be considered, such as a zoning restriction that permits only choices among residential uses. Regulations may also restrict outcomes, such as in the setting of air or water pollution standards for particular cities or streams. Finally, regulations may restrict attributes that a decision maker may use to make choices, such as the restriction against consideration of race in selling houses. The latter two types of regulations restrict permissible alternatives indirectly, but the effect is equivalent. Certain choices are precluded because of outcomes that might ensue or because of criteria implied by choices made.

Origin of a right. The origin of rights is pertinent to pragmatic questions because it defines the scope of acknowledgment of a right. Three origins of rights are most pertinent here: cultural or social legitimation, government, and capture from the public domain. Prior to European settlement, societies in North America claimed communal rights in land collectively as being legitimated by use (see e.g., Cronon 1983; Demsetz 1967), or acknowledged the right of an individual to land because of an investment of effort in clearing and cultivating it. The rights system of Native Americans was distinctly different from that of the European settlers. To Europeans, rights in land were granted to individuals or groups as proprietors by sovereign heads of governments. In practice, physical conquest imposed a European interpretation of rights on North America. Both cultural and legal precedents affect our implicit sense of rights and our legal basis for rights. Rights are sustained by a society through mechanisms of legitimation and enforcement. Specific rights are legitimated by different parts of the social system, some formally from various levels of government and some informally or tacitly as part of a culture. Culturally defined rights may in some cases contradict formally granted rights, as in continuing racial discrimination in the United States.

With the fall of communist governments in Eastern Europe, the question arose of what rights retained legitimacy, or regained legitimacy from previous regimes or previous cultural norms. Did persons or their heirs whose property had been confiscated decades before have any rights to have it returned? Differences in systems of rights may be subtler than the differences between communist regimes and newly capitalist efforts. Despite the long common heritages of England and the United States, golf in England is a middle-class activity carried out on public courses, and fishing in

England is an upper-class sport available only to those who can afford the privately held rights to fish in particular streams. The situation in the United States is reversed. Golf courses are most frequently private clubs with significant social status, and fishing is widely available with public rights in streams.

Systems of rights can be understood as evolving from the capture of rights from the public domain as these rights are recognized to have sufficient value to justify the cost of delineating them (Barzel 1989). It is costly to determine all of the attributes of a particular asset, which means that all of the rights associated with that asset are never fully determined. Barzel describes "transaction costs as the costs associated with the transfer, capture, and protection of rights" (2). Rights are incompletely defined until there is a transaction that requires a more complete definition and thus justifies the costs of such definition. In buying a house, a deed search not only confirms the validity of the title to property being transferred but also checks for other rights, such as liens by contractors who have worked on the property, easements, or mineral rights. The difficulty of measuring attributes of assets creates the difficulty in delineating rights. Opportunities for wealth occur when we recognize possibilities to gain rights from the public domain by defining and making explicit new rights such as air rights over railroad yards. Wealth can be lost when public trust rights in shorelands or wetlands are newly recognized.

Systems of rights are constantly evolving and more complex than we might at first imagine. Barzel (1989, 49) uses a large office building as an example of a system of rights. The rights holders include a titleholder, a mortgage holder, renters, and a janitorial service with a contract. The fire insurer holds rights to the possibility of a fire, which has negative value. Thus, the fire insurer is paid to accept this right, rather than paying for it. Once it holds the right to fire risk, the fire insurer has the greatest incentive to prevent fires and the other rights holders have lowered their incentives to prevent fires. Performance conditions in the fire insurance contract and variations in price of insurance modify this lack of incentives for other rights holders.

In Barzel's argument, formalized privately claimed rights are not inherently better than rights remaining in the public domain because transaction costs—in particular, measuring attributes and policing contracts—may be too high to justify gains in motivation or efficiency from privatizing. Rights in the public domain are by definition not captured by either private or public sector actors; the public domain means something different from the public sector. Governments must also capture rights from the public domain. Governments (the public sector) may claim and compensate rights explicitly, such as rights to areas to build roads, rights to levy taxes on private real estate, or rights to restrict density. The public sector is a collection of rights-holding entities that is in many ways analogous to the collection of owners of rights in the private sector.

Enforcement of a right. Rights must be enforced or sustained over time. They are not inherent in some natural system, so rights recognized or formalized by a society may "decay" if not reinforced formally or socially. Enforcement by government action is familiar, but government action cannot succeed without cultural support from social norms. The Prohibition era in the United States (during which production and distribution of alcoholic beverages were illegal) is one example of a government attempt, based on its established procedures of collective choice, to enforce laws that the society would not sustain. Williams and Matheny (1995) show the importance of such "social regulation" for many environmental problems. Similarly, incompletely enforced laws have occurred in zoning ordinances that restrict the number of inhabitants or the subdividing of houses in neighborhoods with demand for high-density housing, such as near university campuses. Attempts to regulate construction of housing in areas that are not persuasively inappropriate for housing have failed in many countries where squatter settlements are eventually legitimated even though the original construction was illegal (Hopkins 1984a).

Exclusivity of a right. Rights may be acknowledged to belong to individuals or collective entities such as corporations or other types of chartered organizations such as municipalities. Rights are not necessarily exclusive to one individual or entity. The traditional example is the shared rights to graze animals on the town common. A frequent misunderstanding of exclusivity of rights occurred in the willingness of Native Americans to transfer rights to Europeans. Native Americans presumed that they could transfer rights to others and retain the same rights for themselves (Cronon 1983). Additional examples of nonexclusive rights are the right to discharge various things into the air or water, or less obviously, the right to speak at a public hearing. The exclusivity of rights to one individual or corporate body is a crucial characteristic affecting outcomes from a particular distribution of rights because nonexclusive rights are associated with collective goods.

Transferability of a right. Some rights, such as rights in real property, may be transferred from one individual to another through sale. Other rights, such as the right to vote in local governmental elections in the United States, can be gained only through national citizenship and local residence in a geographically defined place. These rights to vote cannot be sold or transferred. The mechanisms of transfer include sale, inheritance, lease (which may or may not be assignable to a third party), and gift. Rights of national citizenship may be inherited by birth, gained through place of residence, or in some countries purchased. Restrictions on transfers of rights in land and property can prevent disproportionate accumulation of rights by more successful (in the evolutionary sense) individuals. Restrictions on transfers by sale may have ethical bases, such as selling a right to vote or selling oneself into labor contracts approximating slavery.

Historically many units of government could make a direct call on the labor of their citizens or residents, called *corvée* in French. Chicago at its incorporation in 1833 " . . . could call out any citizen to work on the public roads for three days a year" (Keating 1988, p. 36). The United States currently relies on a volunteer military, but the military draft might be reactivated. The only widely practiced such requirement in the United States is duty to serve on juries. Social norms against levying labor requirements from citizens, such as the current norms in the United States even against forced military service, can be argued to discriminate against those who are unemployed but must pay taxes directly or indirectly. One might argue that government thus provides backing to provide collective goods of interest to those who pay taxes, but not a mechanism to provide such goods for those who can provide only labor. The opportunity to transfer such obligations by paying a substitute, as was possible for draftees in the Civil War, creates a right both to dispose and a right to acquire the right to provide such work.

It is worth noting that much of the infrastructure (roads and bridges) built in the 1800s in the rural areas of the United States was constructed, or at least maintained, by nongovernment or government versions of such community labor. The concept is perhaps resurfacing in a different form in the recently ubiquitous "Adopt- a-Highway" programs. Signs along highways indicate that a local group has taken responsibility for keeping the roadside clean. Although participation is voluntary, the mechanisms for overcoming the hurdles for such collective action are provided by government. There is benefit in reinforcing cultural norms against littering, which is what motivates the signs that identify a specific group against whom you would be acting if you break the norm. There is also benefit in building community interaction through shared work projects.

Spatial extent of a right. Rights in land are usually identified with a particular parcel or set of parcels and may depend in part on relationships recognized in spatial terms. The idea of authority over a legally described parcel is familiar (at least in the United States). A municipality has authority (jurisdiction) within its corporate boundaries, and in many states has certain "extraterritorial jurisdiction" beyond its boundaries but still defined by spatial extent. Authority to decide about actions on one parcel may be restricted because of effects outside that parcel but attributable to that decision. For example, there are often regulations that prohibit changes in the quantity or quality of water runoff that may leave a parcel. The spatial extent of ramifications of a decision may confound the scope of legitimation from which a right originates, as in air or water quality effects across national boundaries or among social groups with different norms.

Temporal extent of a right. The temporal extent of a right is most obvious in the concept of leasing for a specified time a particular authority to use or decide. Such rights may result from the logic by which rights are legitimated, as in communally oriented societies in which rights to cultivation of particular parcels are granted for life or until there is no direct heir (e.g., Regmi 1976). Such systems achieve efficiency of allocation and social status of ownership, but preclude long-term accumulation of differences by limiting the transferability of parcels to heirs. Temporal limitations on rights are often associated with need or fairness rather than with freedom of individual action.

Rights over time are closely tied to norms and regulations on inheritance. There are two major inheritance strategies. Primogeniture gives all property to one heir, usually the oldest son. This keeps the property size constant over generations, thus maintaining a viable farm unit or an established social status based on size of holding and thus wealth. It requires that other descendants find other lifestyles, in England and Tibet traditionally including serving as clergy or priests. *Per stirpes* inheritance gives property equally to all descendants, thus breaking up farms within a few generations and often forcing family businesses to dissipate in a relatively short time (see e.g., Fukuyama 1995).

The recognition of rights occurs in time, and not necessarily instantaneously. For example, reasonable expectations by a developer about what can be done with a piece of land, called "vested rights," cannot be taken without compensation. How and when such rights become vested is a significant question in land use law. In general, government actions such as zoning or subdivision approvals that developers have relied on as the basis for significant investments cannot later be changed in a way that takes away reasonable expectations for returns on those investments (Siemon et al. 1982).

Allocation Efficiency, Collective Goods, and Externalities

The fundamental premise of neoclassical economics is that if all input resources are unambiguously assigned to individuals (or corporate entities able to act as unitary decision makers), then each will strive to gain the maximum return by allocating these resources to yield the greatest return. Also, each consumer will choose to allocate a budget according to preferences so that these resources will produce a mix of goods that will match demand within the budget constraints of consumers. In particular, each resource will be used in such a way that no amount of any resource could be changed to another purpose and gain an increase in production. This result is thus an efficient allocation of resources. In terms of economic analysis, we would be on the production possibility frontier and the marginal rate of substitution of each input resource would be equal across all possible outputs. There are two partially distinguishable aspects of this claim: motivation and effi-.ciency of information.

Well-defined rights to the fruits of a person's efforts (the decision about how much personal effort to put forth in relation to resulting income) provide motivation. Current restructuring of economies throughout the world suggests that some persons, given the right, will decide to work much harder to gain the resulting extra return that accrues to their own labor and thus raise aggregate production above that from a system of collective returns. This case is a collective goods problem: Individual effort must somehow be monitored and rewarded or it is to each individual's advantage to shirk. Systems of rights that make returns attributable only to large groups in aggregate must find additional means to motivate individuals. Changes in rights of farmers in Russia and China may have increased individual output. Such individual action, however, immediately raises the potential for additional gain through coordinating decisions. Farmers who produced lackadaisically on collective farms during regular working hours produced more effectively on small plots during their own time. Contracts should put in control of a particular attribute of an asset that person who is most likely to manipulate the level of that attribute so as to affect output (Barzel 1989). A share contract (e.g., split revenues 50-50) as in sharecropping in agricultural production gives both worker and landowner incentives to affect the level of output. The worker manipulates primarily labor, and the landowner manipulates choice of crop and capital investments in drainage and lime. Such contracts assume that it is easier for each to monitor output of production than it is to monitor and police the inputs. Many other circumstances of monitoring occur and affect the structure of organizations and contracts.

The second claim for such market systems is the savings in the cost of information because each resource holder need know only the return on his or her own resources. Prices in the market convey all the information necessary for decision makers operating individually to achieve efficient allocations of resources. The efficient outcome of a market system depends, however, on the initial distribution of resources. If the initial distribution were different, the allocation of resources and served demand would be different because the relative demands for different goods depend on the distribution of incomes and wealth among individuals, which determine their budget constraints. For example, a relatively uniform distribution of income might yield a high demand for Fords and Toyotas, but a low demand for Lincolns and Lexuses. An uneven distribution of the same total assets and incomes would increase the demand for Lincolns and Lexuses and thus result in a different allocation of resources to production. The resulting allocation would still be efficient in the sense of being on the production possibility frontier, but at a different point on that frontier because of the different mix of demand.

An external effect of one action affects the relationship between another action and its outcomes. The smoke created by my burning fallen leaves affects the outcome for my neighbor of deciding to work outside if the smoke aggravates a health condition. If I were not burning leaves, the outcome of my neighbor working outside would be different. When external effects are present, an individual acting in response to individual benefits will not make choices consistent with arriving at an efficient allocation of resources because the costs and benefits of these external effects will not be taken into account in making decisions. To achieve an efficient allocation, some mechanism must be created so that individuals consider these external effects. Two responses have been identified: bargaining among the parties and changing the rights of the parties. The latter includes internalization of the effects by placing the right to make both decisions into one organization, imposing a tax or an incentive, or regulating the range of choices that the decision makers have the right to make.

Coase (1960) argued that two firms, such as a laundry and a factory producing smoke as a by-product of its manufacturing, would bargain and agree to produce a quantity of smoke such that the cost of further control of the smoke would be greater than the added cost of soap for the laundry. Even if such bargains would lead to a good agreement, which is unlikely in practice for many reasons discussed in chapter 7, such bargains are unlikely if there are many laundries, many factories, or both. When there are many parties sharing in the same bargain, the effort to achieve a bargain is a collective good. Thus, in general, insufficient effort is likely to be put into achieving a good bargain. Bargaining fails even for small numbers if there are transaction costs for bargaining, in which case the distribution of wealth between parties will also be affected.

In these circumstances in which bargaining is not a good resolution, the task of addressing an externality becomes a collective good. It requires an implicit decision to leave things as they are or to change rights of the parties involved so as to achieve a different outcome. One approach is to create new organizations, such as the metropolitan governments that are intended to internalize decisions among central cities and suburbs so as to bring external effects within the decisions of one body. A second is to establish a Pigovian tax, which imposes on the producer of the effect an additional cost equal to the damage caused to the recipient. In the large numbers case, this is extremely difficult because the relative contribution of each producer and the effect on each recipient is difficult to determine. In particular, the recipients are being asked to value a collective good and have incentives to misrepresent its value to them. The third possibility is a direct change in rights by imposing a regulation, for example, prohibiting the burning of leaves. Such a tax or regulation changes the initial distribution of rights, and thus wealth, of the parties.

Further, Baumol (1972) has shown that in imposing a Pigovian tax, a target outcome must be chosen, at least implicitly, in order to define a set of incentives to account for the externality. We cannot know enough in advance to set the tax at the level it should be once equilibrium is reached without knowing the information sufficient to identify the equilibrium. If we set the tax based on the current situation, it must be adjusted as the market transactions seek the equilibrium. Individuals may choose actions to distort the tax, and with costly transactions there is no reasonable expectation that a particular equilibrium would result. Baumol and Oates (1975) therefore argue for use of financial incentives to achieve chosen targets. The tax implies an equilibrium outcome and an intended equilibrium outcome implies a tax. We cannot choose a level of tax independent of an intention about outcome. Pigovian taxes are not a substitute for a plan, but a regulation establishing incentives and a regulation that requires a plan in order to figure out the content of the regulation.

Such market-based systems of rights are potentially valuable because they require little exchange of information for coordination of decisions to gain efficiency and they provide high motivation for effort. If rights are unambiguously assigned and there are no collective goods, externalities, transaction costs, or dynamic adjustment problems, then efficient outcomes will result. It is much more difficult in any analytical way to claim desirable properties for outcomes when these conditions are only partially met. In urban development interdependence, indivisibility, irreversibility, and imperfect foresight distort both the information advantage and the motivation advantage. In addition, we should not assign rights without considering other criteria, including fairness and dynamics.

Fairness and Social Status

What makes a system of property rights fair or just? Should the social status culturally embedded in the allocation of rights be taken into account in choosing among systems of rights? Should restrictions on transfer of rights be made to prevent a few individuals from accumulating wealth and power over time?

The origin or legitimation of the rights might be argued to be inherently fair. Or, the consequences of the rights might be argued to be fair. The first approach might be exemplified by an argument, which would be consistent with Nozick (1974), that an individual who creates a resource—that is, captures it from the public domain by distinguishing it from a valueless, natural condition—should have a claim to the resource. Creating a resource (identifying an instrumental purpose) by putting in the work required, being the source of the idea, and putting the resulting resource to "good use" might justify a claim to ownership (see e.g., Newby et al. 1978). Converting raw land to agricultural use in some societies justifies a claim of authority over it.

The second approach asks about consequences. Rawls (1971) would ask whether acknowledging such rights would lead to outcomes that are to the advantage of the least well off. Alternatively, a system that tended to yield relatively equal distributions of resources over time, such as the Kipat system in Nepal in which rights revert to the community for reallocation upon death of an individual or head of household (Regmi 1976), might be justified on grounds of intergenerational fairness. A neoclassical economist might argue assignment to those who create it, as in the first approach, but on the grounds that it would yield efficient allocations of new resources. A communitarian might argue that the Kipat system is inherently fitting to the notion that the source of our humanity results from belonging to a community.

Sen (1992) argues that the most important distributional question is the equality of capabilities, not the equality of opportunities or the equality of outcomes directly. Equality of basic goods as defined by Rawls is not sufficient because, as Sen points out, individuals are not equal *a priori* in physical capacity, mental capacity, wealth, cultural norms, social status, and many other attributes. Therefore, equality of opportunity to use unequal capability is not sufficient. The combination of individual differences and compensating social norms can yield equality of capability to achieve outcomes in important aspects of quality of life. Equality of capabilities is distinct from and more appropriate than equality of outcomes because equality of capabilities means that an individual is an intrinsically valued determiner of its own status rather than an instrument for achievement of equal outcomes. Differences in rights can compensate for or exacerbate individual differences. Thus the design of systems of rights is an important opportunity to equalize capabilities.

Differentials in wealth are often attributable to ability or luck in identifying newly valuable resources or creating changes that make resources newly valuable. Land increases in value as cities grow or as infrastructure is provided. Who should benefit from such changes? Henry George (1880) argued that such gains should be taxed. In England, development control that releases land for development by government decisions is based on the argument that these changes in value should accrue to the society, not the individual whose land happened to become valuable by the aggregate acts of society, or especially by the explicit intentional acts of providing infrastructure.

Rights might also be legitimated by an argument of stewardship or altruistic ownership (e.g., Newby et al. 1978). Stewardship implies a client, which might be people, or in Leopold's (1949) argument for a land ethic, the land or ecosystem itself. Stewardship of land for future generations is an argument of intergenerational fairness. Even with merely random success and failure, if transfers of rights are allowed, then those who lose in a given interval may sell or become indebted to those who win. If these differentials are inherited, they are not reversible over time because of the time value of resources—resources invested create more resources (Alchian 1950). This is the basis for taxes on inheritance, which have recently been the subject of active political debate.

The discretion of authority granted by rights is often an indicator of social status. Social status is a quality-of-life benefit for individuals, so systems of rights that create social status yield benefits. This phenomenon may well be confounded by the traditional argument of motivation, but it is clear that a small-business owner or homeowner is granted greater credibility and significance in social interactions than wage employees or renters, other things being equal. Some (e.g., Elkin 1987) would argue that such status and the interests implied are crucial to creating the local government culture in the United States. Regmi (1976) identifies distinct types of land tenure rights in Nepal, prior to 1950, which served particular social purposes and carried different levels of social status. Raikar lands were state lands on which rights to cultivate were granted. These grants allowed persons to collect rents and thus served as a means for paying civil servants, but brought little social status and were not transferable. Birta lands were grants with significant social status somewhat like feudal proprietorships in Europe, but were not transferable or inheritable. Birta holders were required to supply men for war. Guthi lands were used as endowments to sustain religious practices and were operated communally, giving some status to the group.

In Champaign and Urbana, Illinois, until the early 1980s, small independent operators contracting directly with individual homeowners collected garbage. Business owners themselves often drove the one truck they owned. The social status of garbage haulers and the opportunities for entry into small business thus afforded are now gone. Regulations now require closed trucks, a closed landfill has meant longer hauls to distant landfills that are only feasible with large trucks, and flow control regulations to sustain new disposal and recycling options have made single contracts between the municipality and large, nonlocal businesses more viable. A group of small-business operators with the social status and business interests as participants in community leadership has been displaced by professional employees of municipalities bargaining with representatives of large, national corporations to contract for garbage collection services. This change in organizational structure resulting from changes in rights affects the status of individuals differentially by class and race. Do African Americans who might have owned small businesses become employees of large corporations that have no commitment to place or person? Or, do such small-business owners become government employees, which may yield more secure positions with better protection against racial prejudice but yield lower social status than small-business owners achieve?

The distribution of rights distributes the risks on returns. Workers in a one-industry town may want to rent "company houses" because buying a home puts all of their resources in one basket. If the industry folds, people lose their jobs and the equity in their homes. Mining towns such as shale oil mining towns that arose briefly in western Colorado in the 1970s are a recent example. Similar logic may apply in urban areas with little perceived potential for survival. If I am going to live there, I may want to risk my small capital that might go into home ownership in a hedge investment somewhere else instead of in equity in a home affected by the same risks as living in that community.

Rights in Land, Rights to Vote, and Commercial Interests

In the United States, the right to vote comes with residence in a political jurisdiction—the nation, a state, a county or parish, a municipality, and any number of special districts. Although voting rights were once associated with the ownership of land, or in some cases with paying taxes (see e.g., Williamson 1960), owning land is no longer directly tied to the right to vote. An owner of land has no vote except by residing on that land permanently. Neither capital nor land has a vote, nor do persons who hold rights in that land or capital unless they are also residents. Voting rights are an attribute of the right to reside on land in a voting district or jurisdiction, not of the rights of ownership (more precisely fee simple ownership) of land.

Local governments still share strong interests with local businesses and their owners, even if these owners have no right to vote. The claim of economic analysis that assignments of rights can yield efficient allocations of resources requires that all resources be mobile so that they can be moved to their most productive use. The lack of mobility of fixed assets—buildings, infrastructure, business associations—is a primary cause of irreversibility, which implies situations in which plans may be worthwhile. Entrepreneurs can, however, move themselves or move most of their capital, at least in a reasonable time. The entrepreneur's fixed plant depreciates as technologies for industrial production, for retail sales, and for services change. Losses from fixed capital may thus be small, so that moving is feasible. Cities cannot move either their corporate entity, or their assets because both are inexorably tied to place by law or physical nature. This premise is implicit in the Chicago Plan of 1909 and the argument is fully developed by Elkin (1987) among others.

The mobility of capital relative to municipalities is an important characteristic of cities. Thus the elected officials of municipalities are continually in the position of competing for capital. Capital creates jobs and real estate; taxes derive from residents and real estate. Actions by municipalities rely on ability to raise funds through bond issues, and bond ratings that determine the interest rate on these bonds depend on an independent, external assessment of the community's viability. A dying city cannot raise funds. A city can go bankrupt. It is thus in many ways similar to a corporation and has common interests with those businesses in its jurisdiction that create jobs and imply growth. It has even greater common interest with businesses whose assets are relatively fixed.

> These are enterprises whose health is most directly tied to the economic vitality of the city—banks, newspapers, large stores, developers, real estate agencies, real estate law firms, property management firms, utilities and the like. Their behavior is best understood as an effort to enhance the value of their fixed assets by attracting mobile capital to the city. Since many of these fixed assets are themselves parcels of land, such businessmen are naturally drawn to land-use schemes,

and thus a community of interest with officials is born. Not only will they encourage officials in their efforts to induce investment through rearranging land use, but they will also propose projects that the city should undertake. And since they themselves control large parcels of land, many of the projects that they propose will be ones from which they will benefit directly. These land interests, as they may be called, will also work to put in place institutional arrangements that will facilitate inducement of city growth and, to this end, will often cooperate with city officials in securing the necessary powers from state and federal governments. More generally, these businessmen are, by and large, receptive to any schemes—including tax incentives, revenue bonds, and other sorts of inducements—that they expect will enhance the worth of assets whose value is heavily tied to location. (Elkin 1987, 41)

Molotch (1976) made the general argument that the combination of commercial and municipal corporation interests tend to create "a growth machine" because such growth is in their mutual interests. Municipalities have many of the attributes of other corporate entities, and municipalities are inherently fixed in location. Thus cities as corporations and those businesses sharing such characteristics are likely to benefit from plans that address efficient patterns and timing of growth through infrastructure investment and regulations.

This relationship helps to explain why the two most frequent types of plans are plans for downtown development or redevelopment and plans for new development on the urban fringe. Existing neighborhoods, generally, require no newly located or sized, fixed infrastructure that needs to be planned, but these residents are the voters that elected officials must satisfy by creating coalitions of interest to both capital and neighborhoods. These neighborhoods are also the potential opposition for new infrastructure such as highways or landfills built in their neighborhood but primarily for the benefit of people who live elsewhere. Carter Harrison in Chicago in the nineteenth century and Neil Goldschmidt in Portland in the 1970s built such coalitions.

It was as an urban imperialist, not as a social reformer, that Carter Harrison believed he could be of greatest assistance to the average Chicago workingman. He vigorously promoted annexation of adjoining communities, and these annexations created new jobs building and running streetcar lines, laying sewer pipes, hanging electrical wires, putting in new roads and sidewalks, and erecting fire and po lice stations and new bungalow developments. If Chicago continued to expand while guaranteeing labor's right to organize, it would become, Harrison believed, the best place in the world for a working-class family to settle. (Miller 1996, 444).

Goldschmidt built a coalition around quality of life in neighborhoods and revitalization of downtown Portland (Lewis 1996). This coalition addressed the voters in the neighborhoods and the interests of business.

If the relationship between rights in land and rights to vote were different, behaviors and outcomes would differ. In Switzerland, citizenship in a commune, the local corporate municipality, is possible only by inheritance, or rarely by buying membership. Thus, for example, the communally owned common land on which the ski slopes are built was and still is owned by hereditary residents of the commune. No one other than descendants of the original families can gain the right to vote in decisions about these common lands. This arrangement is equivalent to the proprietors of early common lands in the United States. Commoners are those who hold such rights in the common lands. In Zermatt, Switzerland, no one has been allowed to buy into the common holdings since the nineteenth century. Ironically, the last person allowed to buy such rights was the first serious hotelier to begin to develop tourism in Zermatt (Williams 1964). In contrast, in the United States most ski slopes occur on land leased from the federal government, and the resort towns are developed on privately held land that was previously ranches or mining towns. In most cases, the original European settlers, much less any earlier Native American residents, have long since lost or sold all rights in these private lands and have left the area (Hopkins and Schaeffer 1983). In Zermatt, however, the original families are still involved in the tourist trade.

The ski resort comparison is a suggestion that systems of rights can be different and might be designed differently to achieve social changes in the distribution of rights. Two of the most difficult strategies to implement in urban development are to generate tourism development that benefits the existing residents of towns or villages and to generate development in abandoned inner-city neighborhoods that actually benefits the existing residents. Gentrification brings investment by changing who lives there. In Nepal, for example, development of certain tourist facilities requires a Nepali participant, and trekking companies must be majority-owned by Nepali citizens. It is not at all clear that the experience of resorts can be transferred to urban development, but if there is land of significant value once developed, it might be possible to transfer it to a community land trust, equivalent to common lands held by a set of proprietors. The proprietors would be the current residents of the city, but new arrivals could not become proprietors by mere residency. Community land trusts in which local residents collectively become owners of key land parcels for conservation or for redevelopment are one response to these issues. Would development of the riverfront in East St. Louis, Illinois, where a large portion of the population is unemployed and does not own land, work in such a scheme to the benefit of current residents?

These variations in rights in land and rights to vote show that we can consider different systems of rights and use regulations to make changes in rights. Such regulations and investments in capital facilities are the two types of actions usually addressed in plans.

Incentives to Regulate

Why would individuals choose to restrict their own discretion rather than resist all regulations? A decision maker might focus on a particular decision assuming that the rules of the game cannot be changed and that the task is to do the best possible within those rules. Alternatively, a decision maker might consider whether a different set of rules would yield better results: Would the expected value of making choices under a new set of rules be preferred to the expected value of making choices under the old set of rules? When considering regulations, you must take into account that the regulation will apply to you and to other decision makers. Even if for your individual choice you might prefer not to have the regulation, you might prefer to have the regulation because it will affect other persons' decisions as well.

Riker and Ordeshook (1973) define a specific "question of regulation" as distinct from a "question of action." An individual considering a regulation should consider the following:

Is

> my utility from the substitute I would choose given the regulation
> + my utility from the substitutes others would choose given
> the regulation
> − the cost of enforcement of the regulation

greater than

my utility from my use of the action that would be precluded by
the regulation
+ my utility from others use of the action that would be precluded
by the regulation
– the cost of enforcement of the existing rights?

For example, am I better off if all of us are prevented from using septic
tanks for sewage disposal, even though I will also be prevented from using a
septic tank myself? I might be willing to vote for such a regulation, believing
it would be enforced, even though as an individual I would rather build a
septic tank. If everyone built a septic tank, I would be even worse off than if
I had to pay for sanitary sewers and sewage treatment because of the regulation. Thus I am willing to restrict myself in order also to restrict my neighbors. Note that such logic might apply to any aspect of rights. The question
of regulation is one of choosing the system of rights in which I wish to operate, knowing that others will also operate within that system of rights. These
expectations of my own behavior and of the behavior of others depend on my
beliefs about social norms and the likely effectiveness of enforcement.

The logic of regulation presented by Riker and Ordeshook is equivalent to the legal concept of "average reciprocity of advantage," a label used
by Justice Holmes in *Pennsylvania Coal Company v. Mahon*, 260 U. S. 393
(1922). The concept is that if all land in a district is restricted, then in turn
all land in the district will be benefited. I may be prevented from erecting
some use from which I could individually gain but others would lose, but I
and others benefit because no one is permitted to erect such a use. "Where
a court determines that this circumstance exists, it may conclude that there
is no taking because the benefits conferred equal the burdens imposed"
(Blaesser et al. 1989, 14). Thus, the logical explanation of why individuals
may impose regulations on themselves has a parallel in legal precedent
about when regulation is legitimate and does not constitute a taking of
property without compensation. This is, however, only one such legal justification for regulation.

Land developers have a long record of advocating and welcoming regulations that benefit the developers. Weiss (1987) documented such instances
thoroughly. The real estate industry formed real estate boards to lobby for

state legislation requiring subdivision regulations and zoning. Developers first discovered the value of deed restrictions, which they could implement privately within a single subdivision. Deed restrictions are contracts among owners of deeds to particular parcels of land and remain with the land deed if it is transferred. Thus a group of owners can restrict themselves from construction styles or practices that would reduce the value of their properties. They might require minimum house sizes and features. Developers could establish such deed restrictions before selling lots, and developers could retain certain rights to themselves. Surrounding properties were still unrestricted, however, leading developers to argue for zoning.

Although zoning would restrict a developer's own practices, the loss from these restrictions would be more than compensated by the restrictions it would also place on other developers. Developers of more expensive properties had, in general, more to gain from such restrictions than developers of inexpensive property, which led to difficulty in sustaining the collective action of the real estate lobby (Weiss 1987, 107–140). The size of the coalition of support for such regulation was valuable in lobbying, but key individuals who had independent access to the governor could undermine collective action. Richmond (1997) argues that the urban growth boundary legislation in Oregon is "pro-development" because it clarifies up front where development can occur and focuses on increasing density, not decreasing it. Credible regulations reduce uncertainty, which increases expected values for developers. The development process then works more quickly, increasing profits for developers. Developers have been among the supporters of the Oregon growth management program.

This explanation of when and what kinds of regulations are likely to be made emphasizes that regulations should not be taken as fixed. Explaining why plans occur and what regulations they are likely to propose requires considering regulations as among the available actions to be planned.

Plans for Regulation of Land Development

Each of the regulations described here depends on the logic of plans as specific support for implementation of the regulation. The question in each case is, Why do we need to figure out in advance what land uses or facilities should be where and when, and how does this logic relate the regulation to a plan? In addition, plans can provide the basis for substantive due process arguments that a particular regulation serves a legitimate public purpose under the Fourteenth Amendment of the U.S. Constitution (Blaesser et al. 1989). Although such claims may be somewhat more general, their underlying basis should rely on the logic of regulations and the logic of plans.

Zoning, subdivision regulations, and official maps are the three traditional types of local land development regulations. More recent regulations include urban service areas, adequate public facilities ordinances, impact fees, and transferable development rights. Many other types of regulations also affect land development. Health and environmental regulations affect use of septic tanks and sewers. Environmental regulations related to floodplains, coastlines, natural hazards such as landslides, and air quality all affect land use location or transportation between locations. Development impact fees might be interpreted as dynamic externality taxes. Impact fees, transferable development rights, and other similar "incentive" programs depend on regulations to establish them and to sustain their market context. They are thus discussed here along with other types of land regulations. The logic of each type of regulation affects the logic of plans we should expect to observe being made for such regulations and the logic of plans we ought to make. These types of regulations and their dependence on plans are summarized in Table 6-1.

There are at least seven distinct ways in which zoning, as currently practiced in the United States, can address land development issues: externalities (or nuisance), infrastructure sizing and timing, fiscal management, costly or misperceived information, land supply, amenity protection, and development timing. Any zoning action may intentionally or unintentionally have all of these ramifications, but working out a plan for zoning requires recognizing these distinct ways in which zoning might work.

Zoning for externalities. Externalities, as discussed above, result when the actions of one person affect the outcomes from actions of another person. The most thorough study of zoning from this perspective is Fischel (1985). Your location of a business near my home affects the value I derive from choosing to live there. Your business might be a positive externality that improves my accessibility to services. It might be a negative externality that causes noise, congestion, and parking problems for me. It is an externality because you did not consider the effect on me when you made your decision about locating the business.

Table 6-1

Land Regulations and Implied Requirements of Plans

Regulation Type	Regulation Logic	Implied Plan Logic
Zoning	Externalities (positive and negative)	Strategy to address interdependence in advance because of irreversibility of investments and indeterminate adjustment process given imperfect foresight
	Infrastructure capacity	Strategy for capacity expansion and design for capacity at buildout because of irreversibility and indivisibility
	Fiscal objectives	Policy for consistent and fair repeated decisions for fiscal objectives
	Information costs or errors	Policy as means of providing information that is collective good or asymmetric between buyers and sellers
	Management of supply	Strategy to reduce infrastructure costs of spatial substitution of uses as technology changes given imperfect foresight
	Amenity protection	Target, permanent allocation yielding strategy of implementation to acquire rights
	Development timing	Strategy of zoning for non-urban uses until land is ripe for development
Official maps	Protect rights-of way	Strategy for rights-of-way because of irreversibility of investments
Subdivision regulations	External effects of design decisions	Policies to achieve design decisions by developer that have collective good external effects
Urban service areas (Urban growth boundaries)	Timing, resource lands protection, "optimal city size"—depending on how changes in area are managed over time	Strategy of efficient infrastructure provision and interaction costs over time; policy of consistent and fair resource land protection; target design of city
Adequate public facilities ordinances	Timing	Strategy of efficient infrastructure provision and interaction costs over time

(continues)

Table 6-1 (continued)

Land Regulations and Implied Requirements of Plans

Regulation Type	Regulation Logic	Implied Plan Logic
Development rights (e.g., conservation easements, transferable development rights)	Permanent allocation of land to uses	Target design of pattern of uses among, e.g., resource lands and urban development
Impact fees	Timing, fiscal management, and distribution of costs among current and new residents	Policy for consistency and fairness and strategy for infrastructure financing

If zoning is intended to reduce negative externalities, then it should separate uses from each other that would otherwise create externalities. Thus the zoning designations specify land use types or densities perceived to create negative externalities for other land use types. Hierarchical zoning categories allow "higher" uses but not "lower" uses, such as allowing single family in an industrial zone, but not vice versa. Newer zoning ordinances are exclusive to particular uses, recognizing that the single-family house creates an externality for the industry by locating near enough to become vulnerable to noise or air pollution. This reciprocal nature of external effects is inherent in nonseparable externalities.

Nonseparable externalities are those in which the level of output (of the intended product) of one actor affects the level of output (of the intended product) per unit of input for another actor. To take account of the externality, each decision maker not only needs to know the effect of a unit of its own output on the other decision maker, but also has to know the level of output at which the other decision maker is going to produce. Only then can each know the level of output it can achieve from a unit of its own inputs. Nonseparable externalities cannot be resolved by adding an additional cost per unit of output of the externality producer to cover the cost of the external effect as in so-called Pigovian taxes. Therefore, an externality tax per unit of output cannot be set without first identifying the desired equilibrium outcome. That is, the information savings from using pricing fails because we must still know the outcome in advance (Baumol 1972; Baumol and Oates 1975). Interdependence of this type is sufficient in itself to require that we choose a target pattern whether we intend to achieve that pattern by zoning regulations or by pricing regulations. Either type of regulation requires a plan.

Even if Pigovian taxes could work based on these assumptions, they would fail because of dynamic adjustment problems. The dynamic process of adjusting the location of each project to the locations of preceding projects will not lead to an optimal pattern because of indivisibility, irreversibility, and imperfect foresight. Thus, if we accept that the nature of urban development raises these dynamics issues, any kind of interdependence may benefit from working out the pattern of locations before any action is taken. Implementation of zoning as a regulation for externalities or a resolution of dynamic adjustment thus depends on a plan that sets out the relationships among land use types and densities, or whatever attributes affect the interactions among uses.

Externality zoning can protect existing use patterns from land development changes that might reduce the values of current property owners. In this case, there is no need for a plan because the observed development pattern is merely recorded and turned into zoning categories. This assumes a completely static situation. If the externality zoning is to affect new development, either greenfield development at the edge or redevelopment for new uses or densities as demands change, then the pattern must be determined in advance because the interdependence, indivisibility, irreversibility, and imperfect foresight means that the pattern cannot be discovered by costless adjustment to equilibrium. Plans are necessary.

A plan for externality zoning is lumpy—indivisible—because it must address a large enough area to consider the spatial interdependencies that are causing the externalities. Such plans must be done with sufficient lead time to get the zoning in place before structures are built if reversibility costs are to be avoided. Planning such "chunks" of new development area describes the current strategy in Phoenix, Arizona, where neighborhood planning efforts are targeted to areas about to undergo major changes (Mee 1998). The idea is to choose an appropriate scope to incorporate the interdependencies and to get it done before irreversible changes occur.

Plans for zoning based on externalities should make sense of the complex set of external relationships, both positive and negative. To zone so as to separate all retail from single-family residential and to "buffer" them by multifamily may well be based on perceptions that have little basis in defensible criteria. Many zoning practices can be explained as legal manifestations of illegal or unethical objectives. Guttenberg (1993) emphasizes the multiple dimensions of land use classification, which allow regulations to be based on one dimension while affecting other correlated dimensions. Much of the incentive for large-lot zoning and setbacks could be explained as an interest in having neighbors at least as wealthy as yourself, not to mention perceived correlation of social class and race. The New Urbanism focuses more on ensuring the positive externalities from close location of shopping, jobs, housing, and schools than on the negative externality separations of housing of different densities and of housing from commercial and industrial uses.

Zoning for infrastructure capacity. Infrastructure, such as sewers, streets, and schools, is built to serve a specific capacity. Demand above capacity creates at best congestion and at worst system failure. Demand below capacity wastes fixed investments because once built, they cannot be moved or reduced in size. Zoning for particular uses or particular densities constrains the demand for trips, the demand for sewerage capacity, and the demand for school capacity. Thus zoning can be designed to control land development so as to match implemented and planned infrastructure capacities. Implementation of such zoning depends on a plan for infrastructure provision, and the plan for infrastructure provision depends on expectations for land development.

Plans for zoning with respect to infrastructure capacity must consider interdependence of infrastructure provision and land development. We should not expect to see one plan, but rather to see plans by infrastructure providers that recognize the link to land use and by zoning jurisdictions that recognize the link to infrastructure capacity. The many frictions discussed throughout this book prevent production of single plans of such scope. If all newly constructed development is required to hook up to sewers, then sewer capacity, built and planned, has a regulatory effect on development through the regulation requiring such connections.

Zoning for fiscal objectives. Different land uses yield different revenues to local municipalities and generate different costs. Retail, for example, in many states generates sales tax revenues, a portion of which is distributed to the municipality. Retail generates traffic but does not generate school-children. Lower-density single-family housing generates fewer schoolchildren per unit area than higher-density single-family housing. Multiple-family housing may generate more property tax revenue per unit area and fewer schoolchildren, especially if each unit has two or fewer bedrooms. Thus a municipality can use the aggregate mix of land use types for which it zones in order to manage its revenues and costs (Windsor 1979). Given the importance of fiscal viability to municipalities, which as discussed earlier can go bankrupt, fiscal zoning is useful and likely. A plan for fiscal zoning would address the mix of land uses in relation to revenues and costs over time. Such a plan would consider the whole municipality.

Zoning for costly or misperceived information. Buyers of real estate, whether developed or undeveloped land, would like to have information on the many factors affecting their net benefit or value from the investment. Is it in a floodplain or susceptible to landslides? Is there sufficient sewerage capacity? Each buyer could be expected to answer these questions as part of the transaction costs of a purchase. These types of information are in some degree, however, collective goods. If one purchaser in an area is known to have obtained such information and to have purchased a house at a given price, then others can imitate this purchase without themselves checking this information. Thus there is insufficient incentive for each person to expend funds to collect information, which once collected can be shared easily with others at no added costs and no reduction in value to the person who generated it. Further, the seller, who is likely to have this information from experience, has no incentive to reveal this information because it would reduce the value of the property. Finally, for many situations such as flooding, even if people have the information, they are unable to interpret it appropriately in order to make the decisions they want to make.

For all four reasons—cost of information, collective good characteristics of the information, asymmetric information with disincentives for the seller to reveal knowledge, and cognitive errors—zoning can be useful to buyers of real estate. In this context, zoning includes floodplain regulations, hillside regulations, and other characteristics that are not pertinent in the externality, infrastructure capacity, or fiscal management aspects of zoning. Plans to support such zoning must delineate areas with pertinent attributes in sufficient detail to be useful in making decisions.

Zoning to manage supply. Retail services have gone through several technology transformations in the past fifty years, from downtown department stores and neighborhood services to suburban shopping malls, en-

closed malls, big box retailing, and strip centers. In each case, the latest retailing technology is able to drive older technologies out of business, but
in each case also, the new technology has tended to locate on completely
new sites requiring new infrastructure and rendering old sites and infrastructure obsolete and unproductive. In some cases, the differences between
new and old are subtle enough that communities might be able to gain efficiency in infrastructure provision by preventing new technologies from
locating at new sites.

Does it make sense to locate a new, larger supermarket down the street
on newly developed and newly serviced land, knowing that the old supermarket will become noncompetitive and that its site and infrastructure will
be underutilized? A community might try to manage the supply of retail
land to prevent unnecessary relocations of this kind. This strategy is difficult to pursue for at least two reasons. First, municipalities can seldom afford to limit new retail development without risking fiscal consequences,
and the new retailer is always able to argue that the old facilities are unus-
able. Second, a municipality cannot restrict retail zoning for the purpose of
keeping its current retail businesses in operation by preventing new entries
in the market. Anti-trust legislation prevents municipalities from favoring
one set of businesses over another in this way, though this effect may be
achieved by incentives and regulations focused on correlated dimensions of
business activities. A somewhat similar situation arises when a municipality tries to manage supply so as to dampen the swings of boom-bust cycles
in real estate development. Plans for such zoning should consider whether
new retailing technology can be implemented in existing retail locations as
was tried in the downtown Urbana case mentioned earlier.

Zoning for amenity protection. Zoning may also be used to protect ameni-
ties. In general, this must occur in joint benefit with some other purpose,
such as protection of development from flooding by restricting development in floodplains or similarly from landslide or fire danger. Zoning based
solely on restricting land for amenity use, such as recreation, is a taking of
property without compensation under current interpretations. If the intent
is to achieve permanent allocation of land for amenity purposes, then a
municipality should acquire the rights for that purpose. It may not be necessary to acquire all of the rights to a parcel; easements for access or views
may be sufficient. Amenity protection may be a joint product of other log-

ics of zoning, such as the floodplain protection resulting from the costly information argument. Recognizing and using the potential for such joint products expands the capacity of the regulatory actions.

Zoning for timing of development. Land zoned for particular uses is available for development at any time unless other regulations or incentives affect timing. General practice is to zone sufficient land for various uses so as not to increase the price of land or to be vulnerable to charges of monopoly protection for existing uses or particular owners. Land available for development depends on willing sellers and suitability for development. Generally far more land is zoned for development than could possibly be developed within ten or twenty years so that zoning has little effect on timing. This does not mean that zoning is irrelevant to questions of dynamics. Zones can, for example, control the timing of development of a parcel by restricting the parcel to a use that is not yet viable. Thus land zoned for multiple family or higher density is protected from premature development as single family.

Plans to support zoning for land use timing are difficult to explain because zoning is not well suited to control of timing. In the Portland, Oregon, metropolitan region, regulations on land development around light-rail stations were put into effect immediately after the locations for stations were announced. If the time lag for residential and commercial development is short enough, then the developers need not see the information that evolved during the twenty years of planning for the light-rail. If they simply respond to the announcement of committed station locations, they will not commit land irreversibly to inappropriate uses too soon, and they will not build appropriate developments too late. They may need only "unshared" plans, that is, to know that planning is going on and that their best strategy is to hold options open for the land likely to be affected. The plan for light-rail could share the corridor location but not include land use specifics at light-rail stations. In this situation, the specific zoning or development pattern at each station need not be determined until after station locations are committed. Speculation might still occur, but if no irreversible investments were made, there would be no benefit from shared plans.

In addition to these seven aspects of zoning, there are six other types of regulations: official maps, subdivision regulations, urban service areas or growth boundaries, adequate public facilities ordinances, separation of development rights, and impact fees. Each of these depends on plans in a particular way.

Official maps. Official maps specify street rights-of-way to ensure protection of the right-of-way from development. This is an obvious instance of trying to protect the opportunity to build efficient and coherent street networks from irreversible construction in the right-of-way. Reps (1969, 215) reports that in the platting of Philadelphia, rights-of-way were determined in advance of the sale of lands so that "the best routes could be freely selected and would not be blocked by property owners unwilling to allow the road to cross their lands." Such plans for streets are ubiquitous if imperfect. The idea is to identify street rights-of-way sufficient in width for eventual capacities and with sufficient lead time to preclude the need to demolish or move structures that might be built. Mandelker (1989) concludes that official maps are likely to be permissible under the U.S. Constitution if they do not preclude compensation for improvements (e.g., structures) in the mapped street rights-of-way, if the period of reservation prior to acquisition is relatively short, and if there are remedies for hardship cases in which all reasonable use is prohibited. Plans should set out street rights-of-way with sufficient lead time and detail to sustain such regulations.

Subdivision regulations. Subdivision regulations affect the way in which parcels can be subdivided so as to require adequate rights-of-way for streets, to ensure access to each lot, to prevent long dead-end streets, and other such difficulties. Zoning controls the lot sizes and implied densities. Official maps control the street connectivity and protect rights-of-way for major streets. Subdivision regulations focus on site layout at a scale of space and time— five to one hundred acres and one to five years—that is very different from the focus of plans for large areas of cities. Plans for subdivision regulation focus on criteria for good site layout rather than on interactions with other development. Subdivision regulations may also be the legal basis for other pertinent ordinances such as the Adequate Public Facilities Ordinance in Montgomery County, Maryland, which then requires other types of plans.

Urban service areas or growth boundaries. An urban service area is intended to identify in advance the area to be served by sanitary sewers, which is a very long lead time, very lumpy development decision with a straightforward interpretation of spatial coverage and capacity. The urban service area in Lexington, Kentucky, which was implemented in 1959, is an early example (Roeseler 1982). The logic is that a sewer plan has been devised, treatment capacity and a collection network have been chosen and partially implemented, and the jurisdiction thus has a basis for rejecting development at locations not planned for services. The urban service area concept focuses significantly on timing, which zoning does not. The logic of planned services implies that particular service capacities will become available in particular places at particular times. Timing may change if the rate of arrival of new demand is different from the assumptions of the timing calculations. The urban service area should thus be thought of not just as a spatial concept but as applying at particular times, with uncertainty, and with particular capacities. Sewer planning fits the logic of urban service areas almost perfectly. Plans for urban service areas thus follow the logic of the capacity expansion problem discussed in chapter 4.

The more recent focus of most discussion is on the Urban Growth Boundaries (UGB) of Oregon and the very similar Urban Growth Areas in Washington. These carry more claimed "responsibilities" than the urban service area concept because of the political coalitions that have created and sustained them (Knaap 1990). The UGBs could be interpreted as infrastructure-timing areas (Ding et al. 1999), as was the sewer service area established in 1978 in Seattle. Most of the academic discussion of their impacts and the political arguments about their intents and effects, however, are based on other issues. One view is that the UGB is a relatively permanent boundary that will protect agricultural and resource lands from urban development. Another is that it sets a constraint intended to increase the density of urban development and to encourage patterns consistent with the New Urbanism of transit and pedestrian trips. Developers may like it because it increases the certainty of building and subdivision approvals within an area that is legislatively required to have at least a twenty-year supply of land for development. Thus developers gain an advantage over local residents resistant to development within almost all of the area in which they would conceivably be interested in developing (Richmond 1997). The UGB may well have its greatest effect in symbolizing the political will of a coalition, which has gained the backing of state legislation and a metropolitan regional government, to pursue several different purposes for which the UGB is an artifact of an imperfect compromise. Plans for the expansion of the UGB in Portland focus more on the aggregate capacity for development question than on the specifics of infrastructure timing. Therefore the requirements of plans to support UGBs depend on the logic of the UGB. A plan may need to identify agricultural lands, recommend densities of development, focus on infrastructure timing, or all of these.

Adequate public facilities ordinances. Explicit, regulatory consideration of development timing is relatively new in the United States, most of its tools developed since the 1960s (Kelly 1993).[2] Early programs, such as Ramapo, New York, Petaluma, California, and Boulder, Colorado, were driven by concern over the rate of growth. Access to countryside, schools, roads, and sewers were primary issues. Part of the political support was motivated by interest in restricting the size and population mix of these communities, but only Boulder, which used a bond issue to raise funds to purchase land to create a greenbelt, has implemented tools that permanently restrict city size. These early programs attracted legal challenges to the authority of local governments to limit their size and thus interfere with the mobility of persons and rights to develop land. Montgomery County, Maryland, has perhaps the most comprehensive growth management system of this kind (Kelly 1993; Levinson 1997; Godschalk 2000). Montgomery County relies on a long-standing comprehensive plan that identifies a corridor of development, one of the corridors of the Washington 2000 Wedges and Corridors Plan from the 1970s. It uses an adequate public facilities ordinance that makes subdivision and project approvals depend on the availability of services, including schools, sewers, and transportation. It links its capital improvements program to an annual growth policy that sets capacities for new development in "policy areas."

Adequate public facilities ordinances implement directly the strategy aspect of a plan. The ordinance requires that the county calculate available capacity for development areas and use these in decisions about capital investments, although this task is ambiguous at best. Capacity can be used in different ways and in different places, which means that assigning capacity to particular policy areas is ambiguous (Levinson 1997). Plans in support of such growth management programs must address more than simple concurrency of infrastructure and development. A desired spatial pattern of development must also be identified to provide sufficient information to infer what kind and amount of development should go where and when.[3]

Separation of development rights. Conservation easements and "transferable development rights" separate the right to develop urban uses from other rights in the land. Plans to support these types of regulations focus on permanent patterns of land use, not timing of development. Conservation easements are permanent transfers of development rights to a private trust or public body either by purchase or donation. This approach is frequently used to protect biologically valuable lands and to protect agricultural land, especially by The Nature Conservancy and similar groups (Howe et al. 1997).

Transferable development rights works by creating a destination area to which rights are transferred from the source area (Costonis 1974; Pruetz 1997). For example, to reduce density of development in a historic district, strict regulations in the historic district are sustainable legally by allowing landowners in the district to sell what rights to develop they would otherwise have to landowners in a destination area. The destination area must have sufficiently restrictive density zoning and sufficient market demand beyond this zoning level to create a market for these rights to additional density. By purchasing development rights from owners in the source zone, owners in the destination zone can develop at densities higher than would otherwise be allowed. The logic of the plan in this case is a design, a fully worked out pattern of appropriate patterns of density or land use type. For example, Montgomery County, Maryland, uses transferable development rights to protect land that is intended to remain in agricultural use permanently. The design plan is the "wedges and corridors" pattern of the Washington 2000 Plan.

Impact fees. Impact fees that developers must pay in order to develop can be interpreted as regulations. Imposition of such fees involves a regulation that transfers rights to develop from the landowner to the municipality or service provider, which can then sell these rights to the developer. The legal legitimacy of such fees depends on showing that the amount of the fee charged and the location for which it is charged are clearly related to the costs of providing the services for which the funds will be used (see e.g., Nelson 1988; Alterman 1988). The questions of who pays the costs of impact fees and how they affect spatial pattern and timing of urban growth are complex and not fully answered. The character of plans needed to support impact fees as regulations is also unclear. Impact fees may be mostly about who pays and thus affect the cost of housing rather than its location. Setting the amount of such fees requires a fully worked out infrastructure plan as justification that the amount of the fee is closely related to the infrastructure services used by the development project being charged.

Summary: Systems of Rights and Plans for Regulations

Systems of rights set authorities to make decisions and define the scope of discretion in these decisions. Rights in land are best construed as a bundle of rights associated with land, not as simple aggregates such as "ownership." Systems of rights can be modified to achieve goals for allocation of land to uses or to achieve fairness in distribution of returns or uncertainty. Such modifications are regulations. Regulations of land should be assessed on allocative efficiency and fairness over time.

The set of regulations we are likely to observe can be explained in part by the coalitions that have adopted these regulations within a set of interlocking jurisdictions. We should expect people to favor regulations that will yield them benefits from restrictions on others greater than the losses from these restrictions on themselves. We should expect to observe people choosing to regulate themselves, and we should expect to be able to build coalitions to achieve regulations of particular types.

Most land use regulations depend, at least in part, on plans. Regulations should be based on plans appropriate to the logic of the regulation. Adequate public facility ordinances should depend on plans as strategies. Permanent allocations of land among urban and nonurban should depend on plans as designs. Plans as visions may set the context in which the designs and strategies are possible. Agendas and policies may be embedded in the implementation of these.

7

Capabilities to Make Plans

All forms of representation are abstractions from reality which bring some aspects forward to the attention and leave some in the background or eliminate them completely. At one end of the continuum the descriptive meaning of the term *representation* is emphasized; at the other, the political meaning. But because it selects and emphasizes, because it makes a statement about the world, a description has political effects to the degree that people attend to it and are influenced by it. And at the other end of the continuum, the institutions that we call "representative" stand as, and are intended to be, in various ways and according to various not wholly compatible theories, descriptive of the society they represent.
—Lisa Peattie (1987), *Planning: Rethinking Ciudad Guayana*

What capabilities do people have to make plans? What capabilities can professional planners contribute to making plans with and for clients? Do I know what I want? Can I figure out how to act in my own interests? Can a professional planner help me make plans that are in my interest? How is the profession organized so that an individual planner has incentives to plan in my interests? How can groups and organizations contribute to plan-making capacity? This chapter considers knowledge and values, individual and group capabilities to use knowledge and values, the potential of expertise from the planning profession to help bring knowledge and values to bear on making plans, and how planners work in and with organizations.

Intrinsic and Instrumental Values

Intrinsic value is a value of something in and of itself. Instrumental value is value for a purpose, a value as an instrument to achieve some other goal. This distinction is the basis for two fundamental claims. Entities of intrinsic value have the right not to be used as instruments for the benefit of others, and they have a right to be a source of judgments about instrumental values. The simplest statement is that humans as individuals have intrinsic value, but judgments by societies about to whom and to what to assign intrinsic value are much subtler. Slaves are deprived of intrinsic value and used as instruments for the benefit of others. Children are granted less autonomy, and in many societies women have less autonomy as intrinsic beings than men and thus less capability (in Sen's sense, 1992) to act instrumentally in their own interests. Further, some people argue that animals, plants, or land should be granted intrinsic value. Others argue that the evolved state of nature in aggregate has intrinsic value. Actual decision making generally renders the distinction between intrinsic and instrumental much fuzzier than is implied by any simple dichotomy. The distinction can, however, help to explain major disagreements that cannot be resolved without recognizing the fundamental difference between intrinsic and instrumental values.

It is not necessary that intrinsically valued entities be able to express their values or preferences. Parents speak as the guardians for children, and humans speak for other animals. These situations involve representation of one entity by another. This requires that one be able to speak for another without necessarily being able to speak to another, or at least without relying on their statements as decisive or even meaningful. If trees had standing to sue in court (Stone 1973), then who would speak for the trees? A tree would need a guardian, who would have incentives to act in the interests of the tree.

This problem of representing the interests of others is fundamental to the role of a professional. A professional planner is supposed to be able to help pursue the interests of a client better than the client could alone. This problem of representation becomes even more difficult if the clients are persons yet to be born. Plans must at least implicitly forecast preferences of persons not yet able to speak for themselves.

Intrinsically valued entities are much less purely valued than might at first seem the case. People are still used by collective decision as instruments of war. Intrinsic value is in some ways similar to an infinite opportunity cost for instrumental value, but there are instances where human lives are traded off with other objectives, such as in war or to achieve greater speed on highways. It is least acceptable to make these trade-offs when a specific individual is identifiable in advance rather than putting at risk an unidentified proportion of a population. It is seldom the case that entities have pure intrinsic value in the sense of not being traded off under any circumstances with other entities toward some higher end or criterion of value. Many entities have some intrinsic value. In many societies, for example, it is considered unethical to harm an animal or even a tree without sufficient reason.

If one person is treating an aspect of a decision situation in terms of instrumental values and another is treating it in terms of intrinsic values, conflict will be difficult to resolve. If it is inappropriate to build a dam because a fish species, as a species not as individuals, has intrinsic value, then no amount of trade-off in resulting gains will suffice. Most claims of intrinsic value, however, have some instrumental component or underlying instrumental basis.

By asking "What's wrong with plastic trees?" Krieger (1973) elucidates how values can be thought through. If Niagara Falls is valued because it is a "natural phenomenon," should it be left to evolve? If it evolves, the geological formations that create it, it will eventually become a more gradual waterfall, more like a giant rapid than a vertical drop. But is it the vertical drop that is so highly valued? Is the image of a clean vertical drop so strongly impressed on the world as what Niagara Falls is that it should be preserved, even if that means fighting against the natural geological evolution? Is the current equilibrium outcome of a natural system intrinsically valuable because it is the natural outcome? Should we build a plastic Niagara Falls in order to have the waterfall we want? If you cannot tell the difference between a plastic falls and the real falls (as it was), is the plastic falls an acceptable substitute? If plastic trees looked like and provided the functional relationships with other entities that real trees do, what's wrong with plastic? If you argue that such plastic trees are impossible to create, then you have acknowledged that you are making instrumental arguments about the value of trees. That is, substitutes would be acceptable, you just do not believe such substitutes can be created. If substitutes would be unacceptable precisely because they are substitutes, then you are arguing for the intrinsic value of natural trees.

The claim to spiritual values of nature, as represented for example by John Muir, is not a claim to intrinsic value. As Muir's own choice of words belies, it represents a larger utilitarianism.

> The tendency nowadays to wander in wilderness is delightful to see. Thousands of tired, nerve-shaken, over-civilized people are beginning to find out that going

to the mountains is going home; that wildness is a necessity; and that mountain parks and reservations are useful not only as fountains of timber and irrigating rivers, but as fountains of life. Awakening from the stupefying effects of the vice of over-industry and the deadly apathy of luxury, they are trying as best they can to mix and enrich their own little ongoings with those of Nature, and to get rid of rust and disease. (Muir 1901, 1–3, as in Nash 1976)

That wildness in some special sense is essential to this spiritual benefit is in part discovered and in part created by its own practitioners. Its conflict with the multiple-use utilitarianism of Gifford Pinchot's conservation is in its essential requirement of original wildness, which can be created only by identification, not by physical replication (Krieger 1973). We must learn what is wild and identify it as such; in a sense we thus create wilderness by distinguishing it from other areas. We cannot physically recreate wilderness, however, because that would fundamentally contradict the claim of its existence before and beyond the human and thus would remove its spiritual value. This spiritual value is instrumental because it is value for us, but it is made valuable to us by our ability to accept the ambiguity of claiming that we value wilderness in and of itself, that is, that *we* value it for being wilderness.

Leopold's land ethic (Leopold 1949) suggests that there is at least some intrinsic value in land itself. Intrinsic value implies that land should not be harmed without good reason. A wetland could be valued-intrinsically as an evolved state of nature. As discussed above, such a contention shifts the argument to one of intrinsic rather than instrumental value. The following additional arguments about the value of wetlands might be components of a larger explanation of their instrumental value:

- instrumental value as habitat for other intrinsically valued entities, such as birds
- instrumental value as "real" natural environment
- instrumental value for viewing of birds or mammals by humans
- instrumental value for sustaining ecosystem function or hydrologic function
- instrumental value as subterfuge, such as to prevent development that might bring in low-income people, other ethnic groups, higher-density housing, or other perceived costs by claiming environmental risks
- instrumental value as risk-averse strategy to avoid unknown outcomes that might result from disturbing an evolved state

- instrumental value as reserved resource that could not be reproduced if new value for it were found in the future

The current view of wetlands is accentuated by comparison to previous descriptions. The plan developed in 1959 for Berkeley, California, refers to finding productive use for the "submerged lands" in San Francisco Bay (Kent 1964). We have changed our concept of the instrumental value of wetlands through new and more widely shared knowledge. It is no longer acceptable to presume that wetlands are unproductive, even in their "natural" state. In the face of this newly recognized productive value, wetlands would command a higher price; also, with a reduced supply of wetland, the value increases sufficiently that we are now constructing wetlands artificially. All of these are instrumental arguments, but they recognize the importance of intersubjective processes in creating perceived values.

Intrinsically valued things cannot be traded off in instrumental ways because each is uniquely valued and has no substitutes. Only intrinsically valued things can make instrumental decisions and thus count as sources of information about values; they count as decision makers. The intrinsic versus instrumental distinction is thus important on two counts. First, it is a source of confusion in arguments over appropriate actions. An argument in which one person is treating something as intrinsically valued and the other is treating it as instrumentally valued will be fruitless unless this distinction is acknowledged and directly addressed. An approach to resolution that acknowledges the likelihood of a less than fully understood combination of both types of value may be more useful. Second, the distinction determines who counts in having rights to participate in making decisions. Who counts is an ethical question for a society, a question about which individuals in that society may disagree and which may change over time.

Subjective, Objective, and Intersubjective Knowledge and Values

A value or statement is subjective if it is a property of a subject, an intrinsically valued being. An individual's preferences among colors can be determined by asking the subject. A value or statement is objective if it is a property of an object, regardless of who observes the object. In general, people will agree about the observed color of an object. A value or statement is intersubjective if it depends on the set of subjects within which it occurs. Knowledge is intersubjective because what we understand at any one time depends on our interactions with others. Much of what you and I know about the functioning of our bodies or the solar system we believe to be true because people to whom we have granted legitimacy using methods of argument we recognize as credible tell us that it is so.

Recalling the discussion of explanations in chapter 1, objective—that is, replicable—observations linked to currently accepted explanations of how things work are useful because they help cope with the world. Through intersubjective and observation processes, new explanations arise that are more useful in coping with the world. Descriptions or explanations of human behavior, however, affect us, whereas explanations of physical systems do not affect those systems except through effects on our behavior.

> A mistaken view of planetary motion, though held for centuries, had no effect on the motion of the planets. They continued on their elliptical way, undisturbed by human preference for circular motion; and even when men discovered their mistake, they had no means to bring the course of nature into line with their aesthetic predilections. A too restricted view of human nature, on the other hand, even though only briefly ascendant, can significantly alter the expectations and hence the behaviour of men and societies and may thus provide its own bogus validation. (Vickers 1965, 17)

The intersubjectively accepted explanation of the ozone hole over the South Pole is that it is caused by physical processes that could be affected by human choices. This explanation may affect human behavior regardless of whether the explanation is actually correct. Through this effect on human behavior, the explanation may also affect conditions in the physical world. Thus the choice of explanations matters.

Urban development involves physical phenomena, but the behavior of individuals and groups is much more problematic. When establishing our beliefs, attitudes, and accepted facts, we rely on our judgments about whom to believe at least as much as we rely on our own direct knowledge or understanding. We rely on expertise of others with specialized knowledge about how the world works and about how to figure out how the world works. We should be able to rely on planners to have expertise about how urban development works and about how to make and use plans that will increase our ability to cope with urban development. The intersubjective explanation is thus useful because social relationships, individual differences, cognitive limitations, group processes, and specialized expertise create the values expressed and the interests served by the actions chosen. This explanation also emphasizes the importance of the relationship between plans and collective choice, which is discussed in chapter 8.[1]

A subjective value is not something inherently undesirable. If a task calls for information about an individual's values, then subjective values are appropriate. Confusion may arise when the task is to assess values because the subject (person) then becomes the object of inquiry. It is then desirable that a person's (subjective) values be consistent, regardless of who observes or elicits them. That is, the assessment of these values should be independent of the observer, and thus the assessment should be objective. The standard measure of objectivity is replicability. Repeated, independent observations should yield consistent results. My stated voting preference among candidates is subjective because it is a property of my assessment of the candidates and differs from assessments made by other individuals. A pollster, however, claims to be able to elicit my preference objectively; other pollsters would also elicit the same preference, thus meeting the standards of replicability.

Values might be presumed to arise in at least three different ways: as an attribute of individuals, as an attribute of collections of individuals, or as an attribute of interactions among individuals. Should values be derived from some concept of collective social value or by starting from the expressed values of individuals? Do intrinsic entities count only individually? Or, can groups of individuals be intrinsically valued as groups? Alternatively, are individual values so dependent on interactions among individuals that values are intersubjective, residing in the interaction among individuals of a group? Is there a community interest, or merely a community of individual interests?

The notion of a "public interest" is one response to this situation (see e.g., Klosterman 1980), and is central to discussions and ethical statements about planning because the planning profession claims to serve the public interest (American Institute of Certified Planners 1991). The meaning of public interest, however, is elusive at best. It means several different things. It may be an estimate by experts of the "objective interests" of a particular group, implying that experts are better able to estimate these interests than individuals themselves. It may be the interests of the persons that are not actively and sufficiently representing themselves because their interests are a collective good as discussed in chapter 5. In this sense, the public interest is the opposite of organized special interests. It may mean working *pro bono* for groups unable to pay because of a distribution of wealth or income that undermines the capabilities of some individuals to participate fully, as in the idea of "public interest" work by lawyers for nonpaying clients. It is more useful to explain these distinct situations than to rely on a concept of the public interest.

People may not know or be able to determine what actions are in their own best interests. Relationships with other individuals may shape their values inappropriately. If individuals were able to assess a situation independent of the power relationships and without other value shaping, such as advertising, they would express different values or behave so as to reveal different preferences. Ajzen and Fishbein (1980) argue that subjective norms (my perception of what other people think I should intend to do) are important predictors of intentions and thus of behavior. Subjective norms can be shaped, intentionally or unintentionally, through myth, ideology, or selective information. Gaventa (1980) argues that three types of power relations identified by Lukes (1974) accumulate in their shaping of the expressed interests of less powerful individuals or groups. The first type of power is having superior resources to use in bargaining or in other means of resolving conflicts. The second type is barriers against participation, such as avoiding the making of decisions so that there is no decision making to participate in. The "mobilization of bias" (Bachrach and Baratz 1962) may set the formal institutional procedures so as to favor some groups over others. The third type of power results from myths or ideologies to explain the existing order, in particular why the powerless should accept their position as being appropriate. Building on these and other bounds on human capacity to implement intentions or interests, Forester (1989) argues that planners should bring values to the interaction with clients, not merely accept them. Planners must take a critical perspective about what they hear and see in interacting with clients.

Individual Cognitive Capabilities and Processes

Human capabilities to make plans are limited by abilities to express values and to manipulate complex ideas. Can I implement my own values? Can I make choices that are consistent with the logic I intend to use? Experiments suggest that people make choices in ways that they would agree are incorrect once they understand the implications of these choices. These difficulties compound the task of eliciting values from individuals because people cannot always express the values they intend to express. From this perspective, planning experts should help people make decisions they would like to make if they knew how. Memory limitations make it difficult for people to work on complex problems without tools and techniques that recognize these limitations.

Strotz (1956) pointed out that people might not have the same relative preferences for events occurring at two times when viewed from different times. You might decide today that tomorrow is the day to start dieting or that next year is the time to enlist in the military. But when tomorrow comes, you may have changed your preferences. Which is your true preference? Precommitment strategies, such as lump-sum payments in advance for diet or exercise programs, a six-month lead time for enlistment in the military, and savings by payroll deduction, have been developed to take advantage of these inconsistencies. Consistent plans over sequences of decisions become problematic if preferences cannot be forecast.

Psychology distinguishes two types of memory, working and long-term. Although more recent work recognizes a more complex situation, the simple distinction is sufficient for our purposes (see e.g., Wickens 1992). Working memory is what you can hold in active memory for immediate use without taking time to "memorize" it. The capacity of working memory is seven plus or minus two chunks. Chunks are things that you can recall in totality without having to consider their parts. A single digit in a number, a name that you already know how to spell, and a sequence of numbers that has some recognized structure (e.g., powers of two) are chunks. This limitation in working memory is familiar in seven-digit phone numbers and license plate numbers.

Working memory allows very rapid input, very rapid access, but very limited capacity. Its limited capacity explains why long division is difficult to do "in your head"—because you do not have sufficient memory to keep all the active remainders and partial solutions in working memory. When forced to do such calculations in their heads, most people use a method of successive approximations because such iterations require remembering fewer numbers. Working memory also explains one reason for creating hierarchies of elements in order to manipulate ideas. Hierarchies build new things from combinations of small numbers of types of familiar chunks. People imagine a neotraditional urban layout in terms of building placements, streets, and relationships among them, not as a set of lines in a drawing. By using complex chunks, which we can recognize immediately because of frequent prior use, active memory can work on very complex problems. Humans can learn to recognize complex spatial patterns as chunks, which explains why diagrams and structured text are effective representations.

Long-term memory has a huge capacity and a complex associative structure, but requires a long time to memorize things into it. It is also subject to a relatively high error rate on recall. This means that we are better able to use what we already know, that what we know is, in general, based on repeated experiences sufficient to memorize it, and that the associations among what we know may not be accurate. Chunks for efficient recognition in working memory and use in active manipulation come from long-term memory. We know about houses, apartments, streets, people of different types, ways of getting from place to place, and how (we think) the world works from our long-term memory. The associative structure ties together such elements as the name of a place, the person who told us about that place, a person who lives in that place, and a visual image of that place. We may, however, recall these incorrectly and think that the person who told us about it lives there, or that the image of the place is instead the place we were when we learned about it. These errors can be useful by creating unexpected, new relationships and thus prompting new ideas.

Meehan (1989) laments that planning education does not ensure that job applicants know the answers to questions on his employment test: "How many square feet in an acre? How many square miles in a typical U. S. Public Land Survey Section? What is the invert of a sanitary or storm sewer?" (54). One reaction is that these questions are not the meat of planning education. On the other hand, a potential employee who does not have answers for these questions at ready access in long-term memory has not been working on the kind of land planning that Meehan's firm does. The questions are not merely measures of knowledge but indicators of experience.

Memory limits and other factors mean that individuals have a limited budget of attention that can be focused on tasks at any one time and a limited ability to sustain focused attention for long periods of time (see e.g.,

Keele 1973; Wickens 1992). Attention budgets explain why shaping attention can be a powerful way to affect what people do. For example, Forester (1989) frames his interpretation of planning processes in terms of attention: "A critical account of planning practice—as the selective communicative organizing or disorganizing of attention . . . " (11).

People have pervasive cognitive biases that yield choices they would disagree with upon reflection. Kahneman, Slovic, and Tversky (1982) are among the best known of a group of psychologists who have investigated human decision-making biases. Judgments about observable phenomena, probabilities, and preference relations are all vulnerable to such biases. Six types of biases suggest implications for human capabilities in making plans and the relationships of clients and expertise: focusing on what is represented, framing, anchoring and adjustment, ignoring disconfirming evidence (in particular, base rates) by misinterpreting new data to conform to the current hypothesis, and availability.

Given a particular representation or statement of a problem, people tend to focus on that representation rather than on the problem. Any representation for a reasonably interesting problem is likely to be limiting with respect to some responses to that problem. One simple demonstration of this bias is the "nine dot problem." Given nine dots arranged in a regular grid, a way to connect the dots using four straight lines is found only after realizing that the lines can go beyond the perimeter defined by the grid and that a diagonal line need not bisect the grid symmetrically. Peattie (1987) notes that when the planning consultants from the capital or from other countries visited the site for the new town of Ciudad Guayana in Venezuela, they frequently spent their time on a hilltop above the site. The perspective from there was similar to the map representations with which they were thinking about their ideas and similarly distanced them from people currently living on the site. This representation was in sharp contrast to Peattie's perspective, which was based on social interaction with residents.

Even with a single type of representation, the same problem can be framed in different ways and these frames may lead to different solutions. Consider the following problems[2]:

Problem 1: Unless you choose a permanent site for hazardous waste disposal, 900 residents near the temporary storage site will get cancer. You have a choice of two sites. If you choose the first site, 300 people will be saved from cancer. If you choose the second site, there is a one-third chance that 900 will be saved and a two-thirds chance that none will be saved. Which will you choose?

Problem 2: Unless you choose a permanent site for hazardous waste disposal, 900 residents near the temporary storage site will get cancer. If you choose the first site, 600 will get cancer. If you choose the second site, there is a one-third chance that none will get cancer and a two-thirds chance that 900 will get cancer. Which will you choose?

Careful analysis shows that these two problems are identical. In each case, the first site results in 300 saved and 600 getting cancer. Also, in each case, the second site results in a one-third probability of 900 being saved from getting cancer and a two-thirds probability of 0 being saved from cancer. Extrapolating from experimental results, for the first case, most people will choose the first site, perhaps because of its focus on the certainty of saving 300 people. But, for the second problem, most people will choose the second site, perhaps because of the focus on the certainty of 600 deaths. Although the wording is different, and thus the framing is different, the two problems are identical. If answers in such situations are different, then experts who can help resolve such indeterminate situations will be useful. A possible technique in this situation is always to ask such questions both ways and then ask the decision maker to reflect on resolving inconsistencies.

The anchoring and adjustment bias leads people to make insufficient adjustments from their starting position given new evidence. A simple demonstration is to distribute pieces of paper, each with one of two numbers, to a group of people. Then, ask people to estimate some number that they will not know with much accuracy or precision, such as the population of a city or the number of people displaced by a certain highway project. The average of the estimates of the group of people who received a piece of paper with the higher number will be higher than the average of the estimates of those who received the lower number. This result holds even if they are told that the numbers on the pieces of paper have nothing to do with the estimation problem. The anchoring and adjustment bias describes the empirically verified phenomena that persons will anchor, even on a reference point they are told is irrelevant, and fail to adjust sufficiently to account for new information. This bias invites experts who can provide techniques that will increase the weight given to new evidence so that estimates are adjusted appropriately. If a planner provided information about what industries in the local economy yield the most tax revenues and jobs, local decision makers would be anchored by prior beliefs and would not adjust their perceptions sufficiently to fit the actual data.

People tend to ignore disconfirming evidence, in particular the averages for previous instances, such as the average time to complete a Ph.D., the average time to complete a major downtown development project, or the average time to make a comprehensive plan. Even Kahneman, who has written extensively on these biases, notes that he estimated his schedule for an edited book to be well below the average rate. In hindsight, the average rate would have been a better prediction (McKean 1985). People tend to view an instance on which they are immediately focused without regard to historical or contextual probabilities. Another version of this bias is called isolation error. Forecasts of outcomes and estimates of probabilities of success are generated in isolation from historical records of outcomes and probabilities for similar situations. Perhaps we are unwilling to accept that there have been similar situations. The effect can yield either behavior that is too optimistic or behavior that is too pessimistic. Failing to use all of a loan fund for fear of overcommitting the fund might ignore a historical record that not all grantees actually initiate projects and receive the funds. Investing in a private-public partnership project believing it will be successful might ignore the experience that many such projects have failed and that the estimates of benefits from such projects are often grossly inflated. People tend to misinterpret new data to conform to a current hypothesis. Humans have a strong tendency to make data fit the solution, rather than the other way around. If the numbers suggest that our economic development scheme will not generate new jobs, we find a way to reinterpret them appropriate to our particular case so as to confirm what we "know" to be true.

Availability bias arises from the immediacy in memory of particular instances. For example, we tend to think that there will not be another flood right away because we just had one and they only occur with a probability of one year in a hundred. In contrast, we also tend to worry about flooding, fire, or failed projects, or believe in the success of projects, if we have recently experienced a disaster or a success. This bias affects our estimates of the probability of events. We give too much weight to our most immediate single experience, compared to large numbers of other instances that should affect our estimates.

People cannot make reliable (replicable) choices based on multiple attributes. When subjects use different techniques to aid in multiattribute decisions, they arrive at different judgments (Lai and Hopkins 1995). The meanings of trade-offs implied by these techniques are often obscure and are not understood by users (Lai and Hopkins 1989). People cannot rely on available techniques to express the values they wish to express nor make the decisions they wish to make.

Given these cognitive limitations, planners can justify use of their expertise about decision making and values if they can provide techniques and tools that reduce these biases. The techniques must work in complex situations involving combinations of cognitive biases and social distortions of intersubjective knowledge and values. Group capabilities provide one approach but also add additional difficulties.

Group Cognitive Capabilities and Processes

Two heads are better than one. Too many cooks spoil the broth. These familiar sayings frame the question of collaboration. Under what circumstances are group processes beneficial? What makes a group process effective? What are the implications for organizing processes of making plans and taking plan-based action? Research on group processes addresses these questions (Steiner 1972; McGrath 1984; Davis 1992).

McGrath (1984, 61) classifies group tasks into four types, each of which is divided into two subtypes. Generation tasks include generating ideas (creativity) and generating plans. The subtypes distinguish between generating ideas or images (which is pertinent to the vision aspect of plans) and generating actions to achieve ends (which is pertinent to the strategy aspect of plans).[3] Choice tasks include solving problems for which, once found, the answer will be recognized as obviously correct and decision-making tasks in which agreement defines the answer. Negotiation tasks include resolving cognitive conflicts and resolving differences in interests. Execution tasks include performing physical tasks and contests. Most of these types of tasks are pertinent to processes of making and using plans.

First, consider generation or choice tasks in which all members of the group have the same interests and will recognize the same solutions as good solutions. The most extreme form of this is a "eureka problem" in which as soon as someone identifies a solution, everyone else recognizes it as correct or good. Group processes may be more effective than individuals in addressing such problems because of (1) a larger sample of knowledge or skill, (2) parallel processing, (3) specialization, or (4) interactive collaboration. These explanations are based on comparisons between solutions that result from groups and solutions that would result if each individual in the group worked alone.

Groups increase the sample from which a solution, or a skill in finding a solution, can be drawn. As group size increases, there is a greater likelihood that the group will include someone that knows the answer from previous experience or has skills specific to solving the problem. The group size may create costs of interaction and distraction, but if the knowledgeable individual can explain the solution persuasively and focus on it without distraction, then increased group size increases the likelihood of success. The probability of including a knowledgeable or skillful person will also be increased if the diversity of group membership increases. Additional people who know the same things or have the same skills are unnecessary.

Groups may also be beneficial because they allow parallel processing. Members of the group work simultaneously on the same tasks but different parts of the problem, or on different tasks on the same part of the problem. Parallel processing reduces elapsed time, but does not inherently improve quality of the solution. The costs come in the difficulty of decomposing the tasks or problem, managing any remaining interdependencies among the parts, and recomposing the results. The more completely hierarchical the situation, the easier it is to decompose and recompose. These issues arise whether the parallel processors are humans or computers. Parallel processing is having several checkers at the supermarket. Pipeline processing is having a checker to record the prices and a bagger to pack the groceries. Both types of multiprocessing increase capacity per unit of time.

Groups may also gain by specialization, which combines the first two advantages. Each person undertakes a task in parallel with other persons working on other tasks. Each person is assigned a task based on the comparative advantage of skills or knowledge. The difficulties of decomposition, managing interdependence, and recomposition remain and may be even more difficult than in pure parallel processing. In this case, however, the quality of solution as well as elapsed time to achieve it, may be improved because each task is undertaken with more knowledge or skill. An Amish barn raising is a quintessential example of this kind of group process. Pipeline processing—for example, an assembly line—is one case of specialization. The assembly line reminds us that repetitiveness and boredom may overpower the gains from specialization so that specialization becomes a disadvantage in terms of quality. Specialization also implies that a more diverse group membership is more useful in matching persons to tasks.

Finally, group processes may yield benefits from strict collaboration. In this case, interaction among participants working on the same tasks yields results that no individual would have discovered alone. The experimental evidence is that brainstorming is more effective if it is parallel processing rather than collaboration. That is, interaction about ideas inhibits rather than encourages generation of a greater variety and quality of ideas, even if group members are told to generate ideas without evaluating them (Mullen et al. 1991). The Nominal Group Technique, in which ideas are generated individually then evaluated and developed in groups makes more effective use of group processes than does group brainstorming (McGrath 1984). There is little research, however, on focused collaborative processes by professionals.

An example highlights some of the complexities of interpreting group process in practice. Lovelace (1992, 26) recalls the planning for the tunnel under the restored Williamsburg, Virginia. None of the alternatives devised for alignment of a parkway serving the historic town and Jamestown to the south was satisfactory. Three members of Harland Bartholomew's firm were looking at topographic maps of the site. One of them noted that two small stream valleys approached the town from opposite sides. The three of them recognized and developed the possibility and argument for a tunnel under the town. Using these valleys as the access to the tunnel reduced the disruption to both the natural and the historical context of the town. The alignment implied a tunnel over which there were no historic buildings. It also brought cars very close to the town without being seen from the streets of the historic restoration itself. The idea was both compelling and absurd because of the implied expense of a quarter-mile tunnel under such a small town. Although they doubted they could sell the idea, they tried and succeeded. Lovelace does not recall who recognized the possibility or indeed if any one of them did alone. This instance may illustrate the possibilities of true collaboration, both in building the idea into a feasible proposal and in encouraging each other to work on it rather than reject it out of hand. Collaboration may yield benefits distinct from brainstorming.

Sniezek and Henry (1989) report results of an experiment that illustrates these ideas. They asked subjects to estimate the frequency of fifteen causes of death in the United States population. Data were available to assess the accuracy of the answers, but were not available to the subjects to use in making estimates. First, each subject individually estimated the fifteen frequencies. Then the subjects were grouped into teams of three, and each team made estimates. Group estimates were more accurate than the mean or median of estimates made by individuals before being assigned to the group. This result suggests that groups were not simply combining their individual estimates in straightforward ways. Thirty percent of the group estimates were more accurate than the best individual estimate from a member of that group, and 15 percent were better than the best individual estimate and outside the range of individual estimates. This difference suggests that groups were not simply choosing the individual's estimate they judged best or that of the most confident group member. High disagreement among individual estimates within the group and group estimates outside the range of individual estimates of members of that group were each predictive of more accurate group estimates. Thus, diversity in initial conditions was beneficial, perhaps because it countered the anchoring and adjustment bias discussed above. Groups were generally more confident of their estimates than were individuals.

These results suggest that collaboration is occurring because the results of groups are neither the best of the individuals, nor a simple weighting of the individuals, but new estimates, in some cases outside the confidence intervals set by individuals for their individual estimates. This result implies that heterogeneous groups that are made up of individuals whose initial estimates showed greater difference exert more group cognitive effort to work on estimates and thus are more successful in countering conservatism biases of their individual estimates. Such collaboration among heterogeneous members is, therefore, likely to be beneficial in making judgments in situations with incomplete information.[4]

Many group processes accomplish more than one of these benefits simultaneously, and thus may also incur all of the corollary costs. In addition, individuals in a group seldom have identical interests. Groups are often created to bring to the table different interests as well as different skills and knowledge. It may not be possible to separate these phenomena in immediate practice, but it is possible to distinguish them analytically. A group intended to bring different interests to the table may confound the benefits of collaborative problem solving and vice versa. Alternatively, the two may be synergistic. The motivation of different interests provides incentives for individuals to find different alternatives that advance their own interests. The motivation to resolve conflict over interests so as to be able to take action may also provide incentives to find alternatives that resolve conflict. The differences in interests are inherent in the parties in the group, though their understandings of their interests may change in the process of deliberations. In contrast, the cognitive complementarity that is beneficial for group problem solving can be designed into the group.

The critical theory and communicative rationality literature in planning makes essentially the same cognitive argument backed by the ethical aspect of representing interests. Most case interpretations focus on ad hoc panels, voluntary groups, and decision processes within bureaucracy. Forester (1989) concentrates on episodes of planners working with applicants for development permission and neighborhood groups that might oppose the application. Innes (1996) concentrates on ad hoc groups addressing a particular decision situation, usually separately from other decisions. In either frame, the implication is that planners can bring expertise to group interaction to make plans.

Expertise and the Planning Profession

Individuals and groups who want to make plans can gain from planners' expertise in coping with intersubjective values and knowledge, overcoming cognitive limits and biases, managing group processes, and providing specialized knowledge about how human settlements work. The logic of making plans for urban development, as argued in this book, is an area of specialized expertise in the planning profession. Without arguing that it is the only area of expertise within the range of things that professional planners do, it is sufficient to claim that the knowledge involved, combined with knowledge about how human settlements work and embedded skills acquired by practice, constitute significant expertise worth paying for.

The planning profession makes credible a planner's claim to work in the interests of such clients. An organized profession reinforces a moral community and thereby enhances the possibilities for actions. A profession's capabilities will derive in part from community ideals and norms, will rely in part on articulated norms of duties to act correctly and partly on accepted criteria for good outcomes. A profession will thus have norms of behavior and moral commitments to particular outcomes.

A profession consists of individual practitioners with particular relationships to clients. The profession as a whole has an intended function that its individual members achieve by the aggregate result of their behaviors. The professional claims experience and expertise sufficient to know the client's interests better than the client could alone. This yields a claim of professional autonomy from the client sufficient to use professional expertise while still maintaining a responsibility to the client. The aggregate objective of the profession must represent the interests of other parties in a situation besides the primary client of an individual practitioner. Marcuse (1976) explains these ideas by contrasting planning with the legal and accounting professions and the discussion that follows builds directly on his discussion. He presents these concerns in the context of thinking about "system-challenging" versus "system-maintaining" actions. It is insufficient to serve unethical goals ethically.

The structure of the legal profession is that any individual should have professional legal advice (counsel) that advocates the client's interests. Short of perjury, the individual attorney's behavioral objective is to advocate the client's interest, not to seek truth. The legal system's function, however, is to seek truth as a result of the individual behavior of attorneys within it. The system serves the larger interests of protecting the rights of the accused while achieving justice. The accused and the accusers each have advocates of equivalent skill and resources, following the same rules of procedure and with the same motivation to act in the interests of their client. This caricature of the lawyer as loyal advocate misleads by ignoring other roles that lawyers frequently play, such as contract drafter, judge, legislator, or negotiator. In the legal profession, however, the role being played in a given situation and the rules of behavior that apply to that role are clear. In planning, the roles are often simultaneous and the behaviors confounded.

In the accounting profession, Certified Public Accountants audit the records of organizations to validate their financial status for investors and banks. If the accountant were acting directly as an advocate for the client's interest in the same way as an attorney, the audit would be of no value to the client because no one would accept it as a disinterested assessment. It is in the client's interest, therefore, that the accountant not act as an advocate. The client thus hires the accountant not to identify only aspects to the advantage of the client, as if trying to sell stock in the company, but to follow credible, prescribed procedures that have the potential to put the company in a bad light. The ethical system for accountants requires that audits be done in a particular way, regardless of the effect on the client. This possibility is precisely what makes the audit valuable to the organization being audited, which is the immediate and paying client. This requirement of correct procedure is in strong contrast to the open-ended strategies of advocacy available to an attorney.

Again, accountants play multiple roles, but the role being played must be clear. An accountant representing a public utility before a public utility commission is in an advocacy situation similar to the attorney or to a planner submitting an environmental impact report. In representations before a utility commission, an accountant is not sustaining a system of reporting for a large number of individual investors dispersed geographically and temporally who must believe an accountant's report without direct opportunity to interact and whom the client cannot identify in advance. Rather, the accountant is advocating before a body of quasi experts or politicians to gain approval for a proposal that the review panel has the authority to recommend or approve. In this situation the accountant may be successful in winning a rate increase approval by the cleverness of the case in meeting legislative and regulatory guidelines. The accountant may assist in designing a good rate system so that an increase can be won, much as a planner might assist in designing a good project so that an environmental impact report (EIR) will be approved.

Schultz (1989) argues that the strategy of a professional ethical role chosen by the engineering profession advanced its status and opportunities in the late nineteenth century.

> Municipal engineers solidified their growing reputation as problem-solvers in three ways. First, they made themselves indispensable to officials eager to boost their city's expansion. Second, they proclaimed (and apparently persuaded the public) that they were neutral experts who stood above partisan politics. Third, within their own ranks, they created a professional bureaucracy that outsiders came to admire as a model of efficiency. (183)

The engineering profession marketed itself in a consistent way and modeled its claims in its own organizational efforts.

All these systems have in common a dependence on each individual adopting the norms of the profession. The legal system could not function if only some attorneys committed to the system's norms. Underlying this commitment are prohibitions on perjury, conflict of interest, and side payments (bribes), all of which would alter the performance of the system by misrepresenting relationships among individuals in the system. A lawyer need not reveal information that would work against her client, but she may not tell lies or knowingly counsel a client to tell lies. A company may pay for a damaging audit because it is in its interests to sustain a system that is credible to its investors. If a company makes side payments—that is, additional payments to a consultant relative to the audit of a second company—then the incentive system has been disrupted. These systems can be subverted and require enforcement and monitoring to be sustained as credible and legitimate.

The structure of fees compensating a professional must also fit the logic of the system. The most immediate example is the real estate salesperson whose fee is a percentage of the sale price of the property. This approach ensures that the agent's interest is consistent with the client's interest in getting a high price. The agent working on a fixed fee would value any sale equally regardless of price. Ironically, the sales agent often works most actively with the buyer, whose interests are directly contradictory to this fee structure. An attorney working on a contingent fee basis (a percentage of the settlement amount in a civil suit) has a strong incentive to pursue a high settlement, but no motivation to pursue a cause independent of dollars. That federal legislation allows an unusually high percentage contingent fee for attorneys in civil rights cases increases the likelihood that attorneys will take on such cases even in the face of low probabilities of winning because they have to win a smaller percentage of cases to make a desired income.

Professions relate the actions of individual professionals to the goals of the profession in aggregate. The logic of this relationship in planning is diffuse and not clearly established. Instead, planners have stated an allegiance directly to a problematically defined public interest, rather than to a process for achieving it. In contrast, both the accountant and the attorney, in their narrowly defined roles, have an allegiance to a system of achieving an aggregate outcome through behaviors that have the attributes of collective goods.

Like the other professions discussed above, planning has more than one logic for ethical roles and planners have many roles. A planner may be a plan

maker, an advocate, a negotiator, an ordinance drafter, or a regulation en-
forcer. Baum (1983), Forester (1989), Hoch (1994), and Howe (1980) have
described these roles extensively. None of these roles is perhaps as salient
as the adversarial role of attorneys or the independence of certified public
accountants. The planning profession historically has relied on two distinct
ethical claims: progressive reform and expertise in effective decision making (see e.g., Klosterman 1985; Howe and Kaufman 1979). The progressive
reform argument acknowledges a normative agenda and related criteria
about means. The effective decision-making argument tends to ignore the
normative agenda, or assume that it is beyond the planner's realm, and focuses on procedures claimed to yield effective results when confronting interdependent decisions.

The individual progressive reformer finds ways to work within the system to change the system and increase the likelihood that certain outcomes
will be achieved and that less-well-off persons will gain greater benefit. Such
planners may use many of the same methods, including the making of plans,
as other planners, but their success is based on outcomes. Plans may not fit
their interests because investments in the built environment and regulations
of spatial interdependence may not be the most effective strategies to
achieve the progressive agenda. Indeed, progressive reformers may find
themselves fighting such projects and therefore such plans. On the other
hand, the framers of ambitious plans, including the Chicago Plan of 1909,
clearly viewed themselves as progressive reformers and cloaked their plans
in the language of such reforms. Historically, progressive reform has also
included the introduction of professional expertise in decision making and
administration of cities.

Claims linking these aggregate professional objectives to individual professional behavior thus focus on considering appropriate criteria for outcomes and using appropriate methods of analysis. The profession cares what
goals are implied in plans and the profession cares how plans are made.
Were goals of fairness and equitable outcomes pursued? For example, the
profession might "require" an equity report (analogous to an environmental impact report) on plans. Following the perspective of the accountant's
audit, this equity report would reveal to an unrepresented public pertinent
information on which to make choices. Thus the planner might have an at-
torney-like relationship with the immediate client and an accountant-like
relationship with the immediate client *vis-à-vis* its constituencies that are

not immediately represented. The latter would have to bc imposed by professional standards. Were techniques of constituent participation employed in the process? Were these issues appropriately advocated given the particular organizational role of the planner? A traditional test for ethical behavior applied to professional situations is to "rehearse" explanations that justify the behavior to the various constituencies involved.

Organizations and Plans

Planners work in organizations that make plans and act in relation to other organizations. Subunits within organizations make plans and use these and other plans. Plans for urban development are made by organizations and include actions by the same or other organizations. It is thus pertinent to consider briefly how organizations work, in contrast to how plans work, and how organizations make and use plans.[5]

Organizations are useful if and when they can reduce transaction costs compared to the market. This is the traditional argument from economics, as developed by Coase (1937). Rather than contract for services for each task or each day as separate market transactions, an entrepreneur contracts with an employee who agrees to follow the directions of the employer subject to contracted limits. The ensuing internalized transactions are less costly than the set of market transactions that would have been required. Williamson (1975) distinguishes market transactions among autonomous individuals from hierarchical (or organizational) transactions between persons of greater and lesser authority in a hierarchy. Transaction costs of monitoring quality of performance do not disappear within organizations, but the nature of the monitoring may change. Plans are likely to exist regardless of whether a metropolitan area is organized into one government or many. A metropolitan government still faces the problem of dccomposing its scope functionally or geographically to cope with the complexities of plans. Municipal governments take into account actions and plans of other municipalities regardless of whether a regional government exists.

March (1988, 7) argues that limited attention, departmental hierarchies, and excess resources allow conflicting goals and interests to persist in organizations. Organizations do not, and in most instances cannot, resolve all the inconsistencies they incorporate, but they can survive by separating one decision from another sequentially or departmentally so that conflicts are avoided. Limited attention capacity allows decision makers to do one thing today and a contradictory thing tomorrow, but this may be an advantage rather than something to eliminate.

> Despite conventional modern ideologies advocating the confrontation and resolution of conflict, organizational experience with conflict indicates that institutions that would otherwise be seriously threatened by internal inconsistencies are able to sustain themselves for long periods by buffering inconsistent demands from each other. And this is possible, primarily because a fundamental feature of organizations is that not everything can be attended at once. (March 1988, 8)

Plans in organizations can consider interdependent actions without pretending to resolve all internal inconsistencies within the organization. In contrast with a frequent assumption that organizations have unitary and identifiable goals, organizations often make decisions without shared goals or explicit bargaining. They are likely to discover preferences through action as well as to take action on the basis of preferences.

If organizations or relationships among organizations were completely unstructured, then as Pressman and Wildavsky (1973) argue, it would be surprising if programs were implemented or plans were used. As Alexander (1995) points out, however, "organizations involved in a joint task are often bonded by common values, mutual interests, reciprocal obligations over time, or coordination structures that have been mandated or agreed upon" (xiv). Thus organizations bring a history of interaction and activity to their activities and their interorganizational activities, and this history provides significant structure to increase the likelihood of accomplishing programs or using plans.

Coordination among organizations extends these ideas. Chisholm (1989), in looking at transit linkages among several providers in the San Francisco Bay area, emphasizes the importance of informal bilateral agreements and communication in coordinating connections among six transit providers. Passengers are using combinations of these transit services, and each service has some incentive to ensure efficient transfers. One argument would be to internalize these relationships by creating one larger organization. Chisholm argues that the presumed high level of multilateral interdependence that might justify a merged organization can be and is in practice reduced to a small set of bilateral relationships at particular key transfer points. Voluntary agreements—including informal sharing of information about routes and schedules, contracts for services among the different organizations, and sharing the costs of a single dispatcher at a shared terminal to realize the economies of scale—have effectively resolved these interdependencies. The transaction costs of these informally recognized bilateral agreements may be lower than in a single, larger organization that tries to manage them comprehensively. Alexander (1995) elaborates the conditions under which this type of interorganizational coordination and other types are likely to be effective.

Persons in organizations play one of two types of roles. Line positions are division or section administrators with authority over their subordinates, responsibility for the accomplishments of their unit, and authority or discretion to act on matters of concern within their unit. Staff positions, on the other hand, support the activities of a line position and are responsible for advice based on expertise and loyalty. A staff role can be analyzed as a principal-agent relationship. An economist analyzes this relationship in terms of the incentives for the agent's behavior to be compatible with the interests of the principal who is being served. A real estate agent working for a seller should be compensated on the basis of a percentage of the selling price because then the principal and agent have compatible incentives to obtain the highest price. Such incentive compatibility is much more difficult to achieve in other circumstances. A psychologist defines the principal-agent relationship cognitively. The principal must be able to delegate decision rules or to get sufficient information: " . . . agents must decide as they *think* their principals would decide if they were in possession of the same facts, expertise, and emotional calm" (Goldstein and Beattie 1991, 111). The agent may either act directly or give the principal advice to act in this way, even though the principal's immediate inclination may be to act differently.

These ideas are useful in explaining organizational designs. An organizational design will consider departments or divisions, line roles and staff roles, and the relationship between planning as a function and other functions in the organization. Such structure will in any case be an imperfect decomposition of the interactions within the organization. Planning in particular will have complex relationships with other functions and planning in particular complicates the distinction between line and staff roles.

Organizing to Plan for Municipalities

The organization of the planning function in local municipalities can be framed along two primary dimensions: Who is the primary client (principal)? Is planning a "staff" or "line" function in the organization? These two dimensions explain relationships of planners to a planning commission of citizens, city councils, mayors, and department heads.

Walker (1950) sees three possibilities. A planner can be an advocate for a personal view of future development, accept a limited role with issues of land use regulation, or become a confidential adviser to the mayor. The last is the most powerful, if the measure of power is influence on day-to-day decision making, even if there is less influence on land development decisions. Walker favors close association with the mayor in a staff role.

> The problem is one of a tradition and a set of attitudes toward city planning that prevent the proper role of a planning agency from being either clearly perceived or acted upon. Among the obstructions . . . are: (1) too narrow limitation of planning in practice to zoning, public works, and the strictly physical aspects of community development; (2) use of semiautonomous citizen boards, many members of which are amateurs in both government and planning; (3) undue emphasis upon marshalling public opinion for particular proposals rather than working closely with elected and appointed public officials; (4) too great reliance on consultants, with consequent failure to build up experienced permanent staffs; and (5) lack of clear-cut responsibility to the chief executive in the administrative hierarchy, making for uncertain relationships and failure to use the planning agency in over-all policy planning. (Walker 1950, 363)

Walker sees the planning function much like strategic planning for organizations as codified in the 1980s for corporations (e.g., Bryson 1995). From the public administration perspective, such plans (primarily as agendas, policies, and visions) cover all aspects and potential actions of an organization viewed from the top down. "Plans for the future can only be realized if daily decisions are influenced by them and if each operating agency is guided by considerations of overall planning" (Walker 1950, 176–177).

Kent (1964) argues that the plan should be the city council's plan because the council makes capital investment decisions.

> The annual review and amendment procedure should take place just prior to the yearly reformulation by the council of its capital-improvements program. . . .

This timing of the annual review places the general plan in a challenging, practical context. It compels the director of city planning, the city planning commission, and the chief executive to resummarize, restate, and reclarify the main
ideas of the plan. Annual review compels the council to reassert authority in an
area that clearly involves questions of basic policy and that always involves significant controversies and conflicting ideas with which the council, sooner or
later, must deal. (70)

The commission, staff, and city administration are involved to "offer ideas,
initiate proposals, point out problems, attempt to influence the council"
(84), but it is the council's decisions that can benefit most from the way the
plan works.

In contrast to Walker, Howard (1951) defends the role of the planning
commission of appointed citizens. A planning commission creates a buffer
from day-to-day short-term politics to allow deliberation and recommendation from a longer-term perspective.[6] Appointment for fixed terms gives
planning commissioners some independence from the mayor who appointed them. Recommendations by the commission usually require a
supramajority vote (e.g., two-thirds) for the city council to reject them,
which creates a bias in favor of the recommendation. As an appointed advisory body with members likely to be from the real estate industry, architects, or citizen activists "growing up" from their neighborhoods, the commission is justified primarily on cognitive explanations, not aggregation of
preference. This membership is not surprising because these are the persons with sufficient incentive and interest to volunteer their time, to "overparticipate." Even from the cognitive perspective, however, the usual nar-
rowness of membership may be a disadvantage.

In practice there are multiple plans and incentives for many actors to create plans. Transportation agencies, sanitary districts, and school districts almost always have plans quite independent of general plans of a city. The arguments about the relationships of planners to principals could apply to any
of these separated planning domains, each of which may have a citizens'
commission, a legislative body, and an executive. Transportation agencies
and sewer agencies usually prepare plans separately from the general plan
process. These line agencies are generally staffed by engineers and hire engineering consultants to prepare plans. The logic of organization and the
logic of plans still apply, but the substantive expertise is different, and the

scope of planned actions is different. It is thus not surprising to see many separate plans.

These ideas are elaborated in chapter 9 by describing observed instances of how planning is organized. The older references relied on in this section still serve to frame important dilemmas.

Summary: Using Expertise in Making Plans

Plans are meaningless without intentions, and intentions are derived from knowledge and values. Intrinsic values set the basis for deriving instrumental values by determining what values will not be traded off with others. Instrumental values organize means by establishing how much something is worth as an input to achieving these intentions. These values are at least in part derived from individuals and are inherently subjective. Values might be assessed objectively, that is, assessed in such a way as to be replicable if assessed by some other observer of the subject. Values are better interpreted, however, as intersubjective, which implies both that an individual's interests may be distorted and that socially shaped values may lead to desirable behaviors. Shaping attitudes about the consumption of land for urban uses may be more effective toward the survival of humans and other species than either regulations or incentives directed at behavior.

Individuals face several types of limits on their ability to express intended values and to use information and values to make choices. Cognitive biases and illusions distort decisions. Structural biases in social relationships distort knowledge, values, and their expression. Individuals may not know what they want, what is in their interests, or how best to achieve either. Group processes can enhance individual capacities and counter some individual biases, especially if groups include diverse participants and experts. Expertise in the logic of making plans—knowing under what circumstances what types of plans are likely to be useful and knowing how to make such plans—is fundamental to the profession of planning. An organized profession with ethical norms helps to make such expertise effective and trustworthy.

Such expertise is used in public and private organizations. Plans focused on urban development—on investments and regulations—are likely to be made in many organizations and by different departments within an organization in both the public and private sectors. Although these plans are likely to focus on narrow domains of actions, they also are likely to consider implications for a wide range of issues. The temptation to expand the scope of plans so as to encompass all types of actions of even a single organization is unlikely to succeed. Such plans may, for example, focus on the needs of the executive and ignore the specific actions of line agencies or functions. Plans are useful to organizations even though plans do not change authority or control actions directly.

8

Collective Choice, Participation, and Plans

Veiller's faith in expertise, tempered by a concern for acquiring public legitimation but without resorting to democratic forms of control, was to become characteristic of city planning. In this formula, the reliance on expertise cloaked with a mantle of legitimation was regarded as an alternative to the unseen hand of the market system and the populist danger of democracy, setting the pattern for subsequent responses to the capitalist-democracy contradiction. It was in the appointment of park commissions charged with supervising the planning and construction of urban parks that this formula was first institutionalized. . . .
—Richard E. Foglesong (1986), *Planning the Capitalist City: The Colonial Era to the 1920s*

Planning in the United States has a long history of being uncomfortable with both the "natural" free market and the "natural" political process. The reformist tradition sees evil in the outcomes and the behaviors of the players in both systems. Planners wish to make plans for neither private decision makers nor politicians, but rather for some "public interest" of their own creation. This chapter considers the possibility of collective choice, the logic of participation, and the implications for plans. These concepts help to explain the institutions and institutional relationships within which plans are made and used. They also make clear the distinction between problems of collective choice and problems of dynamic adjustment and thus distinguish problems that can be addressed by collective choice from problems that can be addressed by plans.

Groups have been interpreted in several distinct but related ways. Collaboration from a cognitive perspective was discussed in chapter 7. Here the cognitive argument is extended and contrasted with the aggregation of preference to consider how groups can make decisions. As argued in chapter 5 for collective action toward providing collective goods, group membership cannot be taken as given. Incentives to participate, effects of participation, and ethics of inducing participation must be considered.

The Possibility of Collective Choice

Groups of individuals organize to make collective decisions. A group makes a collective decision when it chooses an action as a group despite differences in interests or preferences.[1] A frequent reason is to make decisions about the provision of collective goods because all persons in the group receive the same level of the collective good. The group must decide what level of the good to provide and how to pay for it. Groups may also form to address other types of situations that may legitimate collective action.[2] In any case, the central question is how such group decisions can and should be made. This question has driven much philosophy and political science to a greater depth than can possibly be plumbed here.[3]

The logic of collective action is based on the logic of collective goods, which is distinct from the logic of plans. The decision to plan may be made by collective action and plans may include actions chosen collectively by groups, but neither is necessary to the logic of plans. Working with the beliefs and preferences of individuals and the need for collective actions is, however, a frequent problem in making plans for urban development. Democratic procedures are not a simple solution even in theory, let alone in practice. Public participation cannot resolve the theoretical limitations of democratic procedures because it faces the same limitations. With all their imperfections, these processes frame the situations in which plans are made. They can explain observed behavior in making plans and suggest opportunities to be more effective in making plans.

There are two long-standing claims for democracy. "Social cognition" interprets democracy as a good cognitive strategy analogous to group processes discussed in chapter 7. In contrast, "aggregation of preferences" interprets democracy as a mechanism for turning individual preferences into collective preferences.[4] Some also argue that it is intrinsically appropriate for individuals to partake in democratic processes as part of constituting themselves as autonomous individuals (Hurley 1989, 335). These arguments are distinct analytically, but they are not mutually exclusive as bases for designing democratic institutions of collective choice

In the cognitive interpretation, individuals are sources of evidence about what should be done in the interests of the group. This does not imply agreement; disagreement about beliefs is cognitively useful. The cognitive interpretation values deliberation among individuals about what to do, not just voting. Hurley (1989) argues, based on the cognitive interpretation, that we should focus design of institutions on two principles:

> *First*, they should seek to divide authority on various kinds of issues among institutions and procedures not so much in accordance with positive expertise about what should be done, which may be very hard to identify in the absence of knowledge of the truth about it, but so as to avoid relying on debunked [discredited] . . . beliefs. *Second*, they should actively foster the capacity for deliberation and formation of undebunked beliefs. (326)

Beliefs lack credibility for various reasons, including challenges to the way in which beliefs were formed, such as "self-deception, wishful thinking, prejudice, deceit, propaganda, advertising or some other kind of deliberate manipulation, . . . illusion, common inferential error, etc" (326)[5] The focus is on avoiding the use of beliefs that have been challenged rather than on hoping to identify expertise in specific topics in advance. Such an approach implies institutions that ensure debate and deliberation and divide authority among levels (local, state, federal) and branches (legislative, executive, judicial) of government in order to gain the best cognitive process. Voters are responsible for providing evidence of "what should be done" based on deliberation and "well-considered beliefs" (Hurley 1989, 330).

This argument is distinguishable from the aggregation of the opinions of experts, as in the Delphi process, for example, because those instances rely on narrowly defined domains in which expertise is well defined. The social cognition argument is not merely a statistical argument about averaging estimates of experts.[6] Democracy is a good cognitive strategy in so much as it protects open deliberation and opportunities to express beliefs. Deliberation by legislators is more important to the cognitive interpretation than is strict representation of constituents' interests or preferences. Choosing a representative in the cognitive interpretation is a delegation of deliberative effort rather than a delegation of vote-trading effort as in the aggregation of preference interpretation.

In the aggregation of preferences, individuals are sources of personal preferences to be aggregated. Disagreement is conflict to be resolved by democratic procedures of voting in some institutional structure. Design of democratic institutions from the aggregation of preferences perspective must face Arrow's Impossibility Theorem (Arrow 1951). The theorem states that no social choice mechanism exists that meets four reasonable conditions (discussed below) and that derives transitive social preferences from ordinal preferences of individuals across more than two alternatives. A social choice mechanism is a rule that yields a collective choice as a function of the preferences of individuals. The most frequent rule is that a simple majority—greater than 50 percent of the votes—determines the choice.[7] A transitive ordering is one in which if A is preferred to B and B is preferred to C, then A is preferred to C. Ordinal preferences are expressed only by order of preference among alternatives, not by intensity of preference or degree of difference between alternatives.[8]

Arrow's four conditions are:[9]

- *Collective rationality:* In any given set of individual preferences the social preferences are derivable from the individual preferences.
- *Pareto principle:* If alternative A is preferred to alternative B by every individual, then the social ordering ranks A above B.
- *Independence of irrelevant alternatives:* The social choices made from any environment depend only on the preferences of individuals with respect to the alternatives in that environment.
- *Non-dictatorship:* There is no individual whose preferences are automatically society's preferences, independent of the preferences of other individuals.

The proof is beyond the scope of this discussion, but a simple example in Table 8-1 suggests the problem and frames possibilities to address the situation. Consider a problem of locating a landfill. There are three individual voters (or equal-sized blocks of voters) labeled Urbana, County, and Champaign, and three possible sites labeled Southeast County, West Champaign, and North Urbana. The most preferred is 1 and the least preferred is 3. In this example, Urbana and Champaign prefer the Southeast County site to the West Champaign site. Urbana and County prefer the West Champaign site to the North Urbana site. But, County and Champaign prefer the North Urbana site to the Southeast County site. A sequence of votes among the pairs of alternatives thus creates a cycle. The social preference is intransitive and unstable. Voting does not result in a predictable outcome.

Table 8-1

Collective Choice Illustration

	Voter Preferences		
Sites	Urbana	County	Champaign
Southeast County	1	3	2
West Champaign	2	1	3
North Urbana	3	2	1

There are several ways to break out of the impossibility theorem (see e.g., Stevens 1993; Mueller 1989). Agenda control sets the order in which votes will be taken and the choices to be voted on so as to prevent the cycling problem from appearing. The role of legislative leaders and committees in deciding what will be brought to the floor to be voted on is one way to prevent more than two possibilities from being presented.

The cycling and unpredictability occurs because the preferences of at least one of the three voters are not "single-peaked," meaning that they have more than one local maximum. In other words, if the alternatives are ordered on the x axis of a graph with the y axis measuring preference, a line with two local maxima will be necessary to describe the preferences of at least one of the voters. If the preferences for all voters are such that they can be arrayed on a common dimension, such as from the left to the right in the political sense, so that all voters have single-peaked preferences, then cycling does not occur. Ideology can be used in this way to overcome Arrow's theorem.

"Approval voting" in which each voter identifies all the acceptable candidates in a field of more than two candidates, has many desirable properties (Brams and Fishburn 1983). Experiments with approval voting suggest that it works well in practice and that cycling problems occur infrequently (Regenwetter and Grofman 1998).

Relaxing the requirement for independence of irrelevant alternatives is useful as a predictive explanation of observed behaviors when legislative decisions are made in combinations. It is also prescriptively useful because it suggests criteria for institutional design and strategies for resolving stalemates. Vote trading can be a good thing in an institutional design for democratic procedures. It provides a basis for compromise that allows predictable action rather than the cycling that would occur based on Arrow's theorem. It also provides protection for the minority with respect to its most important issues. Rural legislators can trade their less important (to them) votes on urban mass transit and suburban sewage treatment plants for more important (to them) votes on rural farm-to-market roads and property tax relief for agricultural land. Without the possibility of trades, the rural legislators, now in the minority in the federal and most state legislatures, would be unable to pass any of their most important legislative initiatives. As long as urban or suburban legislators are still short of a majority on their own most important issues, rural legislators can trade their small group of additional votes to turn a suburban (or urban) near-majority into a majority. By joining with suburban legislators to pass items of interest to suburbs or with urban legislators on items of interest to cities, rural legislators can trade for votes on rural issues.

Principles for Institutions of Collective Choice

In Champaign, Urbana, and Savoy, Illinois, the Intergovernmental Solid Waste Disposal Agency (ISWDA) collapsed, unable to locate a landfill or transfer station. This failure was in part because, as a single-purpose legislative body, there were no other issues on which to trade votes to resolve intense resistance to all sites. If the ISWDA had also been able to decide other issues, vote trades for other amenties or important issues might have led to sufficient yes votes on some site.

Although the landfill never has been located and waste is now shipped outside the county, the collapse triggered resolution of a set of issues among the governmental units by putting one more issue on the table: resolution of the debts incurred by the ISWDA. Champaign, Urbana, and Savoy all wanted control over sewer connections and annexation agreements in order to control development. The Urbana-Champaign Sanitary District (UCSD), which provided sewage collection and treatment for all three cities, wanted to rid itself of responsibility for maintaining the Boneyard, a drainage ditch that flows through both Champaign and Urbana. The county was concerned about sales tax revenue losses as commercial properties were annexed to the cities. These governments achieved resolution, in part because there were enough issues on the table to create combinations of acceptable decisions. The agreement included annexation boundary agreements among the cities and the county, payments by the cities and the University of Illinois toward Boneyard maintenance, control by each city of sewer connections, and resolution of shares of the ISWDA debt. Each of these issues had been stalled in part because it was in play separately from any others and, in the case of the ISWDA and UCSD, in play in single-purpose legislative bodies.

Individual voters cannot trade votes because the transaction costs are too high. There are too many individuals to communicate with each other and to establish credible commitments not to defect from agreements. Representatives in legislative bodies, however, can trade votes. They can make credible commitments more easily because they have repeat face-to-face contact on many such agreements. Haefele (1973) shows that in a two-party system with nondoctrinaire parties, each candidate would choose a platform (votes on issues) that yields the same result from individuals voting for parties and the elected legislators trading votes as would result if individual voters were able to trade votes directly. In other words, he shows that if the candidates choose platforms so as to receive the majority vote, they will choose platforms that seek to pass and defeat issues just as voters would if they could trade votes. Note that in this case Arrow's impossibility theorem is circumvented by vote trading in the legislative arena and by the restriction to a two-party system in the electoral arena. Legislators consider "irrelevant alternatives" and voters are restricted to two alternatives.

These electoral mechanisms and legislative mechanisms face many limitations. People cannot always be relied on to express their own preferences or interests. Voting and legislative processes are clearly affected by differences in wealth and power. Plans can and should, however, be informed by electoral and legislative mechanisms. If plans do not recognize when vote trading is likely to occur or how it can be used intentionally, then plans will not correctly predict their own effects or take advantage of available actions.

Haefele (1973) suggests two principles for institutional design. First, legislative bodies should be general purpose, not special purpose, because they need to act on a range of issues in order to have issues about which to trade votes. Second, legislators should be elected based on territorial constituencies (geographical areas) rather than functional or single-interest constituencies. If the only decision that a legislative body can make is where to put a landfill, it cannot trade this decision for a decision about where to locate a school or fire station or whether to create a recycling program. If a legislator is elected to represent a group interested in preserving wildlife through establishing preserves, she will have no basis for trading off a landfill in a given location in return for several wildlife preserves elsewhere.

Using Haefele's example, a functional coalition requires a promise of a park in a majority of districts or a road in a majority of districts in order for legislators to get reelected.[10] Territorial representatives can bargain to get a park in exchange for a road improvement in another district. Territorial districts work better than interest group representation because they are more likely to result in different coalitions around different issues. Different coalitions are necessary for vote trading to work, both to resolve stalemates and to protect the minority. "Log rolling," simply packaging all the individual "pork barrel" projects into a single bill that each legislator supports for a different reason can be deterred by designing the domain of actions of the legislative body and representation districts so that each legislator has some interest in each project. Put differently, if the pork barrel projects are only of interest to one locality, they should not be funded by direct action of a higher-level legislature. The line item veto as implemented in most states is a direct deterrent to such logrolling.

Plans for urban development often deal with infrastructure agencies that are created as single-purpose districts, such as sewer districts, park districts, and school districts, with separate taxing and expenditure powers. Innes (1996) describes several instances of citizen panels with representatives of specific interests to deal with a particular issue. Such groups make sense on cognitive capacity grounds, but create problems for the aggregation of preferences. An ad hoc body with a single issue and members representing individual interests has little opportunity to trade votes or combine issues to achieve resolution of conflicts.

Councils of governments, in which each municipality in a metropolitan region has one representative, may gain some benefit from cognitive deliberation, but representatives are unlikely to be able to trade on issues because each represents the corporate interests of a municipality, not a mix of interests of citizens. Most councils of government have few if any powers of action. Two metropolitan governments that do have significant powers are in Minneapolis–St. Paul, Minnesota, and in Portland, Oregon. The Minneapolis–St. Paul Metro Council includes fourteen representatives from regions of equal population that cross city lines. The representatives are appointed by the governor. The Metro Council has taxing powers for its own operations and is a general purpose legislature that has responsibility over various operating boards and commissions with regionwide scope (Orfield 1997). Portland, Oregon, has a similar regional government, called Metro. Its representatives are directly elected, and it has significant land use regulatory authority through its control of the Urban Growth Boundary (Lewis 1996). These units of government are much better designed from an aggregation of preference perspective and probably from a social cognition perspective than are councils of governments.

Although the two arguments for democracy are analytically distinct, they are neither mutually exclusive explanations nor contradictory in their implications in making plans for development.

> If the content of the agenda is substantially restricted to the proposals of only some political actors in the city, then so is social intelligence restricted. In this sense, the roots of political equality and social intelligence are the same . . .

> . . . In particular, popular control is unduly hospitable to the preferences of businessmen concerned with land use (or to what public officials consider to be their preferences). The result is systematic bias and shortcomings in social problem solving. Moreover, precisely because the roots of political equality and social intelligence are the same, the widespread effort to consider the trade-offs between equity and efficiency is misplaced. There is good reason to believe that systematic bias leads to poor social intelligence: there is no trade-off, only cumulative loss. (Elkin 1987, 5)[11]

Forester's (1989) strategies for planning in the face of power are ways to deal simultaneously with individual cognitive limitations, cognitive arguments for collaboration in groups, and political arguments about inequities of representation. Most of his examples focus on the interactions of planners and constituents in response to specific proposals and in the context of regulations. Similar strategies are needed to interpret how plans are and should be made and used.

The Logic of Participation

"Public participation" is pervasively claimed to be an essential element of good planning. It is required by the AICP Code of Ethics (American Institute of Certified Planners 1991) and in most federal and state mandated or funded planning. In the planning literature "public participation" or "citizen participation" usually refers to some interaction of planners and decision makers with constituencies that takes place outside the formal democratic procedures of voting or party politics. An open meeting to discuss a development project is thus public participation, but voting in an election, working for a candidate, or voting as a representative are not. This separation is inappropriate. Voting and representative government require participation in the act of voting and in deliberation, and public participation in any mode cannot magically avoid the impediments to social cognition and aggregation of preferences that face representative government. Participation in any form is either cognitive deliberation or evidence for aggregation of preferences.

When should we expect to see what sorts of persons participating in making plans? Participation almost always has the properties of a collective good. Incentives to vote, to work for political candidates or parties, to attend public forums, to address the city council, to organize neighborhood actions, or to join public advisory bodies all raise the behavioral implications of collective action.

Direct democracy, such as the New England town meeting in which each citizen has a vote, relies on participation. Meaningful participation relies either on deliberative consideration of what ought to be done or on learning enough about the options to express a preference for a proposal. The outcome in either case is a collective good. That is, the benefit of social cognition or of aggregated preference accrues to each individual in the same way, regardless of whether an individual participated. There is thus an incentive to free-ride on the participation of others. An estimate of the benefit of participating would consider the probability that a vote would affect the outcome, utility from the difference in outcomes, any private benefits from the act of voting itself, and the costs of voting (Stevens 1993).[12] This calculation subsumes in the costs of voting the costs of learning enough about the options to vote in a way that will increase the likelihood of desired outcomes. Private benefits might include satisfactions from being seen by peers to participate, social activities associated with voting, expected patronage jobs, or perhaps illegal incentives such as bribes. The probability that any one voter will affect the outcome of a vote is very small, so based on this explanation there is little incentive to vote. Frank's (1988) "commitment model," discussed in chapter 5, argues that we cannot be who we believe ourselves to be without voluntarily acting consistently with those beliefs. It is therefore necessary to vote in order to sustain a belief that we are empowered citizens. Empowered citizens will have voted even though it is not worth doing so from each individual's perspective. This explanation is not sufficient, however, as evidenced by the explicit efforts by candidates to "get out the vote," by legislative floor managers to be sure that their legislators are on the floor when a vote is taken, and by community organizers to get people to attend meetings.

The difficulties of becoming sufficiently informed to justify direct democracy are addressed in part by representative democracy.[13] Representatives become specialists in learning enough about each issue to vote their constituents' preferences or interests or to contribute a cognitive perspective. Legislators in turn delegate some of these decisions and discretion to the executive branch of government and to appointed personnel, including planners. Public participation is likely to occur in situations in which an individual's interests are so large as to overcome the costs of direct participation. When the proposal is to site the landfill in our neighborhood, we have greater incentive to participate than for the general issue of locating a landfill. We tend to leave that decision to our delegates until they are about to make the "wrong" decision and propose to locate it near us.

An explanation of the "Not in My Backyard" (NIMBY) syndrome is that the immediate concerns are of sufficient worth to some individuals that they can justify the costs, including the leadership costs, of forming a group to take action. Immediate events in our everyday lives make a sufficient difference among alternative decisions that participation costs can be compensated. Often there is an oligopolistic leader who fits the factors identified by Olson (1965) in which groups are likely to form: an oligopoly leader who has a greater incentive than others to lead the group, needed skills, and social affinity among group members. The resident closest to the proposed landfill site has the greatest incentive but can also persuade neighbors progressively farther away to participate. The neighbors are more likely to organize if they are from an affinity group—have organized before or know each other in some way, which is also consistent with Frank's commitment model and Axelrod's repeated interaction model discussed in chapter 5. They are more likely to organize if someone in the group has the skills of leadership and organizing. Many studies have found such self-organization in neighborhoods, especially in response to perceived immediate environmental hazards.[14] Silver (1985) finds many instances in which neighbor-hoods organized implicitly or explicitly to keep out potential new residents who they perceived as undesirable because of lower incomes, different race, or different ethnic or religious heritage. Ability to organize does not nec-essarily lead to better outcomes when external criteria of validity are con-sidered. Thus public participation is not always a good thing.

A major task of neighborhood planning strategies is to develop organ-izations to initiate activities among residents and advocate the interests of the neighborhood before public bodies. These are voluntary groups pro-viding collective goods of leadership and representation. Planners provide skills to jump-start this process, to overcome the frictions to forming vol-untary groups by providing external inducements and reinforcement that would not be available within the neighborhood. When planners refer to neighborhood planning, they often assume that it is focused on lower-in-come, lower-status neighborhoods. Planners' professional skills and expe-rience are more valuable additions to the tasks of forming voluntary groups in neighborhoods where professional skills among residents are scarce and where lack of past successes undermines the confidence of residents in po-tential benefits from collective action.

Once the immediate concern is resolved, a neighborhood organization is likely to disappear, but the experience of creating it makes it easier to recreate it if new concerns arise. The participants have new skills and are acquainted with their neighbors. Community organizers provide external resources, both expertise and money, to form a group where none would emerge on its own, but frequently the organizations fall apart if the exter-nal resources are removed.[15] This implies that their skills and time com-mitment were essential to sustaining the group, not just to forming it initially. Self-organized groups, however, also disappear once the crisis passes. If groups induced by community organizers accomplish immediate objectives, there is no incentive for continued participation. A better measure of the suc-cess of empowerment is self-organization at the next crisis or increased par-ticipation in formal government rather than survival of induced groups.

Saunders (1983) explains possible types of actions, not simply the incen-tives for action. When the formal political system is not acting in a latent community's interests, residents have two types of options. They can act within the system and thus risk incorporation, absorption, and cooptation. Or, they can act outside the system and risk isolation and exclusion. In

Croydon, a suburb of London, England, there was a long waiting list for "council housing," a form of government-funded housing for lower-income families. The long wait implied that not enough housing was being built. The Conservative Party held the majority in the local council and the social service levels were well below the norms of the Greater London Council. Three strategies were available to the council-housing tenants and potential tenants on the waiting list.

- Use the Labor Party in its role as representative of the working class in the formal political process.
- Use tenant organizations that were legitimated within the established institutional framework.
- Form ad hoc community organizations that could function "against" the established institutions by standing outside them.

The elected Labor Party councilors and potential councilors were middle-class persons who lived outside the community (as is possible in English elections). Their perspective was based on ideological principles, not on shared experience with the working class. Their principles were in the right place, but their incentives to take sufficient action were not. These representatives were not representing the tenants' interests as the tenants saw them. The institutionalized tenant organizations were "responsible" organizations tied to the existing system, legitimating it more than motivated to change it. These were reasonable people with a right to be heard. These organizations also had insufficient motivation to act. In contrast, sit-ins, lying in front of bulldozers or trucks, or people tying themselves to trees risked isolation or exclusion as radical actors. Going outside the system is risky for people without the social status to regain their positions inside the system. To argue that some people are more able to get away with deviant behavior, Saunders gives the example of a group of middle-class mothers and children who used "street theatre" to demonstrate for a day care center. The middle-class mothers were in every other way part of the institutionalized order of things. A brief exaggeration beyond limits of usual processes could be tolerated from members of the same affinity group as the elected councilors. As members of that affinity group, the mothers had the skills to do it appropriately. The form of the day care demonstration was unusual for its participants, however, which made clear that the issue was more than usually important.

These actions to "overparticipate"—participate beyond the norms—are worthwhile to individuals in certain situations. In situations of high potential benefit to relatively small groups, they cut across the structures of institutionalized representation as in civil rights demonstrations, apply focused resources as in NIMBYism, and provide information on the intensity of preference as in the day care demonstration. We should expect to see such participation in such circumstances.

How Participation Works

No system of representative government is sufficient in and of itself. Institutionalized organizations will not satisfy all incentives to participate. Under what circumstances is more or less participation useful? How can we work with institutionalized systems of representative government, institutionalized organizations, expectations of "overparticipation" in particular circumstances, and induced participation to make better plans?

The typical claims for participation can be clustered into five themes.[16]

- Participation of more persons and more diverse persons increases group capabilities to make plans.
- Participation of decision makers increases the likelihood they will use the plan.
- Participation of all constituencies avoids later resistance to chosen actions.
- Participation outside of formal democratic processes complements these processes by giving different people access and thus representation.
- The experience of participating helps to create the kinds of individuals necessary to operate a democracy.

Participation of more persons and more diverse persons has already been discussed in chapter 7. The claim that decision makers must be participants is distinct from the usual focus of public participation. Conventional wisdom in strategic planning for private corporations claims that the chief executive should participate so that the plan expresses the intentions of the primary actors (see e.g., Bryson 1995; Mintzberg 1994). In planning for urban development, it is unclear who is analogous to a chief executive. Is the plan for the mayor and executive branch, as advocated by Walker (1950), or for the city council and legislative branch, as advocated by Kent (1964)? Is it for a nonexistent regional government or a number of distinct organizations with distinct leaders? In the latter case, there will almost certainly be multiple plans for these organizations. A plan is about actions. Actions are taken by people. These people should participate in some way in framing and developing the plan in order that it focuses on decisions they expect to make and so that the decision makers are invested in its content.

Participation as a means to achieve support among constituents may take several forms. Constituents might be viewed as if they were decision makers, such as in the case of a corporate board of directors or a set of department heads in a city administration. Participation invests key players. Participation might be viewed as a kind of *a priori* or *ex post facto* legitimation of action. We want to be able to say: You had your chance to speak. Roelofs (1992) argues that people want to have had this chance to be heard "in public," regardless of the outcome. Early participation may be sought in order to learn how to defeat potential opponents rather than to learn their views so as to change the content of proposed plans. In locating hazardous waste sites, to which NIMBY will almost always occur, such strategies may be both ethical and effective. Devising a win-win strategy rests on knowing the interests of various actors. Knowing the basis of likely opposition suggests legitimate ways to compensate the losers.

Bryson and Crosby (1992) present useful distinctions among types of situations in which participation can occur and describe the formation of the Minneapolis–St. Paul Metro Council. In "shared-power, no one in charge, interdependent worlds" there are changing coalitions, legitimate conflicts, and disagreements about how the world works—about action-outcome relationships. Forums create and communicate meaning. Arenas are situations in which decisions are made. Courts adjudicate conflicts and sanction those who break regulations. In the Metro Council case, forums included the many public talks given to many groups while trying to create a constituency for the idea of a regional council. The state legislature was the arena in which the decision could actually be made. The courts resolved disagreements about the implications of the legislation. Participation is pertinent in forums, arenas, and courts. Forums provide a particular opportunity for cognitive deliberations separate from the decision arena. Community visioning meetings work as forums to create ideas and readiness to act by simultaneously creating a group of potential participants. The important point is that participation in a forum can affect a decision even without participation in the decision arena. In some circumstances, participation in forums may have more influence by helping to frame issues and thus constrain the decision arena.

Participation to complement institutionalized democratic processes should be designed so as to represent those interests that are least well represented by institutionalized democracy or by groups that will emerge on their own. For example, incentives should be designed to counter the business bias of local governments or to counter the expected NIMBY response to location decisions. The federally funded Model Cities program of the 1960s created neighborhood mini-governments for those without resources or status to create their own voluntary groups and who were thus not participating in local government institutions for plausible and predictable reasons (Judd and Mendelson 1973). The East St. Louis Action Research Program from the University of Illinois at Urbana-Champaign seeks to increase the organizational capacity of neighborhoods within the city to participate in public decision making as well as private action (Reardon 1994). The state of Illinois has been trying for twenty years to design participation mechanisms, incentives, and modes of incorporating expertise sufficient to succeed in siting a hazardous waste site. It is on at least its third try, not because of general participation problems or issues of democratic governance or access, but because of the effectiveness of "overparticipation" in the NIMBY response to any proposed site. Champaign County, Illinois, has been similarly unsuccessful in devising a process for locating a landfill. Kathmandu, Nepal, faces similar local resistance from residents near its current landfill and to locating a new site despite a much more centralized government and, compared to the United States, little experience with direct citizen action.

It is worth sorting out analytically the different claims about public participation even though they will, in general, provide joint explanations of observed behavior or of good planning. Participation is fundamental to ideas of autonomy and agency and thus is constitutive of being an individual person (Hurley 1989). Participation in some decisions and actions is necessary to the idea of being an individual. There is thus a broad ethical claim for participation. Elkin (1987) argues that "how we carry on our political life helps to define us" (10) and identifies neighborhood issues, especially those related to local land use decisions, as an ideal way to create deliberative citizens (153). In such cases local residents have an immediate and strong incentive to participate because they have some confidence in their knowledge of pertinent facts about their neighborhood.

Thus participation is a way to create citizens, inducing them to partici- pate, to learn to deliberate, to associate themselves with a community of in- terest and support, and to become involved in the institutionalized struc- tures of democracy. In this case participation is designed not simply to improve immediate decisions about plans or to increase the likelihood of successful action, not simply as a substitute or complement for institution- alized processes, but to produce the persons necessary to sustain the insti- tutionalized system. Empowerment planning (Reardon 1994) seeks to en- hance the capabilities of "underpowered" persons to act as self-sustaining equal citizens. Participation is self-amplifying—participation increases par- ticipation. Participation as a means of creating citizens is crucial, and the subject matter of plans presents excellent opportunities for this purpose.

Participation is not a magic solution to the insufficient incentives to par- ticipate in democratic processes. In Seattle, neighborhood groups can ob- tain funding from the city to hire consultants and develop their own plans for their neighborhoods. They use these plans as a basis for negotiation with the city and its plan, which calls for creation of urban villages in particular parts of the city. Participation is costly in any case, as evidenced by this state- ment from the executive director of one of the neighborhood groups: "Our members just don't have the time for all this planning. They're too busy try- ing to make a living" (Goldsmith 1998).

Summary: Making Plans and Collective Decisions

Groups serve cognitive, deliberative, and aggregation of preference func- tions of collective choice. Formal democratic processes and additional forms of participation can complement each other in achieving these functions. Plans can accomplish certain things, but they cannot overcome the diffi- culties of social cognition and aggregation of preference that societies face. Planning processes should not pretend to create solutions to these difficul- ties but should take full advantage of the range of collective choice mech- anisms that have been created. Expertise in the planning process thus should include knowing how to make plans when collective choice is at issue.

9

How Plans Are Made

... the designers' graphic representations, the economists' statistical projections, and the political institutions all emphasized the abstracted city of the future as a perfected implementation of the general welfare and downplayed the existing city of the present as a set of particular problems and interests. All privileged the planners and the corporate institutions—public and private—which they represented as the source of initiative and transformation. My vision, because of my professional background and because of my working situation, was divergent, seeing the city of the future as evolving from the present one and the interests of local institutions as needing affirmation and expression; however, I was not able to represent that vision in a way which made it really usable in the planning framework.

—Lisa Peattie (1987), *Planning: Rethinking Ciudad Guayana*

The behaviors of planners can be explained in terms of tasks that yield plans. The effectiveness of combinations of these tasks—of planning processes— can be assessed by whether they are likely to yield results similar to what would have resulted from highly structured, "rational" processes. One way to explain observed plan making is as attempts to meet standards of rationality in complex ways that go beyond simply trying to approximate directly a prescribed rational procedure.

A language for describing the making and using of plans requires four different dimensions: behaviors, tasks, processes, and standards. *Planning behaviors* are "atomic" things that people do when they are making or using plans. Talking to a constituent, coloring a map, and setting up data for a computer run are behaviors. Behaviors are usually relatively easy to observe, but do not necessarily reveal a purpose. *Tasks* are combinations of planning behaviors that accomplish particular functions or purposes. Forecasting population, evaluating two options by comparing them, assessing land suit-

187

ability for urban development, and teaching a group of neighbors how to run a meeting are tasks. Tasks are generally not directly observable, but tasks can be inferred by observing behaviors, observing outcomes from tasks, or by self-reporting by planners of the purposes of observed behaviors. For example, forecasting population involves data collection and assembly, deliberations about techniques and assumptions, sensitivity analysis, and interpretation of results. *Planning processes* are patterns of tasks; planning processes yield plans. The same tasks and behaviors may also simultaneously achieve other purposes or have other effects. A planning process is difficult to observe because it occurs over a long period of time in different places and in different forms. Processes can be inferred, however, from relationships among tasks or self-reporting of the intent of tasks. Thus tasks and processes help to explain relationships among behaviors and plans, both of which are relatively easily observed.

Standards of rationality provide criteria by which to judge planning processes. Using rationality arguments as standards is different from using rationality as a model of a process. Although these standards are often described as if they were a highly structured planning process, they can still serve as criteria for comparing messy patterns of behaviors or tasks. Observed behaviors can be explained in terms of tasks and processes that would yield plans similar to what would be accomplished if ideal processes could be implemented directly. Behavioral explanations suggest how planners try to achieve good results. Prescriptive explanations then try to improve on such likely behaviors by suggesting how modified behaviors would be more likely to meet the standards.

Behaviors, Tasks, and Processes

Behaviors contribute to tasks, but often to more than one task at the same time or to different tasks at different times. One way to link behaviors to resulting plans is to organize behaviors into tasks.[1] For example, talking to constituents, department heads, the planning commission, and applicants for approvals might contribute to a task of forecasting rates of growth in urban development. Calculating a forecast, designing a survey, and conducting a survey might also contribute to the task of forecasting population. These same behavioral events also serve other tasks simultaneously. To explain the task of forecasting, these various behaviors must be accounted for.

The use of information demonstrates the necessary jointness of behaviors in relation to tasks.

> What is notable in these examples is that the policy result became a foregone conclusion in the process of formulating and agreeing on the information, rather than a later choice after the information was in final form. . . . [T]he managers among the participants not only insisted that the data on the conditions in the estuary be thoroughly discussed and accepted by everyone, but also made sure that, along with the data, management options to deal with problematic conditions were presented. To the managers, these options were what gave the data meaning. They regarded the status and trend reports as meaningless unless the policy implications were made clear. (Innes 1998, 58)

Data cannot be collected or analyzed independent of the generation or testing of options because the data have no meaning independent of their ability to distinguish among available actions. This jointness does not mean that the tasks of data collection, verification, option generation, option testing, and option evaluation cannot be interpreted as tasks in relation to standards of rationality. It does mean that it is impossible to observe tasks directly or infer them from separate behaviors at different times. Observing data being used in deliberations about available actions implies that data were collected and validated. These tasks, which are evidence of meeting standards of rationality, were thus performed. In at least some cases, behaviors can be observed that are sufficient to explain how these tasks were performed. For example: Who talked to whom about what when? How many copies of a draft or analysis were distributed to whom, when, and with what response?

Tasks can be identified as generic types or at increasing levels of specificity. Harris (1965) identifies three general tasks: prediction, invention, and choice. Others frame three questions as general tasks: Where are we? Where do we want to go? How do we get there? Explanations of behaviors in relation to plans, however, require more specific tasks. Forecasting population growth over the plan horizon, for example, is often identified as a task required in making a plan. Tasks may be made up of subtasks but not hierarchically because subtasks may serve more than one supertask simultaneously. Observable behaviors can serve multiple tasks jointly and more specific tasks can serve more general tasks jointly.

Actors who are self-reporting intended tasks may identify only one task in association with a behavior, even though the behavior might serve several tasks at once. A forecast task, for example, contributes to a planning process in several ways. A normative forecast creates an idea of what could be. It simultaneously tests this idea for feasibility and desirability. The forecasted population frames the comparison with other ideas, affects what people believe about how the world works, communicates the idea to many people, and may frame negotiations. When a community organizer presents an idea at a community meeting, all twelve elements of Checkoway's description of a planning process (as shown in Table 9-1) may be occurring simultaneously. The idea may develop in real time; it may serve as the focus around which to build a coalition, and so on. Tasks cannot be linked one-to-one to prescribed processes or to standards.

Despite this complexity, plan-making processes are frequently prescribed by listing tasks. Several such prescriptions are shown in Table 9-1.[2] Most of the authors cited say that the order of tasks matters, but is subject to iterations. Tasks may be repeated before completing the entire list and after completing the entire list. In Table 9-1 the tasks all fall in the same order except the first two for Checkoway's, which are therefore numbered. The processes described by Patton and Sawicki and by Black are typical of what is called the rational or rational comprehensive method. The process described by Bryson is the now conventional strategic planning method for organizations, whether private or nonprofit. Checkoway described the community organizing perspective. All of these descriptions can be arranged with reference to the three general questions identified in the first column.

The table shows that the descriptions are in many ways similar and in only a few cases directly contradictory. They vary in level of detail from three tasks to twelve. They emphasize different generic tasks by identifying different numbers of detailed tasks. "Where are we?" is covered by Patton and Sawicki in one task: "verify, define, and detail the problem." Bryson, however, describes four detailed tasks. Checkoway identifies nine detailed tasks for "How do we get there?" Almost all of these nine tasks involve creating an organization or institutional context in which to act. The processes described in the other columns take an institutional context as given and leave any changes in it outside their process. These descriptions are useful in different situations where emphasis on different tasks is necessary because of different initial situations. Tasks could be further disaggregated to describe processes in much more detail, and research on how tasks are accomplished or could be accomplished requires such greater specificity.

Table 9-1

Planning Processes*

Wetmore	Patton and Sawicki	Bryson	Black	Checkoway
Where are we?	Verify, define, and detail the problem	Initiating and agreeing on process Assessing the internal environment Assessing the external environment Identifying strategic issues	Data collection Analysis of data Forecast future context	2. Identify issues
Where do we want to be?	Establish evaluation criteria	Identifying organizational mandates Clarifying organizational mission and values Establishing an organizational vision	Establish goals	1. Set goals
How can we get there?	Identify alternative policies Evaluate alternative policies Display and distinguish among alternative policies	Formulating strategies	Design alternatives Test alternatives Evaluate alternatives Select an alternative	Develop constituencies Select tactics Build organizational structure Activate people Develop leaders Educate public Establish relationships with influentials Build coalitions Advocate political change

*Order of tasks is top to bottom except in the last column where steps 1 and 2 are reversed as indicated by numbering.

Rationality as Standard and Process

The rational method, exemplified in Table 9-1 by Black and described in the first column of Table 9-2, is not a description of observable planning behavior. It is, however, more than just a description of tasks. In its strictest form, it sets a standard for the quality of plan making that can be applied even to processes that do not rely on implementing a sequence of steps directly. Few planners have been able to ignore this standard completely as a set of attributes by which to judge good planning processes, despite constant attacks on simplified ideas of rational procedure.

The essence of the rationality standard is to claim exhaustive inclusion of all relevant elements: (1) that the purposes of all tasks have been accomplished, and (2) that for each task all pertinent variables were considered. Good performance measured by this standard might be achieved indirectly without implementing these tasks directly. Considering all goals, assessing the present and future situation in all its dimensions, identifying or inventing all options, testing options for all effects, evaluating with respect to all interests, and selecting by appropriately combining all criteria constitute the standards of rationality regardless of method or process. Recall the arguments about evolution and optimality in chapter 2. If the emergent criteria of survival are accepted as appropriate and an infinite period of evolution is assumed, then an evolutionary process will tend to yield optimal results by the same logic claimed for procedural rationality. In simple terms, the practical problems with this formulation as a standard, much less as process, are the external validity of goals and the requirement for infinite time.

Rationality as a standard of performance rather than a process makes coherent sense with communicative rationality, critical theory, and observed planning behavior. Communicative rationality focuses on one aspect of planning behavior. Critical theory emphasizes external validity. Observed plan-making behavior can be explained in part as planners trying to achieve a rationality standard given cognitive and collective choice limitations, concern for external validity, and limited resources.

Communicative rationality argues that given a set of conditions about the persons communicating and the nature of communication, a rational choice of action will result. Table 9-2 shows an approximate pairing of the conditions for procedural rationality and the conditions for communicative rationality.[3] The table is divided into three strata because the middle four aspects of each

Table 9-2

Procedural and Communicative Rationality

Rational Comprehensive	Communicative Rationality
All goals considered	All interests represented
All aspects of current and future situations assessed	Interests informed and able to present
All options considered	Interests equally empowered
All effects of alternatives tested	Good reasons, good argument
All alternatives evaluated by all criteria	Allow all claims and assumptions to be questioned
Best alternative selected	Consensus reached

argument are consistent as combinations of aspects rather than individual ones. This statement of communicative rationality is based most directly on Innes (1998), who builds on Habermas (1990) and Forester (1989). If all interests are represented in the conversation, each interest is informed and able to present its arguments, each interest is equally empowered in the give and take of conversation, arguments are based on reason, and all claims and assumptions are questioned, then the situation will be fully assessed, all options will be considered, and all alternatives will be tested and evaluated. If the conversation yields consent for action, which may be less strict than the claim for consensus, then an alternative will be selected for which action is enabled. Thus communicative rationality turns the standards of rationality into standards for communicative processes that would achieve them. This transformation may be helpful in that conversation may be a more concrete way to consider these standards, but they are still not directly attainable.

Forester and Innes each start from Habermas, but derive different planning responses. In simplest terms, the critical practice or deliberative planning approach of Forester (1989, 1999) takes the boundedness of rationality as applying to communicative rationality as well. Neither careful design of specific institutions nor reliance on the goodness of persons is likely to yield morally sufficient communication. Thus, planners (and others) must be individually and collectively responsible for bringing moral commitments to the table and for acting in ways that are intentionally likely to counter cognitive, institutional, and structure-of-power biases. Recognizing that not all interests will be represented, that capacity to represent will not be equal, that communication will not be sincere and grounded only in good reason, a planner should act so as to counter these biases. The likelihood of good actions depends on critical reflection and on prior, external moral commitments.

Innes (1996, 1998) emphasizes a direct implementation of communicative rationality as process. She focuses on cases involving consensus-seeking groups, usually created as ad hoc institutions to deal with a particular problem or issue. This approach leads to a focus on how to design such conversations to approximate the conditions of communicative rationality. A full range of interests must be invited to the table. A forum must be created in which they can deliberate with sufficient time and with sufficient "reason giving" to arrive at consent for action. Rationality of conversation within the group is the primary basis for claiming validity for the group's conclusions. The activities of such groups are events in a larger context in which other issues and other interests are playing, and how the activities of such groups relate to these other interests must still be considered.

These two tacks reflect two different kinds of optimism. Forester is optimistic that it is worth the effort to act critically to counter a fundamentally problematic world.[4] Innes is optimistic that it is possible to design approximately rational institutions, if only as a particular kind of deliberative group focused on a particular situation. These two tacks approach the difficulties of standards of rationality in familiar ways that are also used by those who work directly from procedural rationality. Forester accepts that goals must be in part external, but will be formed or reproduced in the actions themselves. He also focuses on problem framing, debiasing tools, and decision process. Innes decomposes the situation into a more manageable subset of issues and then tries to approximate an institutional design in which goals and actions emerge simultaneously.

As in most adaptations to the standards of rationality, these approaches come into significant conflict with the attributes of situations in which plans are most likely to be worthwhile: interdependence, indivisibility, irreversibility, and imperfect foresight. Forester's cases tend to focus on interactions about specific project approvals rather than on the making of plans. Innes's cases tend to focus on policies or specific regulations, not on plans for urban development. Two kinds of reasons may explain this selection of cases, one methodological and one substantive.

Observing talk in relatively well defined arenas is easier than inferring a great variety of tasks over long periods from observable behaviors. It is hard to observe one person working on an analytical task because people don't give running commentaries on what they are doing unless the task inherently involves communication. It is therefore not surprising that the observation of planning practice has focused on negotiation and mediation tasks in which behaviors are more readily observed rather than on plan creation or analysis tasks in which behaviors are harder to observe. An individual planner with fairly direct responsibility for review of a particular project application, with its interests implied and made visible by the immediate controversy, can be observed and interpreted. A defined, task-oriented group, meeting on a predictable schedule, can be observed, and its relationships with the larger context can be followed outward from the group's visible deliberations. There is seldom so obvious and visible a single forum or arena focused so heavily on observable talk from which to interpret the making of plans for urban development. Johnson's (1996) thorough description of the creation of the Regional Plan of New York and Its Environs, for example, covers a period of ten to fifteen years and many forums and arenas in order to create such an interpretation.

Substantively, plans for urban development must confront the Four I's: interdependence, indivisibility, irreversibility, and imperfect foresight. Plans for urban development must address at least two and generally many interdependent actions over several years. Cases described in the communicative rationality literature usually take such plans as given and focus on one action or decision that may use information from a plan. The complexities of considering many actions are the essence of the purposes of making plans. Cases that avoid the underlying logic for making plans give little basis for generalization from such cases to the making of plans. The remainder of this chapter considers how to interpret cases that do confront the Four I's.

Lindblom's (1959) critique of plans and Harris's (1967; Harris and Batty 1993) advocacy of plans represent two optimistic responses to the difficulties of directly implemented rationality in complex systems. Lindblom is optimistic that we can ignore these complexities and still cope effectively. In essence, though not using these words, Lindblom argues that the problems of interdependence, indivisibility, irreversibility, and imperfect foresight can be ignored and that incremental (marginal) responses will be both sufficient and cautious in useful ways even when the Four I's are present.

He argues that equilibrium-seeking behaviors under the assumptions of continuity and reversibility will work better than trying to plan. In contrast, Harris is optimistic that attempts to deal with complexity by making plans, though necessarily constrained, can lead to better actions. The difference between these optimistic views is the degree to which plans that will matter can be made and at costs less than the potential benefits. The logic of such trade-offs is clear, but the implication for the scope of plans is an empirical question for which there is little evidence.

The following dilemma emerges. Should planners focus effort myopically on issues, solutions, and choice situations that happen to float near each other in a natural stream of events? Or should planners focus effort on ways to expand the scope of actions considered in decision arenas in order to plan? The second approach necessitates prior effort in order to maintain the timing of actions and requires scanning farther across and ahead in the stream of events, thus necessitating forecasts of systems behavior and intentions.

Branch (1981) argues for "continuous city planning," building on the situation rooms created to plan and monitor military actions. His proposal for a "city planning center" to organize and make available the information pertinent for decisions emphasizes the perspective of plan users rather than plan makers. His descriptions of continuous city planning are arguably closer to daily planning practice than are the prescriptions for comprehensive plans. Branch found only one instance of intentional use of the continuous approach (Kleymeyer and Hartsock 1973). The norms of good practice, however, make it hard to claim that a continuous process is being followed intentionally, even if it is a good description of much observed practice.

Many plans are made in situations in which they are likely to be useful. What behaviors interpreted as what tasks and processes yield such plans? Observed plan making can be explained as responses to recognized limitations in meeting standards of rationality because of cognitive limitations and difficulties of collective choice. These responses include decomposition, representation, using expertise about interests and participation, and using ambiguous line and staff roles in organizations.

Decomposition

Observed plan-making processes are feasible because they decompose plans functionally, organizationally, spatially, and temporally. Observed choices of scope seem to be based more on historical convention, however, than on carefully considered explanations of the logic of plans. Decomposition based on interdependence is central to choosing a scope for a plan. Decomposition must simultaneously take into account the functional, organizational, spatial, and temporal dimensions, which are often in conflict and must be traded off.

The watchmaker analogy used by Simon (1969) illustrates the principle of decomposition. Imagine two watchmakers (prior to the advent of electronic watches, when watches actually had mechanical parts). The first uses a design in which the parts remain assembled only after all of them are put together. If this watchmaker is interrupted before completing a watch, it falls apart. The second uses a design based on stable subassemblies. The watch is decomposed into subassemblies that are interdependent within themselves and remain assembled if put down on the workbench. These subassemblies can later be assembled into watches based on interdependence among the subassemblies as units because there are no interdependencies from within one subassembly to within another subassembly. In a world of interruptions, the second watchmaker is likely to complete more watches than the first.

The same principle is at work in the ideal of object-oriented programming for computers. Each object is a unit of computer code that has encapsulated all its internal workings, and interacts with other units of code only through inputs and outputs to the entire object. There are no relationships directly among elements that are within different objects. Friend and Hickling (1987) have developed a graphic language and collaborative group protocols for identifying interdependent decision areas in plan-making situations. Their techniques are described further in chapter 10.

Observed plan making is decomposed functionally. The particular process to achieve the function of treating sewage can be changed independent of the design of the function of collecting sewage through a network. Treatment plant design and sewer network design each involve high levels of interdependence within the separate functions—"intradependence." Treatment plant design and collection network design, however, are independent of each other except in the aggregate inputs and outputs—how much waste of what kind is output from the network and thus input to the treatment plant. Such decomposition yields subassemblies that can be planned independently of each other, keeping track of only inputs and outputs. These inputs and outputs can then be planned at another level of plan making without reconsidering the internal workings of each part.

Plans for schools, transportation, sewers, and water are usually separate from each other and from so-called general or comprehensive plans. General plans usually address land use for the purpose of establishing zoning regulations and some consideration of the relationships of these to investments in transportation, parks, and sewers. Transportation and sewer decisions, however, are seldom included in the set of choices being planned in a general plan. They are often taken as given, as much because they are decisions of different organizations as because of functional decomposition. Local and regional parks are sometimes included in general plans and sometimes separate, but decisions about parks are usually made by a different department or a separate political jurisdiction.

Such decomposition creates feasible problem scopes and allows group processing based on specialized expertise. Sewer and transportation plans are made by engineers, school plans by school administrative personnel, and general plans by urban planners. General plans for urban development sometimes operate on two levels. The first focuses on land use and the second considers the integration across functional plans, which are usually made by others. Plans mandated by federal legislation or state legislation generally require certain elements, such as housing, land use, and transportation, which also imply a degree of decomposition within the general plan. Integration into one plan of these required elements seldom overrides in practice, however, the decomposition of plan making that arises from limits of cognitive capacity and organizational structure.

Observed plan making is decomposed organizationally or jurisdictionally. Plans for a city focus on the actions such as zoning that are available to that jurisdiction. Thus, plans are defined by decomposition into the interdependent actions of one city and the aggregate inputs and outputs to the actions of other cities. Metropolitan area plans address input and output interactions among the plans of cities as well as the agencies that provide other functional elements at a metropolitan scope such as sewers and transportation, which are often provided by geographically distinct jurisdictions. Decomposition makes sense whether or not there is a centralized authority at the metropolitan level as in Portland, Oregon. If there is such authority, then the strategy of any one city will take this into account. A city will still need a strategy as a municipality, however, whether it is dealing with peer municipalities, a mix of jurisdiction types, or a regional author-ity. The decisions of metropolitan scope will be considered either by the combination of plans of several agencies and municipalities or by a regional authority if it exists. The Portland 2040 Plan (Metro 2000) occurred more easily because the Metro regional government was able to plan for decisions over which it had authority, but counties, municipalities, and infrastructure providers still made their own plans as well.

Observed plan making is decomposed spatially. Land use locations are interdependent because of access, amenity, and disamenity relationships. These relationships operate over different distances. Visibility of industry may be undesirable within an eighth of a mile and sound from a freeway within a quarter of a mile. Access to work may be desirable within distances up to 20 miles. Land use plans can be decomposed spatially at several levels: subdivision design, area plans, downtown plans, city plans, urban expansion plans, and metropolitan area plans. Each focuses on different interactions but each is a useful decomposition, making it feasible to confront the Four I's while treating other plans of different scope as yielding only inputs and outputs in aggregate.

Area plans set the framework for subdivision plans by considering the traffic flows and land use relationships among subdivisions. An area plan need not consider the layout of each residential street or the layout of lots, but it must consider how the traffic from each subdivision is handled by collector streets and directed to arterials and freeway interchanges. An area plan might set policies for subdivisions so as to encourage patterns that would feed transit rather than automobiles and thus might address transit access from subdivisions.

Chicago plans from the 1960s illustrate these ideas of functional and geographic decomposition. Transportation planning was carried out separately by the Chicago Area Transportation Study (Chicago Area Transportation Study 1959, 1960, 1962), an agency separate from the agency doing the comprehensive plan. The comprehensive plan developed by the city had two levels: (1) a set of principles (policies) applying to all geographic districts and the relationships among districts, and (2) a separate booklet for each district showing how those principles resulted in specific choices in that particular area (City of Chicago Department of City Planning 1964; City of Chicago Department of Development and Planning 1966). Figure 9-1 shows the recreation proposals at the citywide and neighborhood lev-

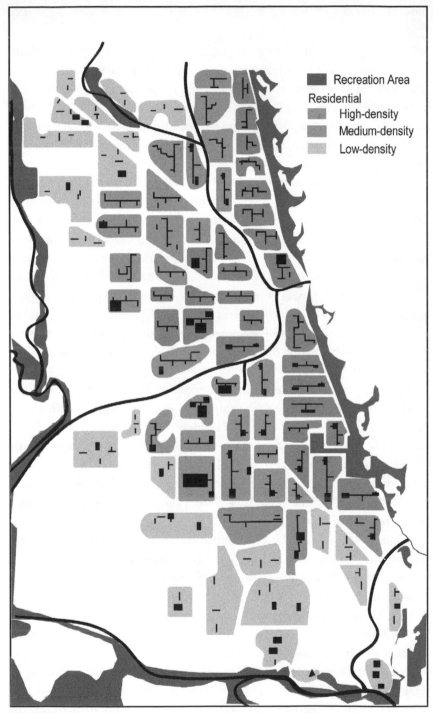

Recreation Area
Residential
  High-density
  Medium-density
  Low-density

Figure 9-1
Diagram of proposed recreation areas by neighborhoods (adapted from City of
Chicago Department of Development and Planning 1966, 41)

els. The general scheme in each neighborhood is similar, but its details are worked out based on local characteristics largely independent of the local characteristics of other neighborhoods.

Observed plan making is decomposed with respect to time. Target years are often identified—for example, Washington 2000 or Portland 2040—but this approach often masks other decomposition dimensions. Recall that spatial decomposition focuses on neighborhood units, a mix of land uses that are interdependent in spatial location and site suitability and are also relatively independent of other neighborhood units. Such spatial decomposition suggests an area sufficient to support a local park and a school and neighborhood shopping. Another level of plan considers the collector street linkages, the interceptor sewer capacities, and other relationships of the neighborhoods or districts to other parts of the city. Note, however, that this decomposition is independent of the rate of growth for the area and is independent of time period or target year. The decomposition into these units of plan making does not depend on time. Plans must address appropriate spatial units and must address them at appropriate levels of detail whether it will take five or twenty-five years for the area to be completely built out.

Similarly, a sewer plan considers at least the entire geographic area that could plausibly be served by the alternative plant locations, whether buildout might occur in ten or a hundred years. Once the plant is located, it is unlikely to be moved and it will set the context in which any other plant in the same metropolitan region will be located. Thus sewer plans have different geographic scope from other plans while also focusing on different functions and levels of detail about these functions, but these differences in scope are based more on functional and geographic decomposition than on temporal decomposition. Larger geographic areas may result in larger times until buildout, but the logic of decomposition is not time but functions and space. Time periods and target dates are frequently artifacts of decompositions on other dimensions.

Plan making in Phoenix, Arizona, illustrates this logic. Plans were developed for geographically defined neighborhoods based on expected incentives for community participation and expected "intradependence" of actions in these areas. The planning agency chose the order in which these plans were developed specifically to get them done before irreversible development or redevelopment occurred (Mee 1998). Functional and geographic dimensions determine the scope of each neighborhood or area plan.

When to make a plan is determined by the lead time necessary before the first significant irreversible actions might occur in the functional or geographic scope of a chunk to be planned.

Representation

As Peattie notes in the quotation at the beginning of this chapter, planners use representations that focus on spatial patterns, physical systems, economies, and networks of interaction, not on people as individuals or as communities. Would it make more sense to represent neighborhoods as sets of persons rather than as streets and buildings?

Observed plan making uses data maps and tables, issues and forces maps, sketch maps, comparative evaluation tables, and explanatory and persuasive text. These types of representations are used in figuring out the plan and in presenting what is often viewed as the final product—a plan document. Some kind of land suitability analysis and map is usually used to identify areas suited to various land uses. These suitabilities are typically judged by experts or interpreted from standard reference materials. Maps of existing land use and population distribution may also be used to identify developable land. Issues and forces maps describe the current situation in a loose combination of graphics and text that is able to incorporate a wider range of perceptions about the situation than are more formal maps. Sketch maps build on issues and forces maps by recording ideas of how development might occur and how such development might respond to or be affected by the issues and forces. As possibilities are identified, comparative tables are created that describe each idea in terms of a common set of attributes. Such comparisons are most likely to be created to bracket the recommended plan rather than for a range of plan possibilities early in the discussion. Text explains these representations and builds an argument for stages of agreement on choices in the plan. These representations are consistent with the processes described in Kaiser et al. (1995) and the content of many plan documents. Sewer plans or transportation plans have different but analogous representations, focusing on networks rather than land areas and with much greater emphasis on cost because of their primary focus on investment in contrast to the primary focus of many land use plans on regulation.

These conventional representations tend to frame plans in terms of outcomes in physical space and attributes of these outcomes. In contrast, representations seldom frame plan making in terms of available actions, connections between actions and consequences, interdependence among actions, or relationships among different decision makers. If models are used, they tend to focus on predicting patterns of activity given an infrastructure network or land use pattern, not on connections between investments or regulations and their consequences. Beliefs about how the world works are seldom represented or tested in any explicit way.

Where local institutions are newly established, plans for development have been more explicit about some of these elements. Integrated Action Planning arose among international development planners and has been codified for applications in Nepal (Irwin and Joshi 1996; Joshi 1997). Integrated Action Planning focuses on decisions that local government councils actually make by showing how decisions about capital budget projects in one year might relate to capital projects in another year. Two representations are important: (1) maps of current infrastructure and the environment, and (2) maps and tables of infrastructure investments such as water supply, roads, and other public service facilities by year and political ward. These representations are used in direct collaboration with local council members, who are elected from wards. The representations thus address the political basis for investment decisions based on wards and investment strategies over several years and several investment categories.

These representations are not much different from capital improvement budgets that might be used in the United States, but they link plans more closely with budgets and they explicitly keep track of who can make what investment decisions from what source of funds and with what political motivations. In contrast to the frequent focus on outcomes, this approach works outward from a set of actions available to a client to make a plan for those actions. There is also less focus on forecasting of demand and more focus on relationships between available actions and possible outcomes by considering interdependent decisions. One motivation is to encourage commitment over several years to phases of major projects so that large infrastructure projects can be implemented that are not possible in a single year. Explicit recognition of ward-based politics and the value of building coalitions around distribution of project benefits among wards are central to this task. The Integrated Action Planning approach connects actions to outcomes by representing sets of local council decisions that result in infrastructure, but it does not represent these connections explicitly for consideration of difficulties or opportunities for new approaches. Connections between actions and consequences are taken as given.

Connections between actions and consequences are sometimes considered through the use of scenarios. A frequent approach is to propose a set of regulations, a pattern of infrastructure investment, or both, and predict the land use pattern that would occur under these conditions. In many historical plans, such scenarios have been constructed by hand based on generalized interpretations. In a planning study for Portland, Oregon, in 1966, these scenarios were labeled "Trend City, Lineal City, Regional Cities, and Radial Corridors" (Metropolitan Planning Commission 1966). The focus, however, was on comparing the outcomes rather than on justifying relationships between available actions and these consequences. More recent planning in Portland for the 2040 Plan relied on more explicit modeling and analysis, but still assumed that actions can be found to achieve desirable outcome patterns rather than testing whether such actions are likely to yield particular results. A great deal of work has been put into developing models to make these kinds of forecasts, but such models are still seldom used in actual plan making.[5] Finding usable representations and tools to connect available actions and consequences remains an opportunity for improvement.

Finding or creating sets of actions that fit available decision situations is an iterative process that seldom represents more than a few alternatives explicitly. A direct approximation of the rationality standard suggests inventing and considering as many alternatives as possible so as to get as close to all as financial and cognitive resources will allow. Observed plan making tends instead to focus on representing and developing one alternative by elaborating the level of detail, the level of performance assessment, and the level of evaluation. This "progressive deepening" (Mintzberg et al. 1976) process may discover that the primary alternative is internally contradictory and infeasible or that expected performance is less than for other known alternatives. Then the process backtracks to modify the primary alternative, or to develop a new alternative. Harris (1967) describes this process by analogy with various systematic search strategies such as branch and bound.

That progressive deepening is frequently observed as a search strategy is not surprising given the limitations of memory and attention and the conservatism biases. As previously argued for long division, when capacities are limited, a process of hypothesis testing by successive approximations is less demanding than keeping a large amount of information active for consideration. It is easier to think about relationships among several actions and their consequences by focusing on representing, modifying, and elaborating one basic idea than by keeping track of several alternatives simultaneously. Observations and interviews of successful architects suggest that they follow a progressive deepening approach. One explanation of this process is that designers identify early in the design process a "prime generator," a fundamental idea that focuses their thinking and that remains unchanged throughout the design process (Darke 1979). In some cases designers or planners identify alternatives that bracket the primary alternative, with one alternative having less and another having more of some critical attributes. For example, a metropolitan land use pattern based on light-rail might be bracketed by one based on high-speed rail and another based entirely on buses. These alternatives serve as means to understand the primary alternative and as reference points for evaluation rather than as alternatives for serious consideration and elaboration in their own right. Such behavior is understandable. Even in situations in which many alternatives could be generated easily, it is still very difficult to elaborate them, assess their performance, and evaluate them—to think seriously about them. Such behavior is also understandable because of the difficulty of communicating many alternatives to others and achieving agreement on one alternative after presenting many. A primary alternative and its bracketing alternatives not only ease the task of making a plan, but also ease the task of selling the plan.

Connecting actions to consequences requires not only forecasting effects but also valuing those effects so as to determine preferences among options. Techniques for eliciting values and preferences independent of specific options—either alternative actions or alternative outcomes—are notoriously difficult to implement. Either people respond in ways that do not express their intended preferences or they refuse to respond at all (Lai and Hopkins 1989, 1995; Lindsey and Knaap 1999). The questions often used to elicit preferences in practice do not yield valid information, even assuming that people know what their preferences are. Valid methods are either too costly to implement for practical use, or people refuse to use them because the questions are simply too difficult to answer. Computing tools may be useful in reducing the number of such trade off questions needed to make a choice (Lee and Hopkins 1995).

The most frequently observed representation for evaluation or assessment is a table comparing alternatives on a set of attributes. A familiar format is a table with the alternatives listed as rows and the attributes listed as columns. This format is used even if the alternatives were created explicitly to bracket a primary alternative. In selecting a car, choosing among faculty candidates, or selecting students for admission, such comparison tables are frequently used. *Consumer Reports* product reviews, computer magazine product reviews, political candidate profiles in newspapers, and some step in almost all systematic evaluation techniques involve such tables. Many plans include such tables in their working documents if not in their final recommendations. Such tables arise for two primary reasons. First, evaluations involve multiple attributes and usually more than we can keep track of in working memory. Second, none of the many methods for aggregating preferences across attributes is widely accepted or applied in practice. These tables are external memory devices, representations with which to think through comparisons in various relatively ad hoc ways. A crucial implication is that for such tables to have meaning, they must include more than one alternative because the transformations of measures of the attributes into preferences, even if only implicit, can only be accomplished in relative terms.

Such comparison tables do not come at the end as implied in many prescriptions of processes for making plans. Frequently, for example in the 1966 Portland study (Metropolitan Planning Commission 1966), a few alternatives and a comparison table are created early in a plan-making process to frame the situation, suggest additional attributes that relate to objectives, define forecasting tasks, and highlight information that would actually help distinguish among choices. Such comparison also prompts modifications of alternatives or creates openings for invention of new alternatives. In a progressive deepening process, evaluation tasks are included from the beginning even though there is a focus on a primary alternative.

When compared to explanations of the logic of plans and the standard of rationality, observed plan making and conventional prescriptions make surprisingly little use of representations that connect available actions to consequences in other than superficial ways. This affects what actions are considered, whether interdependence among actions and decision makers is considered, and whether consequences are evaluated in a way that compares outcomes diagnostically. Such diagnostic evaluations are needed in order to discover how to modify actions in relation to preferred consequences.

Participation and Expertise About Interests

Some planning behaviors can be explained as behaviors to counter the limitations of available collective choice and organizational institutions. Sedway and Cooke's (1983) criteria for successful downtown plans focus on conditions that increase the likelihood that a plan will be carried out. They explain plan making by recognizing which persons and organizations have incentives to plan because of the actions and resources they control, and thus which persons are likely to gain from making and using plans. Keating and Krumholz (1991), on the other hand, focus on what should be done to change such situations so that other persons have incentives to plan for other objectives. Other instances, including Austin and Atlanta, focused on large numbers of public participants. These instances of plan making can be interpreted using collective choice, collective action, and organizational explanations.

Electoral politics, whether considering the cognitive or aggregation of preference explanations, are flawed in practice. Direct public participation is similarly flawed. One response is Krumholz's approach to equity planning (Krumholz and Forester 1990). The Cleveland Policy Report set a policy "to provide a wider range of choices for those Cleveland residents who have few, if any, choices" and gave four reasons: "(1) the urgent reality of conditions in Cleveland, (2) the inherent unfairness and exploitative nature of our urban development process, (3) the inability of local politics to address these problems, (4) our conception of the ethics of professional practice" (Krumholz 1982, 163–164). Planners chose the central criteria for choosing among situations on which to focus and for developing recommendations for actions. Planners took responsibility for advocating these criteria and actions to and beyond the planning commission, mayor, and council.

This professionally adopted policy highlights a paradox of progressive policy. The policy derives from principles, not from political mandates of either the current power structure or the powerless. It is articulated from fundamental cultural values, usually by middle-class or upper-middle-class persons. The basic premise was consistent with religious traditions and claimed moral ideals. No constituency, however, gave the Cleveland Planning Commission this policy. Nor did the appointed citizen members of the planning commission create it, though they did ratify it. The professional planning staff formed it, framed it explicitly, and applied it to each situation they faced or created by their own initiative. Race was often an implicit issue as in the Euclid Beach case. The commission advocated the establishment of a public beach, but neighbors opposed the beach, expressing fear of crime. A proposal to locate public housing on the all-white west side of Cleveland brought forth claims of environmental problems and infrastructure shortages. A highway proposal ignored its destruction of African American neighborhoods. In each case the professional planners made recommendations consistent with their policy of focusing on the interests of the least well off, whether or not they could win the day and even though city council and neighborhood citizens opposed their views in each specific instance. As specific situations arose, the policy was a constant reminder of fundamental social commitments.

In light of some implicit external standard, the planners used the backing of the profession's commitment to "seek to expand choice and opportunity for all persons, recognizing a special responsibility to plan for the needs of disadvantaged groups and persons" (American Institute of Certified Planners 1991). In Cleveland the planners articulated and committed themselves to this policy without direct backing from electoral politics or citizen participation. Whether their external standard was a standard of rationality or of more fundamental standards, their response is a direct attempt to counter the limitations of collective choice mechanisms. The Cleveland Policy Report was different from conventional plans because such plans would not serve the objective of these planners. Other responses by planners to limitations of collective choice have been much less direct. Most focus on inducing public participation by underrepresented groups as a counter to electoral politics and to "natural" citizen participation, such as NIMBY responses. Commitment by the profession to a standard process of analysis that must include consideration of distributional effects and a broad range of effects also counters the limitations of collective choice and organizational structures.

Advocacy for equity as used by Krumholz takes direct responsibility for changing actions without seeking to change the situation that justifies such an approach. Empowerment planning as elaborated by Reardon (1994, 1998), on the other hand, takes as a primary objective empowering those whose lack of power justifies counteracting electoral politics and citizen participation. Empowerment acknowledges cognitive and constitutive (who is dignified as being a person to be listened to) limitations as well as collective choice limitations. It uses current situations to increase the power of underpowered persons and groups to augment the cognitive basis for initiatives beyond the capabilities of planners, and to engage persons as worthy of citizenship. Such an approach prompts plans appropriate to its purposes. Underpowered persons are seldom initiators of investments or regulations. Their actions do not face the issues of interdependence, irreversibility, indivisibility, and imperfect foresight that benefit from the design or strategy aspects of plans. Visions change aspirations and beliefs, and agendas organize action and create trust. These aspects of how plans work are better explanations of plans made when empowerment is a primary objective.

Berkeley, Burlington, Hartford, and Santa Monica in some degree elected their progressive agenda setters. Clavel (1986, 16–17) identifies three factors creating the possibility for progressive administrations that had substantive agendas. Central cities were dying as middle-class whites moved to the suburbs, so arguments that the growth and economic development agenda was helping central-city residents lost their credibility. Opposition movements of several sorts—civil rights, antiwar, environmental—provided a context in which local political opposition could arise. Planning, primarily in the sense of agenda setting, occurred both by opposition groups and as mediation between government and direct participation of citizens. Planners' roles were prescribed sufficiently loosely that they could operate within the potential contradictions of established government and direct participation from neighborhood organizations. This ability to handle contradictions within organizations is consistent with March's arguments discussed above. The progressive political coalitions in Berkeley, Burlington, Hartford, and Santa Monica formed in opposition and took the time before they gained power to form their agendas. In Berkeley they framed "an agenda of possibilities that the city could think about until action became possible" (Clavel 1986, 187). These agendas were supported by professional analysis by highly educated individuals who were attracted to these progressive ideas.

These agendas did not look like the Chicago Plan of 1909 because they were not for the interests of the commercial elite or about infrastructure investment. Rather than the Chicago Plan's idealized claims of indirect benefit to the moral and material interests of the broader community, the progressive coalitions and professionals conducted specific analyses that addressed the direct distribution of tangible benefits to their claimed constituents, the underrepresented poor residents. Rather than calculating totals for bond issues, they calculated dollars coming to city residents.

Progressive reformers may act inside or outside the system. Krumholz in Cleveland worked from within a particular position as an employee of the city. Others worked for neighborhoods or citizen groups with independent sources of funding for support, the best-known being Saul Alinsky (Horwitt 1989). Most plans for urban development are now made by agencies within city or other government institutions or by consultants hired by these institutions, but instances of citizen groups forming to make plans largely independent of government institutions are still important.

As explanations of observed behaviors, these approaches provide useful ideas for particular situations. Planners such as Saul Alinsky, Norman Krumholz, or Ken Reardon, who bring strong prior commitments to particular goals that are significantly related to cognitive, institutional, and structural biases, tend to behave so as to counter aspects of these institutions and structures. These commitments have usually found the agenda, vision, and policy aspects of plans more useful than the design or strategic aspects. Investments and regulation of physical development are unlikely to be central to these commitments because the underpowered are unlikely to be making such investments.[6]

Planners also use expertise about participation and interests to design systems of ad hoc participation in plan making. The "Austinplan process" as interpreted by Beatley et al. (1994) illustrates the issues well. The ninety-four-person steering committee represented specific interests: "business, culture, environmental, ethnic minority, human services, neighborhoods, public sector, real estate, and community at large" (187). Fourteen task groups addressed functional areas, and twenty-two geographic areas each had their own area councils. These participant groups totaled more than a thousand people. Thus decomposition, functionally and geographically, was part of the structuring of participation. The process resulted in a plan, but it was not adopted by the city council because the electoral process changed the makeup of the council dramatically and the economic situation changed.

Beatley et al. (1994) focus on the question of whether the thousand participants were representative of the larger citizenry. The participants were different in demographic attributes from the general population, had similar attitudes, but were more likely than the general population to believe in the potential of government action to solve problems. From a deliberative cognition perspective, this may have been an effective process given that the purpose was to plan for government actions. These participants were likely to help and willing to participate. As representatives of the population, they may have been good trusted delegates, representatives entrusted to learn and deliberate about what should be done rather than simply be a mechanism for encoding the given preferences of a population. Perhaps more problematic, the process did not mesh with the parallel electoral process that identified the legal representatives with authority to act on the actions being planned. Keating and Krumholz (1991) report other instances of contradictions between electoral politics and induced participation in plan making. These instances suggest a need to combine induced participation and institutions of government.

Organizational Roles

Two responses to limitations of organization are frequently observed. First, planners do not assume that organizations that could exist do exist, or that collective action that could occur has occurred. The major difference between Checkoway's planning process and the others described in Table 9-1 is that Checkoway includes the tactics necessary to create an organization to carry out goals and the others take the existence of organizations as a given. In his approach "we" is not known or given *a priori*. The frictions to collective action and thus to organization, which yield inequitably distributed capabilities to act, beg differential interventions to prompt collective action and create organizations.

Second, plan making for urban development occurs in an uneasy ambiguity between being a line department focused on planning for actions for which it has responsibility versus having a staff role to decision makers with authority over a wider range of actions.[7] Aspirations to a staff role for the full scope of city organizational functions have seldom been successful in sustaining a responsibility for making plans for urban development. The plan commission as buffer from politics was useful even to Krumholz in shielding his appointment from immediate political actions. He was useful to mayors in part because he had a somewhat independent platform from which to advocate particular interests.

The planning function often swings back and forth in its balancing of a staff function and a line function. If the planning director is closely associ-

ated with the mayor or chief executive and thus closely tied to political actors and their agendas, the planning function may be carried out largely in
a staff role to the executive. Seattle created, in its executive branch, an Office of Policy Planning (OPP) in the 1970s. Dalton's (1985) analysis of this
case provides evidence to clarify two roles: (1) central staff to the entire city
administration focused on the mayor, and (2) land use planning for a land
use line agency. As a staff agency, the OPP had directors with local experience and political ties to the mayor, as expected in a trusted, general staff
position. The OPP analyzed projects, managed projects, and became a
lightning rod for line agencies concerned about centralization of authority
in the mayor's office. The OPP's land use planning tasks, on the other hand,
were neglected and fewer professional planners were hired. As the agency
transformed back into a line agency to administer the land development
process and long-range planning for regulations and capital improvements,
it changed character. It hired as its new director a professional planner who
was neither from Seattle nor connected politically to the mayor. It focused
on land use duties and coordinated its planning with, but did not presume
to plan for, other line agencies. The types of plans and analyses appropriate to the different roles are different. Analysis of the mayor's agenda and
policies considers their feasibility and consequences in the short term and
their political implications. Plans for land use regulations and capital investments consider strategies and impacts on a wide range of issues, but may
not address immediate concerns of the mayor.

In Philadelphia in the 1950s and 1960s, Edmund Bacon (1974) claimed
success by expressly focusing on the longer term and avoiding conflict on
day-to-day issues. His vision of future development focused on decisions
others were ignoring. As planning director in San Francisco, Allan Jacobs
(1980) had a more complex relationship with the mayor's office, mixing staff
role access with line agency functions. The Boston Redevelopment Authority combined redevelopment and planning into one agency under the
leadership of Ed Logue in order to have capital investment actions under
the control of the planning agency (King 1990). Plans, and thus planners,
must influence some actions that are actually available to take. Mayoral
terms are short. The situations most likely to benefit from plans are infrastructure investment and land use regulation. Therefore, influencing a wide
range of day-to-day decisions facing the mayor may not be the most powerful use of plans because plans may not be effective in addressing those de-

cisions. It may be more important to influence decisions about capital improvements, which are likely to result from proposals by departments and actions by the council. This claim argues for plans oriented to the line functions of departments and to the city council.

Planners may be the agents of civic organizations, as in the Chicago Plan of 1909 or the Regional Plan of New York and Its Environs of 1929. Johnson (1996) describes how the primary client, the funding "principal" was a committee of prominent private citizens. The resulting plan responded explicitly and implicitly to the interests and beliefs of the members of this committee. At the same time, both the committee and the staff believed that the plan would be useful to the many municipalities and agencies making major infrastructure investments and setting land regulations in the region. They were planning for the actions of others. They assumed that the plan was a collective good from the perspective of the municipal governments (as well as from their own perspective). Thus the municipal governments and agencies could jointly "consume" the plan, but would be unable to organize themselves in collective action to create it.

Plans for urban development seldom have sufficient salience in the activities of government to sustain an agency or department that does not also have an implementation role in regulating land use or programming capital improvements. The organization of most planning departments confirms that, despite the uneasy balance, having a primary responsibility for land use and unfulfilled aspirations for wider influence is a fairly successful combination, even if it does not fit neatly in organizational logic and roles.

Diagnostic Evaluation of Plan Making

In chapter 3 the discussion assessed plans based on effects, net benefits, internal validity, and external validity. Knowing that a plan yielded good outcomes is not sufficient to improve plans, however, unless there is a way to relate this success to available behaviors that will lead to improved plans. Recall the canoeing metaphor of chapter 2. I can choose how hard to paddle and in what direction to point the canoe; I cannot just decide not to hit a rock in the stream. We can choose how to behave in making a plan; we cannot just decide to have a good plan.

There are two general approaches to assessing plan-making tasks: (1) comparison to rationality as a standard, which yields claims that the tasks operate as substitutes for direct implementation of a rational process; and (2) experimental assessment of tasks in relation to resulting plan quality (Hopkins 1984b). Explanations of tasks inferred from observed behaviors as attempts to achieve a rationality standard can be extended to consider what further improvement might be possible. A convergence of observed processes and prescribed processes can be sought by adjusting the prescriptions when they do not make sense of what is possible or adjusting processes when they fail to take advantage of what should be possible. The preceding discussion of observed plan making suggests some such opportunities.

The second approach is to test tasks in relation to resulting plan quality directly, but it is difficult to assess the quality of a plan and to link plan quality to particular plan-making tasks inferred from observed behaviors. In general, the quality of a plan can be judged only after it is created because the situation for which the plan is created is incompletely defined. Thus the specific measures of success are discovered in making the plan rather than known *a priori*. Plan quality can be judged after the fact by a panel of judges or by the persons who made the plan and thus now understand how to judge its success. Either approach is difficult to implement (Hopkins 1984b). There is very little research on the effectiveness of tasks in making plans, and there is even less research that relies on explanations of the relationships between observed behaviors, inferred tasks, and plan quality.

Using the problem-solving participants as a panel of judges, Brill et al. (1990) tested the effects on solution quality of difference among the alternatives considered. They showed that subjects given a set of four alternatives that were more different from each other were able to find better solutions than subjects given four alternatives that were more similar. This suggests that in some situations, generating a small number of very different alternatives may yield better solutions. It also appeared that a computer support system that made it easy to investigate many alternatives could compensate for starting with only one alternative. This result also suggests, however, that being able to generate alternatives is important. These results are consistent with conventional wisdom about desirable processes, but they contradict observed behavior in making plans for urban development, in which alternatives are seldom generated except to bracket a recommended alternative as a basis for arguing in its favor. Equally pertinent, these results suggest that it is effective to use small sets of different alternatives rather than trying to implement procedural rationality directly by trying to generate as many alternatives as possible.

Bryson et al. (1990) used the lead participants in project planning as judges of the degree to which goals of a project were achieved. They considered the context in which projects were developed—the plan-making situation—and tasks: communications with affected groups, effort in identifying the problem, use of conflict resolution techniques, and effort in searching for solutions. The data were coded from secondary source reports of the cases. They found that attributes of the plan-making situation affected the degree of accomplishment. Thus results of plan-making research must be generalized with care. Effort on problem identification increased accomplishment of goals, but search for solutions did not. They acknowledge that this result may arise from the participants seeing their work as reframing the problem until a solution arises rather than as searching for a solution. Searching for a problem definition may be just a different perspective on searching for a solution as implied by the now familiar phrase that a problem is defined by its solution. This research focused on single projects rather than on sets of interdependent decisions that might comprise plans, which limits its generalizability to plans for urban development.

Helling (1998) looked at the plan making and outcomes for a visioning effort in Atlanta. Although the process followed conventional claims about how visioning should be done, there was no evidence that it achieved its intended results or met the claims for the process. Participation alone could not compensate for a situation in which the process seemed to seek consensus without having access to any available actions that could be taken and without a way to affect attitudes through a vision. A high-participation approach involving ten teams and over a thousand people resulted in little more than a great deal of interactive participation.

Evaluation of plan making may require consideration of interactions between how a plan was made and how it was used. The effectiveness of use may depend on the process by which it was made. For example, if public participation leads to better plans because these plans are more likely to be used, why does this occur? Does the increased use of the plan result because it becomes a better plan or because the users who participated in making the plan become invested in using it regardless of how good the plan is? If plan use increases with participation in plan making regardless of any increase in plan quality embedded in the plan itself, then the effects of participation would have to be determined by measuring plan use, not by measuring plan quality. Or conversely, if there is a problem of plans not being used, it matters whether anything done to improve quality will increase use or anything done to increase participation will increase use even at the expense of quality.

Summary: Opportunities to Improve Prescriptions for Making Plans

Explanations of how plans work, how plans are made, and how plans are used suggest contradictions between conventional prescriptions and observed plan making. Either the prescription should be changed or the logic of the prescription should be reinforced so as to be more persuasive in trying to change practice. Such contradictions and systematic evaluation of plan-making behaviors suggest five opportunities to adjust conventional prescriptions so as to yield better plan making.

Observed plans are seldom implemented in the sense implied by conventional prescriptions. A focus on using plans when making decisions makes more sense than a focus on implementing the plan. Observed plans are seldom up to date. Inferring opportunities to make plans from the decision situations in which they are being used makes more sense than time-driven revision. The prescription for a comprehensive plan for twenty years of forecasted growth fits neither observed plans (except when constrained by legislation to meet the prescription) nor the logic of making plans. Choosing efficient scopes for plans based on appropriate criteria makes more sense than a prescribed standard scope. Neither the prescription of a sequence of steps nor the rejection of any systematic process, has succeeded in improving plan-making processes. The internal logic of a plan depends on linking actions and consequences, which should be the focus of plan-making procedures. The prescription for extensive public participation also fits neither observed plan making (except when constrained by legislation to follow the prescription) nor the logic of making plans. A combination of formal democratic institutions and direct participation is more effective and fair in bringing collective choice to bear on making plans and on using plans to make decisions.

10

How to Use and Make Plans

Therefore it is quite possible that when particular portions of the plan shall be taken for execution, wider knowledge, longer experience, or a change in local conditions may suggest a better solution; but on the other hand, before any departure shall be determined upon, it should be made clear that such a change is justified.

If many elements of the proposed plan shall seem familiar, it should be remembered that the purpose has not been to invent novel problems for solution, but to take up the pressing needs of today, and to find the best methods of meeting those requirements, carrying each particular problem to its ultimate conclusion as a component part of a great entity—a well-ordered, convenient, and unified city.

—Daniel H. Burnham and Edward H. Bennet (1909), *Plan of Chicago*

The planning-as-canoeing metaphor in chapter 2 highlights the importance of recognizing opportunities to use available actions as they emerge in the stream of events and of recognizing how these interdependent actions fit together in a plan. To create strategy, imagine using it. When I pull into that eddy on the river, what might I wish I had considered before arriving there? Strategy emerges from its use. In contrast, conventional descriptions of plans conclude with discussions of how to implement the plan (e.g., Kaiser et al. 1995; Kelly and Becker 2000). Implementation suggests that the focus starts from the plan and looks to actions, that the focus is on one plan, and that there are tools for implementing plans. Limited human attention capacity, however, suggests that people will focus on decision situations, issues being raised, or solutions being suggested, not on plans.

Pressman and Wildavsky (1973) argue that the many steps between program design and implementation, each step having some probability of failure, make program implementation unlikely. Alexander (1995), in contrast, argues that because organizational settings include a great deal of structure and history of interaction, implementation is actually much more likely than the assumption of independent statistical probabilities would imply. Implementation of plans is analogous. If we assume that plans are created and implemented independent of their context, then the likelihood of implementation is small. If a plan emerges from its context and is used in the daily activities of that context, then the plan has much less work to do. Using such plans is likely to yield improved outcomes.

The logic of plans as presented here suggests that plans can and should emerge from their context and be used from the decision-making perspective rather than implemented from the plan's perspective. Learn ways to recognize opportunities to use plans in the stream of daily activities. Make plans that can be viewed from the perspective of decision situations. Opportunities to use plans are also triggers to make plans. Such plans should be of efficient scope, relate consequences to actions, and use formal as well as informal institutions to deliberate and make choices. These prescriptive implications are logically developed in reverse by considering first how to use plans, then how to make them.

Interpretations of observed plan making in chapter 9, based on the logic of making plans developed in the preceding chapters, show that conventional prescriptions are not consistent with observed practice. Analytical and empirical evidence argues for modified prescriptions. These arguments are framed here as five claims. None of these is entirely new, but each directly contradicts a conventional prescription that is frequently, if not universally, advocated. These claims remain, however, within the norm that plans for urban development are worth making in certain situations and in certain ways.

1. *Recognize opportunities to use plans* by looking at plans from the perspective of decisions about available actions. Do not implement a plan working from the perspective of the plan.
2. *Create views of plans for decision situations.* Do not present plans only from the perspective of plan making.
3. *Recognize opportunities to make (revise) plans* by considering decision situations. Do not make plans at fixed time intervals for fixed time horizons.
4. *Make plans of efficient scopes* by choosing the functional, spatial, and or-

ganizational scope of a plan so as to be useful in shaping and making decisions. Do not strive for a comprehensive plan on the premise that the closer to this ideal, the better.

5. *Link consequences to interdependent actions* that are available and recognize uncertainty in these links and these actions. Do not allocate a chosen, forecasted demand to locations as if this could be directly achieved.

6. *Use formal and informal institutions* to deliberate and act. Do not privilege direct participation as if it were inherently more effective or fair, and do not presume that plans are or must be collective choices.

Observed planning practice follows some of these prescriptions, even though they contradict conventional prescriptions for making plans. These claims may, therefore, be more persuasive to people who use and make plans.

Recognize Opportunities to Use Plans

Mandelbaum (1990) argues that plans should be read as opportunities to discuss and deliberate in public, but the reading style he suggests is not immediately related to decision-making situations. The argument that plans are hard to use is not new.

> The conclusion is unavoidable [based on interviews and looking at consultant-generated plans] that a city plan is of little or no value unless there is a full-time planning official to keep it constantly before the officials who must carry it out; for, whereas the latter will frequently consult a planner who is part of the governmental organization, they but rarely consult a ready-made plan. (Walker 1950, 210)

Plans are more likely to be used, even by planners, if pointers are provided from decision situations to plans rather than only from plans to decisions. Using plans when making decisions suggests that the focus is on decisions, that one decision can point to many plans, and that there should be tools for indexing plans from decisions. This difference in perspective has important practical implications for the format of plans, which is the focus of the next section.

The process of making plans is usually the major determinant of the format of a plan, not the process of using a plan. Plans are made from the perspectives of visions, targets, strategies, agendas, and policies. Plans make sense as plans from such perspectives, which determine the scope of decisions, issues, and solutions that should be considered. When focusing on decisions—including deliberations and negotiations to shape issues and create solutions—it is difficult also to focus attention on a plan from the perspective of the plan. The information in a plan is needed in a different form. Rather than asking how to implement a plan, ask: "Given the current understanding of this decision situation, what information in what plans is pertinent to deliberating about and choosing an action?" Two examples of using plans illustrate this idea.

The 1958 Master Plan Supplement for Lexington, Kentucky, sets out the logic for the urban service area.

> The Urban Service Area map delineates the location of this additional urban land in portions of the surrounding drainage areas. They range in size from 1.4 to 5.9 square miles. Sewer systems in each of these drainage areas can reasonably and economically be provided by an integral trunk sewer system leading to a single sewage treatment plant in each drainage area. Land development based on this concept will operate most economically if residential subdivision development, as it progresses, were directed to and encouraged in each of the several drainage areas successively. (Segoe and Associates 1958, 18–19)

The accompanying map, simplified to a diagram, is shown in Figure 10-1. The shaded area of 6.6 square miles in the center is the area then served by sewers as represented by the arrow pointing to the square, which is the location of the treatment plant. The remainder of the central area within the gray outline was planned to be served by new interceptors to the existing plant. The surrounding areas outlined in gray are the upper parts of watersheds, each draining away from the city in a different direction.

If we interpret this plan as implementing a design, then we should ask whether a treatment plant was built in each watershed and whether the watersheds were developed in succession. If we interpret this plan as implementing a policy, we might think of the service areas being different from those shown, but we should still ask whether a plant was built in each watershed and whether the watersheds were developed in succession. Was the plan implemented as design or policy? Not exactly, but it was used.

The plan interpreted as strategy was to build collection networks that would take advantage of gravity, build treatment plants of efficient size, and

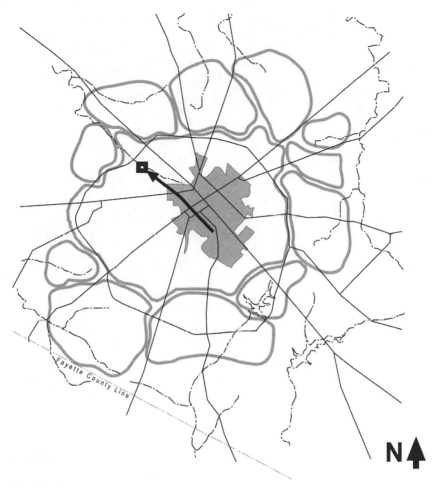

Figure 10-1
Sanitary sewerage strategy for Lexington, Kentucky, 1958

sequence development to take advantage of available capacity. Areas to be sewered were identified as being within an urban service area, and only outside that area was development permitted to use septic tanks and then only on lots of ten acres or more. This strategy thus supported both investment decisions and regulatory decisions. Another major problem in Lexington at that time was to connect large areas of existing development, which was still relying on septic tanks despite inadequate soil conditions and lot sizes. In 1958, the planners believed that treatment plants serving small watersheds of one to six square miles and relying on gravity flow would be efficient.

Figure 10-2
Sanitary sewerage strategy for Lexington, Kentucky, 1963

Figure 10-2, which shows the situation as of 1963, and Figure 10-3, which shows the situation and plans as of 1972, suggest that the plan was used as strategy. These diagrams were constructed from planning documents from the City-County Planning Commission, Lexington and Fayette County, Kentucky (1964, 1973). By 1963, additional interceptors had been built to serve the southwestern part of the central area, using a force main (dashed line) to take flow uphill to the existing plant. New interceptors were also built to the north, which served parts of two of the outlying watersheds,

Figure 10-3
Sanitary sewerage strategy for Lexington, Kentucky, 1973

including a lift station (circle) and a force main to bring sewage back from
outlying watersheds to the main plant. There were also two small treatment
plants each serving a subdivision in the same outlying watershed on the
south side. There were three small private plants as well, which are not
shown in the diagram. Progress was made, but rather than treating the plan
as a design, it was used as strategy to ask whether a lift station should be
built instead of a separate plant, or whether separate small plants would be
efficient in the interim before sufficient development occurred to justify a
large plant.

By 1972, much larger treatment plants, force mains, and lift stations were financially feasible because of new Kentucky legislation (Bahl 1963). Federal legislation in the early 1970s made large plants the norm nationwide. In 1973, as shown in Figure 10-3, a new plant has been constructed just south of the county line, and the two small plants that were in operation in 1963 have now been eliminated. In addition plans are underway, as shown in the gray, to sewer additional areas. A proposed third plant is shown to the southwest, but even then an alternative of pumping that waste through a force main back up to the divide and then by gravity to the southern plant was also being considered. The 1973 plan actually suggests three alternatives, not shown here, as contingent strategy to serve the urban service area, which in 1973 was as shown by the dotted line.

As decisions arose, the logic of the plan as strategy and the underlying information were pertinent and apparently used to derive new specific actions. Compared to the 1958 plan, fewer treatment plants were built, the second major plant was built in a different location, and the network was different, which resulted in a different sequence of chunks of sewered land. The internal logic of the plan as strategy held: an urban service area in which connection to sewers is required, extension of sewers in efficiently sized chunks, and permission for septic tanks only outside the area for which sewers were planned and on larger lots.

On the regulatory side, rezoning decisions relied on the logic of the urban service area as a basis for making decisions, but the direct implementation of zoning as a timing device is always problematic. Again it is difficult to argue that the plan was directly implemented through zoning, but it was used in making zoning decisions. Some of these decisions relied on the service area boundary explicitly and were sustained in court; other decisions resulted in developments outside the urban service area (Haar 1977, 581; Roeseler 1982).

In making rezoning decisions, consideration of the map of drainage areas, map of future land uses, and designation of the urban service area would not have been sufficient. Consideration had to be given to the internal logic of the strategy and information from which these spatial patterns were derived and the method for deriving them—to the logic of the plan based on interdependence, irreversibility, indivisibility, and imperfect foresight. A strategy is a contingent path through a decision tree, which means that when each decision is taken, the current state of the system should be considered. If the assumptions on which the strategy was derived have changed, then the strategy should be recomputed. A policy about re-zoning is a presumptive rule. Each time it is applied, there is discretion to determine whether the policy fits the specifics of the situation. And each situation may in turn suggest refinements in the statement of the policy.

In the San Ramon Valley of Contra Costa County, California, planners focused on a particular target outcome: establishing an employment node on the Bishop Ranch as described in detail by McGovern (1998). The initial plan in 1958 envisioned complementary areas of residence and employment, and the Bishop Ranch of 464 acres was targeted for manufacturing employment. The site was finally developed for a different kind of employment in the mid-1980s after several early projects fell through and planners had resisted proposals to use it for residential development. In the end, "To implement their vision for Bishop Ranch, county planners sought out the developer and tenants that eventually came to the site." (McGovern 1998, 252). By the strict definitions used here, this case fits better the carrying through of a design than the fulfilling of a vision by changing attitudes. Indeed, the vision of a balanced community was lost because the employment located was not consistent with the cost of surrounding housing. Was the plan implemented? Not in the conventional sense. From the plan perspective, implementing it meant zoning the parcel for manufacturing. The project finally occurred when planner's put on their work agenda a focused effort to carry out the design by attracting and working with a specific developer.

To recognize opportunities to use plans:

- When making decisions, shaping issues, or reacting to proposals that emerge in the stream of daily activities, look for information in and the underlying logic of the variety of plans that may be relevant to that decision.

This principle applies to all five ways in which plans work.

1. Vision: What attitudes and beliefs of whom could I shape today?
2. Agenda: What can I cross off my list today?
3. Policy: What policies apply to this decision situation?
4. Design: Does this action, as elaborated for execution, still fit logic of the design?

5. Strategy: Of what strategies is this decision situation potentially a part?

Using plans in this way is difficult given the way plans are typically presented, which suggests that we need different views into plans.

Create Views of Plans for Decision Situations

Ideas about how to organize and access data are highly developed in information science and computer database design (see e.g., Date 1995). Rather than make copies of information reorganized into many different forms, the preferred approaches are to create indexes to point to information from many different perspectives or to create alternative views of the same information. Conventional plans do not have indexes that point from particular types of decision situations to the pertinent visions, strategies, designs, policies, and agendas that relate this decision to other interdependent decisions and issues.[1] Plans are not available as alternative views for different kinds of decision situations. Using plans requires such indexes or views, at least implicitly. In order to consider indexes and views, we need to consider first how plans are typically organized.

Kelly and Becker (2000, 186) outline one conventional table of contents for a comprehensive plan.

1. Background (including community history)
2. Existing conditions analysis
3. Issues and goals developed from citizen participation
4. Alternative scenarios and policies
5. Final plan and policies
6. Implementation strategies

This table of contents follows a plan-making and plan-adoption perspective. It is organized to justify the plan by explaining it in terms of rationality as a standard. Other plans are organized by functional elements, following a functional decomposition of the plan-making process as described in chapter 9. In either case the plan is organized to justify its adoption by reflecting the process of making it relative to a rationality standard. Such plans are not organized to be used when decisions are made. Kelly and Becker (2000, 183) suggest other formats to make the plan "user friendly, accessible, and short," generally by including only the adopted policies, implementation tools, and related maps. This approach eases the search by making the document shorter and easier to read, but it still keeps the plan's organization in the perspective of the plan and its implementation. Indexes are even better than a shortened plan because they are sorted by decision situations and they can point to many plans.

Kelly and Becker (2000, 177–181) also point out the difficulties of presenting future land use maps. If a plan map is an attempt to describe the future pattern of land use, there is a dilemma between specificity and generality, between being too precise to be credible and being too general to be pertinent. Such maps again focus on the plan's perspective, not the user's perspective. One way to break this dilemma is to think of maps and diagrams as indexes to and representations of the internal logic of the plan. Geographic location and spatial patterns are among the most pertinent ways in which users think about their decision situations. Plans are pertinent in decision situations that face the Four I's, and the Four I's are likely to occur when locational aspects matter. Thus a location-oriented index is especially valuable.

Cincinnati, Ohio, developed a "Planning Guidance System" in the early 1970s (Kleymeyer and Hartsock 1973). The key components were a library of plans by government and nongovernment actors and "situation boards," which displayed up-to-date information on available plans and actions to implement them. This approach was highly unusual in recognizing the existence of many pertinent plans and the need for some way to monitor them. The use of this system, however, focused on bringing " . . . the diverse pieces of planning going on in the city into an integral whole from which planning needs may be derived . . . " (11) and "to show the relationships between parts; to adjust the individual parts; to make the effort to bring together the agencies which are involved in conflict, or which need coordination, to try to reconcile differences; and to summarize the current status of existing plans in a simplified document . . . " (1). Although a major innovation, the expectation was still that a high degree of integration and coordination could be achieved by a planning mechanism. Rather than trying to bring all the plans together in a planning agency, it makes more sense for the many actors to index the relationships of their own and others' decisions to their own and others' plans.

An index can be constructed in three tasks. First, give meaningful labels to concepts in the situation of interest. Second, organize these labels so that searching for the concept of interest will be efficient. Third, provide pointers from the indexed concepts to information pertinent to these concepts. A book index is a list of concepts described by key words, ordered alphabetically for easy searching, and followed by page numbers to point to locations in the text. Indexing is a more general concept, however, than this familiar instance. An index could be a map or a diagram, for example. Creating indexes to use plans begs several questions. First, what concepts should be included in the index and how can they be labeled? Second, how can these labeled concepts be organized for efficient search or even to "push" them into the focus of attention without a user taking the initiative to search? Third, how can pointers be constructed that point to pertinent information in the typical formats of plans?

A comprehensive plan document and a capital improvements program are (or should be) two views of approximately the same information. Views, in the context of computing system design, are alternative ways of looking at the same data, which is stored only once for efficiency and ease of maintenance. If you have access to a computer database of names and phone numbers, you can view that data sorted alphabetically by name or sorted numerically by phone number, depending on which is more useful for a given task. These are two views of one database.[2] New computing tools make it possible to access the content of plans in different ways so that, for example, we might view the same information (or parts of it) as a comprehensive plan or as a capital improvements program. If we wanted to access information in these ways frequently, it would be efficient to set up an index to the data to create these views efficiently.

Rather than refine a plan in the plan's perspective by making it shorter or more readable, it makes more sense to create and maintain a user's manual, index, and views to your own plans and to the plans of others. Different indexes and views will be needed for different types of users and situations.

Staff developing recommendations, executives engaging in negotiations, and plan commissioners or city council members deliberating or deciding how to vote share similar requirements for an index to plans. They need pointers from a decision situation, issue, or proposal to the internal logic of plans that may be pertinent to that situation. These situations include capital improvements programs in aggregate and commitments of funds for individual projects, changes in requirements of a particular zoning category and rezoning of particular parcels, annexation policies and individual annexation agreements, tax increment financing districts and forgiveness of fees or taxes for individual economic development opportunities, and neighborhood preservation and reinvestment proposals.

An immediate implication of the stream of opportunities metaphor is that planners must allocate time and attention, for which they use two primary tools: work programs and daily calendaring. These tools should be used to focus attention by deciding what to do and, perhaps less obviously, by deciding what not to do. How should staff spend time? Which invitations to speak, requests to attend neighborhood meetings, requests to meet with developers, suggestions to investigate proposed "solutions" should be accepted and which rejected? The best daily calendaring includes making appointments with oneself to work on the agenda aspects of plans. Implementation sections of traditional plans are sorted by plan element and identify who is responsible for taking initiative for that element and with what priority. An index should be sorted by actors and priority and point to plan elements for which they are responsible. In accepting tasks requested externally, compare them with the work programs and explanations pointed to in plans to decide priorities. Table 10-1 summarizes how these indexes could be used and created for various situations.

In each of these situations, relying on pointers to text is insufficient and inefficient. An index in the form of a schematic diagram can show how one location relates to other locations through interdependence of decisions. The index diagram, labeled for efficient searching from the perspective of decision situations, may point to other diagrams that show interdependence through potential consequences of related actions. This diagram is not the same thing as a future land use map; its purpose is not to describe a future land use pattern, but to describe the relationships among various likely possible future actions. If there is credible talk of a future bypass, it is more useful to diagram the competing locations than to pretend to choose one, when that choice is not really being made yet. In deciding whether to annex parcels, approve a subdivision, rezone a parcel, buy a parcel for development, buy a home, organize a neighborhood group, it is more useful to index the range of likely options for future actions and their relationships to other decisions than to check ideas against a future land use map, which conveys only a conclusion, not the relationships on which it was based.

The example in Figure 10-4 is a combined index and plan concept map

Table 10-1
Indexing Opportunities to Use Plans

| | Opportunity Type | | | |
	Decision Situation	Issue Raised	Solution Proposed	Work Resource Available
Example	City council vote to request bids on capital project for street extension	Neighborhood group complains about persistent flooding	Developer proposes big box retail on site at edge of town	Receive budget to hire new senior planner
Labels in index	Capital projects, Council votes, Streets, Location by Neighborhood and Ward	Flooding, Drainage, Runoff regulations, capital projects; Location by neighborhood, Ward, Watershed	Developer negotiations, Site plan review, Economic development	Work programming elements
Format for search and pointers	Alphabetical list pointing to page numbers and map coordinates; map location pointing to street network and accessibility	Alphabetical list pointing to page numbers and map coordinates; map location pointing to drainage network capacities	Alphabetical list pointing to page numbers and map coordinates; map location pointing to interdependent actions and infrastructure networks	Alphabetical list pointing to page numbers for elements of plans requiring planner initiative
Concepts pointed to	Related items in Capital Improvements Program, recent and planned actions in location or on network; policies on street extension; internal logic of plans for expansion; state DOT plans, financing possibilities	Runoff regulations, drainage system plans of various jurisdictions, capital improvements program budget options, . . .	Annexation policies, site plan review criteria, adjacent existing and planned land uses, infrastructure capacities, locational strategy for retail services, . . .	Action elements, key projects or actions involving public sector initiative

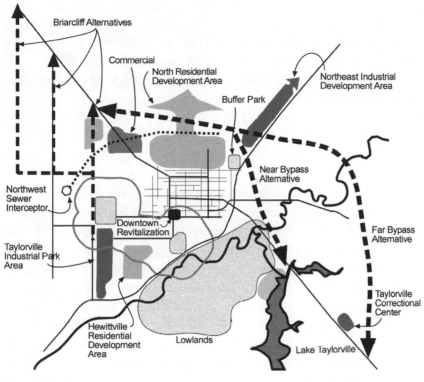

Figure 10-4
Overall strategy diagram for Taylorville, Illinois

adapted from a map in color from a plan for Taylorville, Illinois.[3] It shows
two possible routes under consideration for a bypass to the northeast rather
than pretending to choose one. It shows that residential expansion to the
north, which would be feasible and appropriate given the new sewer interceptor, must work in some relation to either bypass route. It shows that
parks are sufficient in the southwest and lacking in the northeast, and that
a park location could be used as a separation between residential and heavy
industrial uses. On the west it highlights three plausible north–south roads
that might be upgraded to access industrial sites on the southwest and that
protection of these rights-of-way interacts with subdivision approvals near
the new sewer interceptor. In general, it focuses more on highlighting interdependent choice situations and issues that may arise and less on de-
picting an agreed future pattern.

Investment, to which other instances are similar, illustrates concretely how to create and use an index. Similar descriptions apply for zoning changes, official map designations, annexations, subdivision approvals, economic development packages, or responses to neighborhood protests. Relationships between various land use regulations and the plans that affect them were discussed in chapter 6. To create an index, scan plans for content implying capital investments; identify potential projects; and create pointers to plan content related to these projects, including other interdependent decisions. For example, if the plan suggests residential growth in a particular direction, infer street projects necessary for such growth. Point to parts of the plan that explain logic and interdependence of this growth direction. Use the index when adopting the capital improvements program (writing staff recommendations, negotiating among departments, voting in council) to reference plans. Use the index to reference plans when making individual project commitments, especially when issues or proposals arise (budget shortfall, neighborhood opposition, fast-tracked economic development opportunity) that call into question the adopted capital improvements program. For example, if a federal grant could be obtained because of a political opportunity, check interdependence among proposals and issues as indexed to plans from the closest equivalent project in the capital improvements program.

An index for residents ought to include a locational map index and a topic index. These indexes should point to aspects of the plan affecting decisions to buy homes, to react to regulatory and investment proposals, and to opportunities to pursue issues of major interest. Although a planning agency might create such an index for its constituents (because it is a collective good to the individual users), the index should point to information in any pertinent plans, not just to the agency's own plans. For example, from the location of a parcel that might be purchased, pointers should identify street, sewer, drainage, and other investments that would affect its services, accessibility, tax rates or fees, and proximity to major project proposals, including alternatives under consideration. They should also point to zoning criteria, recent zoning changes and zoning changes that might be inferred from plans.

A developer or owner of undeveloped land has interests similar to a home buyer, but focused on larger parcels, options for development, and regulations that might change. In addition to items identified for homeowners, pointers should be provided to impact fees, plans of infrastructure providers such as the state department of transportation, and annexation agreements and policies. A developer is likely to want to rely on secret or unshared information and to hire staff or consultants who will search for information or create a private index. The value of an index is less a collective good for developers than for residents, but a planning agency might still provide such an index as an inducement to developers to consider its plans.

An agency should also create an index pointing to its plans from the perspective of other governmental units, such as a county or special district, that serve the jurisdiction making the plan and adjacent cities. In this case, the perspective is not, "What might we want to know from this decision situation about the plans of others?" It is, "What might we want others to know from their decision perspective about our plans?" Because other agencies do not normally make such indexes, an agency may also want to index the plans of others from the perspective of its own decision situations.

To create views of plans for decision situations:

- Create indexes to your own plans and plans by others and share these indexes to encourage use of plans by others.
- Use indexes to access information in plans and create views when making decisions, shaping issues, or reacting to proposals that emerge in the stream of daily activities.

These principles apply to all five ways in which plans work. Whether a plan is working as vision, agenda, policy, design, or strategy, we need pointers to its internal logic in order to bring it to bear on daily activities.

Indexes can make it easier to use your own plans, to use the plans of others, and to encourage others to use your plans. Indexing the relationships between plans and actions—that is, indexing in the opposite direction—can point out opportunities to make plans.

Recognize Opportunities to Make Plans

An index is asymmetric. It can be searched from only one perspective and point in only one direction. In deciding whether to revise a plan or, in general, whether to make a plan, an index pointing from the plan perspective to the user's perspective would be useful. What decision situations have occurred and what actions have been taken, what issues have emerged, what solutions have been proposed that are pertinent to the continuing validity of a particular component or aspect of a plan?

As discussed in chapters 4 and 9, plan-based monitoring should trigger action with sufficient lead time to avoid irreversible actions that will later be regretted. Recognizing situations for which existing plans are inadequate is difficult because they must be recognized in advance. It is less pertinent to know whether commercial development of five acres or one hundred acres will occur in five or twenty-five years than it is to know before development begins what road layout will work, what configuration will fit coming technology, and which locations in a metropolitan area might be good or bad. For example, locations of commercial centers and job nodes depend on technologies of retailing and transportation and thus these locations may change regardless of changes in population. Automobile dealers have relocated from downtown to the urban edge even in small towns with little population growth. The reversal costs to change configurations of previously built-up areas are a more important explanation for such relocation than is population growth. If these questions are considered and commitments made before the first development in that area occurs, then development will avoid creating new problems of irreversibility in the newly developed areas. If the first development occurs before this is worked out, the configuration will be deflected from a desirable configuration by the high costs of reversing earlier actions. Metropolitan form, land use configurations, and lead time are more important than land supply and population forecasts because decisions about where, when, and how much investment to make are more sensitive to the former than to the latter.

Revising plans, which is just a particular situation of making plans, can and should be based on the record of use, which can be recorded as actions are taken and then indexed from the perspective of plan making. If plan making is functionally decomposed, then an index from revising the plan for street networks must point to decisions about sewer extensions, zoning, and other interdependent actions that have occurred, not just to the record of street investment decisions. It makes sense to create and maintain an index from the plan-making perspective to the decision-making perspective as one basis for making plans. Plans can in part be inferred from past patterns of decisions and in part from expected patterns of future decisions as imagined from previous experiences.

Computing tools provide new opportunities to create and provide such user's manuals and indexes. The conceptual problems of designing and implementing indexes are highly developed aspects of information science. The kinds of manuals and indexes proposed here can be produced in hard copy, but they could be much more powerful if implemented using the technology of the World Wide Web (Shiffer 1995). On the Web, clicking on a pointer takes you directly and instantaneously to the information rather than merely identifying the document and page numbers. Many cities now have Web sites that point to documents or to available data, but they are not indexed with reference to decision situations or issues in a way that points to the internal logic of plans.

To recognize opportunities to make plans:

- Infer from decision situations the validity of plans to continue as guides to decisions.
- Infer the content of revised plans from the record of decision situations, actions, issues, and proposals.

These principles apply to all five aspects of how plans work. Complementary pairs of questions associated with each of the five ways plans work illustrate the potential of indexes pointing in both directions, to recognize opportunities to make plans as well as to recognize opportunities to use plans.

1. Vision: What attitudes and beliefs has this vision changed through what efforts by whom?
   What attitudes and beliefs of whom could I shape today?

2. Agenda: What actions have been completed by whom based on using this list?
   What can I cross off my list today?

3. Policy: What decisions have been made based on this policy and how many contradicted the policy or raised issues of interpretation or concern?
   What policies apply to this decision situation?

4. Design: What actions have been taken and, based on these, is the design still valid?

Does this action, as elaborated for execution, still fit the logic of the design?

5. Strategy: Is the strategy still valid given the decisions and uncertain outcomes that have occurred?
Of what strategies is this decision situation potentially a part?

Make Plans of Efficient Scopes

Many cities make a comprehensive plan for the entire municipality, or through some organization, for an entire metropolitan area. The empirical norm is that these plans are based on twenty years of forecasted growth and revised every five years. These norms are codified in legislation in some states and to some degree in model legislation advocated by the American Planning Association (1998). Conventional prescriptions recognize that these attributes are only ideal reference points from which practice will deviate, but these prescriptions give little guidance for choosing the scopes of plans in specific situations. The Four I's, the characteristics of investments and regulations, uncertainty, and the principles of decomposition provide justifications on which to base choices of scope and time horizon. In general, the implications are *not* to plan for twenty years of demand, *not* to plan comprehensively for all functions for an entire metropolitan region, and *not* to rely only on plans made by or for the public sector. Many plans of different scopes made by different organizations will be more efficient. A plan for some functions may have a metropolitan scope geographically, but this should be the result of the logic of interdependent decisions, not the presumed prescription. Per unit of planning effort, such plans will have greater effect on choosing actions so as to achieve intentions by bringing to bear the implications of interdependence, indivisibility, irreversibility, and imperfect foresight.

Consider the following example.[4] The Urbana-Champaign Sanitary District (UCSD) is responsible for sewage treatment for the municipalities of Champaign, Urbana, and Savoy. The municipalities are responsible for the collector sewers within their jurisdictions, but the UCSD is responsible for all major interceptor sewers and for collector sewers outside of municipal boundaries. A recent interjurisdictional agreement set these responsibilities and prohibited the UCSD from providing sewer service to any development that does not have an annexation agreement with one of the municipalities. In making decisions about available capacity for development proposals, the UCSD recognized an impending constraint on capacity relative to demand at one of its two treatment plants, which triggered the making of a revised plan for treatment plant capacity.

In the world of ideal comprehensive plans, there should already exist a metropolitan region plan that would tell the UCSD where growth is intended and likely to occur and thus how much capacity to add where and when. But no such plan exists in Champaign-Urbana. When plans that fit this ideal do exist, for example in the Portland, Oregon, metropolitan region, the metropolitan plan does not directly answer the question of where to add sewer capacity and when (Metro 2000). Even in Portland, the Tualatin Basin Sewer Plan (Stevens Thompson and Runyan 1969) and the lack of similar plans for the eastern side of the metropolitan area were major determinants of the Urban Growth Boundary, rather than the growth boundary determining sewer plans. In any case, the Champaign-Urbana situation without a metropolitan government is more typical. There is a sewer provider separate from the general purpose governments. There are three separate municipalities and unincorporated land within the UCSD service area. In addition, there are several suburban towns within commuting distance, each with its own sewer provider. Ignore for the moment all the other special districts (two park districts, forest preserve district, private water supply utility) because they only complicate the example without changing the point of the argument. Who should plan how much, of what, for whom, and with what foresight?

Organizational decomposition, as discussed in chapter 9, suggests that each actor should develop a plan for its own actions, cognizant of the plans of other actors. Thus each of the cities and the county should plan for its land use regulations and street, collector sewer, and other infrastructure extensions, while the UCSD should plan sewage treatment plants and interceptor sewers. Functional decomposition, however, suggests that all of the components of the sewer collection and treatment system should be addressed in one plan, all the extensions of streets in another, all the land use regulations in another, and so on. Spatial decomposition suggests that all elements within each area should be addressed in one plan. The spatial decomposition should define areas that encompass many interdependent actions and that interact with other areas only in aggregate without regard to patterns within each area. By spatial decomposition, a plan for all functions should be made for each of several areas of new development or redevelopment. A comprehensive metropolitan plan for twenty years is an unrealistic aspiration; it is likely to be a bad compromise rather than a useful combination of the plans implied by these principles of decomposition. As discussed in chapter 5, in some situations plans will be collective goods, which affects who should plan for whom. Careful choice of scope based on this multidimensional decomposition, as elaborated below, should yield more effective and more efficiently made plans.

A plan should address a set of sufficiently interdependent actions that are indivisible, irreversible, and subject to imperfect foresight. What do we need to know to locate sewage treatment capacity? What are the crucially interdependent actions? What are the indivisibilities—the magnitudes of the economies of scale—involved, and thus what range of sizes of treatment plants should be considered to balance these economies of scale against uncertainties? What interdependent actions are irreversible? What uncertainties will remain? In a particular situation, approximate answers to these questions can be used to choose the scope of a plan. Recall also from chapter 4 that the benefit of a plan as strategy is the difference in value between what you would do with a plan and what you would have done without it. How much precision about which decisions when is worth achieving in prediction or commitment before taking action now?

Sewage treatment plants can be located only near lakes or streams. The potential set of locations is thus greatly restricted. The question for the plan can be narrowed initially to where, along which lines (streams or lake edges), a plant of what size might be located. Expansion at existing locations may have so many advantages (less neighborhood opposition, robustness of sewerage network, economies of scale in operation) that other sites need not be seriously considered. With these feasible locations in mind, interdependent actions that should be considered include land development patterns and densities implied in zoning decisions, transportation network investments, and park acquisitions. For each of these interdependences, the necessary level of precision should be considered. To decide whether an area should be sewered or not sewered, it may be sufficient to distinguish among plant locations without regard to density of development or use based on zoning. Locations of regional park acquisitions will matter, which suggests focusing on uncertainties related to such locations. A time horizon is not very important in choosing the scope of such a plan because, regardless of when development occurs, the urban pattern in the area potentially served from the sewer plant location must be considered.

The plant location question, framed in this way, begs consideration of key determinants of the overall urban form. The question of where sewers should be provided is interdependent with questions of where major park acquisitions and roads should occur. The UCSD, however, cannot make decisions about park acquisitions, roads, or land use, so it cannot decide where these will be. It can only ask where municipalities and the department of transportation are currently considering locating them and how UCSD actions would influence and interact with these uncertain possibilities. The UCSD can share its developing information about sewer strategy and hope to receive similar information from other actors. It can and should negotiate, informally and formally, for commitments from other actors that would be consistent with actions the UCSD in turn commits to carry out. Significant uncertainties will remain, however, because these other actors have only imperfect foresight of their own actions and their actions do not completely determine private sector development actions. Even if private developers participate in negotiations, they are unlikely to make credible commitments to actions with sufficient precision to be useful in sizing treatment plants. Thus the UCSD should make plans about its future actions in order to choose its immediate actions. It should consider others' plans and share its own plans in order to increase the likelihood that others, acting to their own advantage based on this information, will take actions that are consistent with actions of the UCSD. The UCSD should consider flexible, robust, and just-in-time delivery as aspects of its strategy.

Though the scope of plans should not be decomposed on the basis of time, time matters because the UCSD must decide when to build a plant and of what capacity. The economies of scale dictate that it must build a larger plant than immediately required and it must thus balance the time during which this capacity is not used, and does not generate revenue, against the economies of scale gained later when the plant is more fully utilized. This trade-off depends on economies of scale, the rate of arrival of demand, and the discount rate and the burden over time of financing these investments. This specific question frames an analysis for pertinent forecasting of scenarios, which will not be the same kind of generalized forecasts of population used to drive conventional comprehensive plans. The decision on sizing the plant should depend on a distribution of expectations of population sizes over time and risks of over- or undercapacity relative to uncertainty in the realized population, as discussed in chapter 4. These considerations cannot be embedded in a single population forecast and still be pertinent to a wide range of different, individual infrastructure investment decisions. The demand forecast needed for sizing the treatment plant is not the same in spatial scope or time sensitivity as that needed to size a road or choose its time of construction, even if the road and sewer are in the same geographic location. The road will serve through traffic as well as local traffic and the sewer may serve future extensions, but they will not serve the same geographic service areas because road networks and sewer networks have different physical characteristics. An efficient scope of plan for sewers will consider its interdependence with plans for roads and plans for land use regulations, but these plans are, for good reasons, most likely to be made separately.

None of these timing questions affects the location of the road or treatment plant because their *locational* interdependence is the same regardless of when either is built. The UCSD has to think through the entire sewer collection network associated with a new plant and the general urban form that would result in relation to roads whether the buildout occurs in five years or fifty years. The decomposition of that interdependence is primarily spatial, not temporal. The benefits from such a plan based on the interdependent, indivisible, irreversible decisions in the spatial area accrue regardless of when the projects are built.

Friend and Jessop (1969) and Friend and Hickling (1987) developed planning tools to implement their "strategic choice" approach. A brief description of the methodological implications makes clear the similarities between their approach and the logic presented here. Strategic choice recognizes that plan making arises from a focus on particular decision situations that raise uncertainties about related choices, uncertainties about the environment in which these choices will play out, and uncertainties about values that should be used in making these choices.

The tools focus on Analysis of Interconnected Decision Areas (AIDA). These tools do not assume that the scope of a plan is given. One of the first tasks is to figure out which decision areas (decision situations, choice opportunities) should be addressed in a particular plan. The tools also focus on how interdependence among decisions affects the available choices and the preference among choices. Decision areas are represented as circles linked to other circles with which they are interdependent. A sewer plant expansion might be one decision area and the zoning categories for a newly annexed area might be another. In the AIDA graphic vocabulary, a line should connect these two decision areas to show that they are interdependent. Decision areas that are highly interdependent should be considered as a group, which is shown by drawing a circle around them. Within the circle of each decision area, options (alternative actions) for that decision are listed.

The tools of representation focus on working with these relationships. These representations thus leave a history of the logic for a particular plan that can be relied on when using the plan to decide what action to take in a contingent strategy. For example, in using the plan, we could ask: Which other decisions was this decision interdependent with? Are these interdependencies still valid? Were options for other decision areas carried out as assumed in the strategy? Did they have the expected consequences? Despite these potential advantages, the strategic choice approach is seldom used in making plans for urban development.[5] The logic of making plans and its implied modifications to conventional prescriptions suggest additions to the tools of the strategic choice approach.

The explanations of these decompositions based on the Four I's, are reinforced by explanations based on specialization of expertise and knowledge with respect to organizations, places, and functions. Sewer plans, transportation plans, land use development plans, neighborhood development plans, and environmental protection plans rely on different informal and formal knowledge held by different people in different organizations.

To choose efficient scopes for plans:

- Identify and create actions available to your client now and in the future based on likely streams of opportunities. At least some of these will have been identified when the client recognized the opportunity to plan.
- Identify interdependence among these actions and interdependence with the potential actions of others.
- Identify indivisibility, irreversibility, and imperfect foresight affecting these actions.

- Group these actions based on interdependence, indivisibility, irreversibility, and imperfect foresight.
- Make a system of plans, one for each group of interdependent actions and perhaps others for groups of interdependent groups of actions. Take into account actions by others, but treat actions as uncertain.
- Expect others to make plans, both formally and informally, for multiple scopes, horizons, and revision intervals.

These implications apply quite generally. They are consistent with plan making in California, Chicago, Phoenix, Seattle, and elsewhere as described in chapter 9. In contrast with the conventional prescriptions, however, they prescribe criteria to choose the scope of plans for each situation rather than prescribing a standard scope.

The above explanations focus on the strategy aspect of how plans work, which is in many ways the most demanding. The recommendations hold, however, for the other aspects of plans.

The design aspect of plans differs from the strategy aspect by articulating outcome patterns rather than contingent sets of actions. Plans for outcome patterns can and should be decomposed based on these same principles. A design of regional scope should focus on elements of urban development that are interdependent at that scope—major park acquisitions and major infrastructure locations—for the same reason as for the strategy aspect of plans. This commonality is a reminder that one plan can work through more than one aspect.

Vision also depends on choice of scope. Although the vision aspect is much more likely than other aspects to focus on outcomes rather than actions, it must still motivate actions. Visions for neighborhoods can be imagined and used distinct from visions for metropolitan areas. This does not mean they are completely unrelated, but they are definitely decomposable. They seek to affect the attitudes of different people and to motivate different actors and actions.

The agenda aspect of a plan relates primarily to organizational scope because it works as a memory device for a list of actions and trusted commitment to constituents. For an agenda, the revision interval and time horizon depend on the reporting interval required to maintain credibility. How many objectives can we commit to accomplish or how many actions can we commit to taking so that we can report success in time to sustain the credibility of these commitments? The number depends on the particular situation, but there is a logical explanation as a basis for choosing the scope and revision interval.

The policy aspect of a plan affects the scope through the question of decision costs, consistency benefits, and frequency of repetition of the decision. How frequently must a category of decision occur to justify the setting of a policy? The answer depends on costs of individual decisions compared to costs of policy setting and on the benefits of commitment to consistent decisions. The choice depends on the particular situation, but there is a logic for choosing when to commit to policies of what scope.

Link Consequences to Available Actions

Where are we? Where do we want to be? How can we get there? Most conventional prescriptions for making plans treat these three questions as separate tasks, implying separate representations. In caricature, the answers are presented in an existing land use map, a future land use map, and a zoning ordinance and capital improvements program. An action should help move us from where we are to where we want to be. Plan making should focus attention on the connections of current situations, actions, and consequences rather than on each separately. It should focus on the interdependence among decision situations because the interdependence is fundamental to creating plans that work. Forester (1989, 11) argues that what planners do is communicate so as to focus attention. The logic of making plans argues that, compared to conventional prescriptions, more attention should be focused on interdependence and on connections between consequences and actions, and less attention on describing present and future states and general frames of implementation.

The tasks of making plans, as discussed in chapters 7 and 9, exceed the cognitive capacity of individuals without external representations. Such representations also enable communication for collaboration in groups. These representations strongly affect the focus of attention, and thus choosing representations and ways to use representations is essential to focusing attention on links between consequences and available actions. The strategic choice approach (introduced in chapter 4 and described in more detail earlier in this chapter) and Integrated Action Planning (described in chapter 9) suggest good tools for dealing with interdependence. They generally lack tools for linking consequences and actions, however, other than formats for recording consequences of combinations of actions. Sketch maps and scenarios based on models are possibilities for making such connections.

Sketch maps, which are used and suggested in several prescriptions, deserve further elaboration. Consider again the sewer planning case described earlier. The feasibility and costs of locations of treatment plants and sewer networks depend significantly on the locations of outlet water bodies and on the topography that constrains gravity flow of the collection network. A sketch map can focus attention on this information. A symbol for a treatment plant location allows locations of the existing plants and possible additional plants to be easily modified to record ideas or share them with collaborators. Scaling the symbol size can loosely represent treatment plant capacity. A terrain representation gives clues to possible collector network configurations and to watershed boundaries that may be significant. Network design is slightly subtler. In Champaign-Urbana, the limits requiring lift stations are likely to be long stretches of very flat land with insufficient gradient to support gravity flow. In most urban areas, however, the limits will be ridges that separate watersheds. In any case, a terrain representation provides the information needed to imagine possible plant locations and areas served. The map can also include other information about existing development, existing plans for expansion of the transportation network, boundaries of jurisdictions competing for revenue, and so on. Such maps are not, however, just maps of existing conditions. The point of such diagrams is to organize ideas about how potential actions are linked to consequences and other actions.

It is easy to imagine such a map as generated by a Geographic Information System (GIS), but it is crucial to think of such representations as much looser and more easily modified (Hopkins 1999). The representation should be a sketching device, a manipulation of possibilities and relationships, not merely a compilation of data. As illustrated in Figure 10-5, annotations, symbols, questions, and relationships should keep track of ideas because the sketch map is an external memory device and a collaboration device.[6]

One type of sketch map is an issues and forces map, which incorporates actions that might be taken by others, relationships among actions, and descriptions of consequences, implications, and contingent relationships among interdependent actions. The spatial referencing is one powerful way to consider actions and consequences simultaneously. It is not, however, suf-

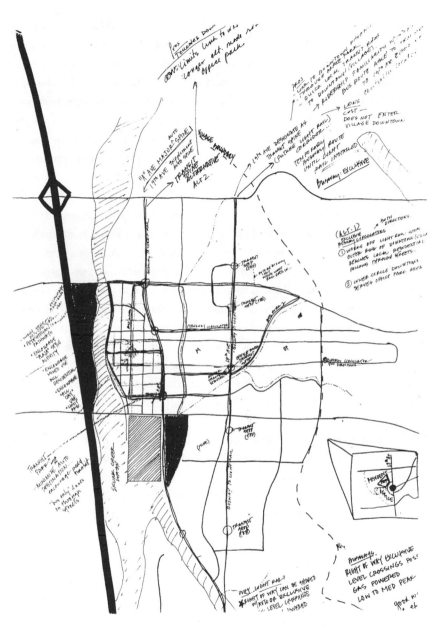

Figure 10-5
Sketch map from community planning meeting in Phoenix, Arizona

ficient and its power can lead to cognitive anchoring and biases. Counters to these biases include collaborating in making such maps, sharing such maps among planners for different clients, and using such maps as a changeable medium for continuing interaction with constituencies and collaborators rather than as a fixed report of information. Such maps can, however, overpower the real situation so that the map representation becomes the focus of attention. Sketch maps and diagrams can seldom represent causal mechanisms that link consequences to actions. Other representations should also be given prominence in deliberations.

"What if?" scenarios as contingent forecasts are a tool for iterating toward plans by asking either of two kinds of questions with respect to various combinations of actions and various consequences: What consequences will occur if we take these actions? Or, if we desire these consequences, what actions would achieve them? Contingent forecasts are most useful to discover strategies and to build arguments about what to do rather than as tools for choosing among forecasts of population as the primary input to a plan.

In conventional plans, population forecasts are usually used as input data for an allocation process, albeit with sensitivity analysis based on high and low forecasts. The most important forecasts, however, are those that depend on the choice of actions and are thus endogenous to the making of the plan. If a new highway is built, what will the population be? Or, if the population should be two hundred thousand, what new highways should be built? If minimum lot size zoning is implemented, what will the pattern look like? Or, if a compact pattern is desired, would minimum lot size or maximum lot size zoning be more likely to achieve it? It is better to ask such questions in both directions—to connect consequences to actions—rather than only to ask what the consequences of a given set of actions might be as in conventional prescriptions.

Working out such implications requires some sort of model, which is at best problematic because participants are likely to differ in their beliefs about how the world works. To make matters worse, it is often difficult to determine what a model assumes about how the world works. For both these reasons, it is important to use more than one model, each based on a different view or emphasis about what matters. The range of economic structure, demographics, urban structure, transportation, housing, and municipal revenue models is far too great to consider here.[7] In any case the models should be used to consider how consequences relate to interdependent actions so as to discover possible actions and possible consequences.

Interdependence among land uses and hydrologic consequences for flooding illustrate how this might work. A study of the Hickory Creek Watershed in Will County, Illinois, considered the effects of increased urban development on flood peak levels and on levels of flood damage from increased development in the floodplain (Hopkins et al. 1978; Hopkins et al. 1981). Water flow depended on land use patterns, and damages for a given level of flooding depended on land use patterns. A "modeling to generate alternatives" technique was used to generate land use patterns that were very different from each other but that kept total land value net of flood damages relatively similar (Hopkins et al. 1982). From such analysis it became clear that what mattered was the timing of the arrival of flood peaks on different branches of the stream; if the peaks on the two major branches reached their confluence at the same time, then the downstream damages were much higher. Any land use pattern that delayed the timing of one relative to the other was approximately as effective. Thus many land use patterns, but not just any land use pattern, were equally good for this criterion, and a decision among them could be made based on other criteria.

Rather than just taking as given that more impervious surface is bad, the explicit consideration of how actions related to consequences suggested different strategies. The analysis also considered the implications of regulations that might not always yield planned land use patterns. Thus the connection to available actions such as zoning was also made explicit (Goulter et al. 1983). Making use of such tools in the time frame of specific plan-making situations is still difficult. Working with one or a small number of aspects in a way that the results can be used to consider other aspects, as in this case, will be more effective than trying to consider all aspects in one model.

The example of sewer system development in Lexington, Kentucky, described earlier in this chapter also illustrates the importance of focusing on actions and consequences rather than on allocations of land use types. If the basic principle of expanding in efficient chunks and utilizing available capacity is understood, then decisions can be addressed as they arise. If the focus is on designations of land areas, then the internal logic of the plan—its basis in links between actions and consequences is lost.

Choosing a plan requires comparisons of alternative actions based on consequences. Such comparisons should yield cognitive feedback, information useful in figuring out how to modify an idea into a better plan. It is more useful to learn how to modify a set of actions to increase the likelihood of desirable consequences than it is to learn only what consequences are likely to occur from given actions. Explaining how cities work is thus fundamental because such explanations not only link actions to outcomes but also recognize what differences in actions would be required to achieve different outcomes. Operational models that give such cognitive feedback in making plans have been devised for electric power generation capacity by Andrews (1992) and for bus routing by Lee (1993). In the bus routing case, one of the diagnostic feedback reports shows graphically the loading of each bus route between each bus stop. This information highlights opportunities to move routes so as to eliminate links with light loads or double up routes on links with heavy loads. This kind of feedback suggests how to make changes to improve plans. Similar tools are needed for urban development plans.

To focus attention on linking consequences to available actions:

- Use more than one representation to cope with complexity and avoid cognitive bias.
- Use representations that relate actions to each other and connect actions to consequences.
- Embed multiple forecasts in multiple representations of related actions and consequences rather than using forecasts as the *a priori* basis for plan making.
- Compare alternatives on the basis of consequences so as to discover cognitive feedback about how to modify and create available actions and build arguments about what to do.

These principles apply to all five aspects of how plans work. Although strategy most directly emphasizes the link from available actions to outcomes, designs and visions must also connect actions to the envisioned or designed outcome. Agendas and policies are justified in terms of the consequences of committed or consistent actions, which are thus the basis for judging performance.

Where are we? Where do we want to be? How do we get there? These traditional questions should not be taken to imply separable planning tasks or representations. Inventing, discovering, and choosing actions becomes possible by considering consequences and actions simultaneously rather than separately.

Use Formal and Informal Institutions of Collective Choice

The logic of participation explains what formal democratic institutions and ad hoc participation can accomplish for social cognition or aggregation of preference. Conventional prescriptions for making plans emphasize the importance of public participation as direct involvement of ordinary citizens or organizational stakeholders in the process of making plans. As Lucy (1988) argues, the American Planning Association ethical principles emphasize direct public participation without adequately recognizing the role of formal political processes and organizations. Plan making should recognize relationships to both direct participation and to formal mechanisms of collective choice. The two approaches are not, however, perfect complements. Critical judgments about what should be done still matter.

Highly participatory plan making, such as reported in chapter 9 for Austin and Atlanta, may not lead to better plans or to plans taken seriously by government or other organizations. Plans driven by governments may advantage commercial interests over others. Participation in forums to frame decision situations will be most effective if it recognizes that the decision arena in which authority resides should be the target of such efforts (Bryson and Crosby 1992). Participation in forums that frame electoral politics is thus also pertinent. Plans that do not recognize departmentalized organizations with distinct line responsibilities, ward-based versus at-large election of legislators, and separation of authority among general purpose municipalities and special districts will not be pertinent to actions regardless of how much public participation has occurred.

Plans should recognize what formal mechanisms of collective choice will be used, but not necessarily take the preferences of participants in these institutions as given. The selling of the Chicago Plan to voters in order to pass bond issues for major public improvements is a classic example (Moody 1919). If the plan is the city council's plan, it should recognize that the decisions are individual votes of council members conditioned by political affiliations and a history of coalitions. Integrated Action Planning (Irwin and

Joshi 1996) as implemented in Nepal makes this explicit by including tables of distribution or projects and expenditures by wards by year to show ward representatives how their ward is being served.

Using formal and informal mechanisms of collective choice for deliberation and aggregation of preference also emphasizes the relationship of collective choice to the ways in which plans can work. Any decision, including a decision about plans or implied in a plan, may involve collective choice. Collective choice is thus not an attribute that distinguishes plans or plan making from other types of decisions or activities. The process of making a plan may focus attention on questions about which collective choices should be made. Plans may serve as a vehicle for deliberation, but only in the same way that any decision could. The logic of how plans work is analytically distinguishable from collective choice. Explanations of how plans work make sense whether carried out by an individual, an organization, or a government. Recognizing the distinction between plans and collective choice makes it possible to use these mechanisms more effectively as complements for related tasks when appropriate.

To use formal institutions of representative democracy and informal institutions of direct participation for both social cognition and aggregation of preference when making plans:

- Choose organizational scopes for plans based on formal choice mechanisms and the motivations, advantages, and biases they contain.
- Induce participation that is likely to increase cognitive capacity by advantaging ideas and perspectives otherwise disadvantaged in formal institutions.
- Induce participation that is likely to advantage persons and communities insufficiently represented in representative democracy, the market, or the organization.

These recommendations apply to plans by private developers as well as by municipalities and to all five aspects of how plans work. Agenda and policy aspects of plans are particularly pertinent because they increase consistency and public commitment to proposals. Thus they can counter both inappropriately narrow direct participation in particular decisions and inappropriately narrow formal processes that ignore local circumstances. Including a policy to invest in neighborhoods in the public agenda of a political leader, for example, counters the tendency, discussed in chapters 5 and 8, to focus on the commercial interests of downtown landowners and businesses. The cognitive advantages and justice advantages of induced participation to complement formal institutions of collective choice can improve design, vision, and strategy aspects of plans. Vision aspects of plans can change attitudes and beliefs and thus change the outcomes of collective deliberations or aggregations of preference. Visions can counter defections from collective action toward collective goods by motivating people to participate, which means visions can substitute in part for regulations imposed by collective action.

Summary: The Logic of Making Plans Matters

These prescriptions, taken together, suggest including plans within the stream of opportunities metaphor. As presented in chapter 2 and paraphrasing Cohen et al. (1972), the metaphor was elaborated to frame plan-making situations: A plan-making situation is a collection of interdependent, indivisible, and irreversible decisions looking for issues; a collection of issues looking for interdependent decisions in which they might be pertinent; a collection of solutions looking for issues to which they might be an answer; and a collection of planners looking for work. Using the metaphor to frame urban development as a complex system requires adding to this mix a collection of plans that are co-evolving with other elements, meaning that decisions are looking for plans in which they might be pertinent and planners are looking for opportunities to make plans that are pertinent to decisions and issues. The metaphor is a system of interacting elements, but a system does not imply simplicity or the potential of control. Think of an ecosystem, not of systems engineering. Ecosystem brings to mind more easily the level of complexity and the idea that plans and plan making are within the system rather than controlling it from outside. This perspective on using and making plans depends on each of the key arguments in this book.

Plans can be useful in complex systems, in "natural" systems, if plans are recognized as elements within complex systems rather than as external mechanisms for achieving control. Plans can affect the world in certain limited ways, and explanations of how plans can work are persuasive backing for claims that a plan with particular content will be useful in a particular situation. Explanations of how plans work also make clear in what situations we should not expect plans to work well and which other approaches are more appropriate.

Plans can incorporate uncertainty. The lament "We can't make plans because we don't know what other people are going to do" demonstrates a misunderstanding of how plans work. Plans are made by individuals, groups, and governments. Plans are not inherently a government activity or a shift to more central control. Just as with many other activities, however, when plans are collective goods, it makes sense for governments to provide plans. Plans are not regulations, but land development regulations are likely to depend on plans to decide what the regulations should be. It therefore makes sense to make plans about regulations.

Human cognitive capabilities and social interactions frame explanations of how plans can be made and justifications for how plans should be made, including expertise about analytical techniques, collaboration, and values. The difficulties of collective choice cannot be overcome by plans because plans are not a decision-making mechanism. Plans organize information pertinent to decisions, which may be made individually, through negotiation, or through deliberation and voting. A plan might be chosen by mechanisms of collective choice, but the plan is not the decision mechanism.

The logic of making plans for urban development matters because it is useful in figuring out how to make better plans and how to use them more effectively. It makes sense of much of observed planning practice and justifies parts of conventional prescriptions for making plans. Through careful interpretation of observed practice and conventional prescriptions, however, the logic of plans also suggests changes in such prescriptions, changes that should result in improved practice. Practice is thus not only the beneficiary of better interpretations of the logic of plans, but also a major source of wisdom on which to build that logic.

The principles used to organize this chapter—recognizing opportunities to use plans, creating views of plans from decision situations, recognizing opportunities to make plans, making plans of efficient scopes, linking consequences to interdependent actions, and using formal and informal institutions to deliberate and act—bring plans within the system. We can use our plan-making (canoe-paddling) abilities in combination with the forces of the streams of opportunities we face if we work from the logic of interdependent, indivisible, irreversible actions in the face of imperfect foresight. These attributes characterize the decisions that can benefit from plans and provide the basis for making plans of efficient scope. We must be able to use plans while making decisions in the stream, which requires ready access to the internal logic of the plans from the perspectives of decision situations. Plans will be useful, usable, and used if they make sense of and from the stream.

Notes

1. Plans for Urban Development: Why and How?

1. Kieran Donaghy proposed a "coherentist" approach to planning research in a seminar discussion of these issues, and his views have had a major influence on my perspective.

2. Plan-Based Action in Natural Systems

1. If you wish to cross a river, you cannot go directly across by pointing your canoe directly across. The combination of your paddling directly across and the current moving downstream will land you downstream of your starting point. In order to go directly across, aim your canoe at an angle upstream. The combination of your paddling and the current will lead you directly across. The angle you should set depends on the strength of the current and your strength in paddling. See e.g., John T. Urban, *A Whitewater Handbook for Canoe and Kayak*, Boston: Appalachian Mountain Club, 1965.

2. The literature on behavior of systems includes works that address systems in the abstract, such as Ashby (1956) and Beer (1966), who develop the concepts of cybernetics in more accessible form than some earlier authors. In addition, these concepts are developed within the context of particular disciplines and their focus on particular types of systems, such as Botkin (1990), Dawkins (1976), Holling and Goldberg (1971) in biology, and Alchian (1950) in economics. McLoughlin (1973) has developed these concepts most completely with respect to urban planning.

3. The market system conditions are explained in any economics textbook, such as Nicholson (2000) or Varian (1992).

4. The Law of Requisite Variety (Ashby 1956) says that a system must have as much variety in responding to disturbances as there is variety in disturbances.

5. See Anas et al. (1998) for a review of urban models based on equilibrium, dynamic adjustment, and imperfect foresight.

6. Alexander (1992b) considered transaction costs as an explanation of planning in a slightly different way. He focuses on the substitution of hierarchical organization for the market as a response to reducing transaction costs. Here we are including transaction costs as one additional friction in the dynamic adjustment

process. The irreversibility of costs of construction is a much greater component of the argument for plans. Organizational questions are considered in chapters 5 and 7.

7. Economic analysis claims that persons or firms use the prices of land and transportation as signals that indicate beneficial opportunities to change location. Even with the restrictive assumptions in neoclassical economics, however, these signals will not equal the prices that would occur at equilibrium except when equilibrium has been reached. There is a path of changing prices and a path of changing location actions, each responding in turn to the other. If there are no transaction costs and decisions can be made in infinitely small increments, the sequence of changing prices can be shown to result in a sequence of location choices that will lead to the predicted equilibrium, as explained in any advanced economics text, such as Varian (1992). Conversely, when actions face interdependence, indivisibility, irreversibility, and imperfect foresight, and thus transaction costs, even this iterative adjustment process fails because the prices at any given iteration will not be appropriate signals. See also Hopkins (1979) for an explanation based on mathematical programming.

8. The term "indicative" is also used by some authors in the urban planning literature (e.g., Alexander 1992a) in a slightly more general way to mean plans that work by persuasion rather than regulation.

9. Plans are often explained as a response to "market failure" or to "political failure," in particular to the failings of market to account for externalities and collective goods and for the failure of political systems to account for expertise and unequal capacity to participate. Plans, at least in the sense addressed in this book, cannot directly resolve these failures, which are discussed in chapter 5. The classic discussion of planning in market and political failure terms is Dahl and Lindblom (1953). Moore (1978) argues the case for collective goods, which is really a case for government and regulation, not a case for plans. Klosterman (1985), in a thorough review of the arguments of market and political failure, acknowledges that these arguments do not distinguish planning from government, but provides no alternative explanation of plans.

10. Alex Anas suggested adding imperfect foresight and the label "the Four I's."

11. The scope of work on organizations is far too vast to address here. March (1988) is the collected work of one major contributor. Williamson (1975) leads another perspective. Chisholm (1989) and Alexander (1995) focus on interorganizational structure and behavior and provide accessible interpretations of organizations pertinent to planning.

12. Lai (1998) extended the formal structure of the garbage can simulations directly to the question of plans and their effects in organizations by specifying intentional ways in which elements of the process would be looked at ahead of time.

3. How Plans Work

1. There are many typologies of plans more or less pertinent to the explanations presented here. Kent (1964) identifies five uses of plans: policy determination, pol-

icy effectuation, communication, conveyance of advice, and education. Alexander (1992a) classifies plans on several dimensions. His distinctions among indicative, allocative, and regulatory fall within the categories used here in a crosscutting way as described in the text.

The standard textbook in land use planning (Kaiser, et al. 1995) identifies three purposes of plans: "One is to provide a process to make policy, that is, a process by which people of a community can take part, with elected officials and appointed boards, in generating and debating policy ideas. A second purpose is then to communicate that policy and intended program of action to property owners, developers, citizens, elected officials, appointed officials and other affected parties. The plan should educate, inspire, and convince those parties. A third purpose is to help implement policy. Advance plans do that by becoming guides to elected and appointed public officials as they deliberate development decisions. Regulations may even incorporate plans as formal criteria for reaching decisions in the issuance of permits. Plans also document the legal, political, and logical rationale behind the development management measures that implement policy" (251).The second is mostly equivalent to the vision explanation, though it may also include strategic use by parties other than the government. The third purpose is the strategy explanation or some variation of it.

Bryson (1995) describes the corporate perspective on strategic planning. My use of the term "strategy" here is distinct from the idea of "strategic planning" for organizations. The "Vision of Success" associated with "strategic planning" is similar to my use of vision here in that it is a motivator and an organizer of an aggregate image of good outcomes.

Garvin (1996) describes comprehensive plans as three types: compelling visions generally of one person, strategies, and visions constructed collaboratively. His examples are the 1909 Chicago Plan, the 1947 St. Louis Plan, and the 1961 Philadelphia Plan, respectively. Even these three examples suggest that the distinction is imperfect. My approach describes ways in which plans can work and interprets cases as working in more than one way. The focus is thus more on explanation and less on classification of plans themselves.

2. See Shipley and Newkirk (1998) for discussion of the use of the term *vision* in planning literature. Baer (1997) identifies his "Plan as Vision" with two somewhat distinct roles: " . . . to stimulate thought and elicit comment . . . " and "The reader should be attracted into the exercise, lifted to the prospect envisioned, convinced as to its possibility (or that of one like it), and provided enough 'realism' to convince the natural skeptic in us all to at least momentarily suspend disbelief" (333). My use of the term focuses on the latter. Bryson and Crosby (1992) describe three venues of action: forums, arenas, and courts. Forums are opportunities to frame issues and discuss ideas. The development and creation of the vision aspect of a plan fits this role while it is being developed, which is similar to the dual roles of vision suggested by Baer.

3. Such explanations are easier to test in the case of regulations than in the case

of plans because we can observe whether regulations were binding. For example, Knaap (1990) finds that local zoning decisions were indeed changed to meet regulatory conditions established by the state of Oregon. The state-level regulation constrained the observed decisions of local governments.

4. Strategy, Uncertainty, and Forecasts

1. Stokey and Zeckhauser (1978) provide a brief introduction to subjective expected utility theory and risk aversion; Keeney and Raiffa (1976) provide a more complete explanation. These elaborations acknowledge that increments of outcome measures may not yield constant increments in utility and that different people have different attitudes toward risk. Hirshleifer and Riley (1992) is an up-to-date and comprehensive advanced treatment of the economics of information.

2. For simplicity this illustration does not differentiate among years in which housing is sold by discounting revenues or years in which things are constructed by discounting costs. Schaeffer and Hopkins (1987) develop a description of a similar situation using probability density functions over outcomes and also include the uncertainty of obtaining the right (for example, zoning approval) to construct the intended uses.

3. These probabilities can be interpreted in several ways. They could be subjective probabilities devised by an expert to express the relative likelihood of alternative future demands. They could be frequencies of these levels of demand based on previous years in the same or similar communities or situations. See Klosterman (1990) for a textbook on conventional population forecasting techniques.

4. Calculations of total revenues in Figure 4-4 follow the same logic as in the earlier figures. For the top branch, $600 \times \$15 + 600 \times \$50 = 39{,}000$. For the next branch, $300 \times \$15 + 300 \times \$50 = \$19{,}500$. In this case the revenue per unit is based on the number of units built, but these revenues are received only for the number of units sold to meet demand. Using these same principles, the remainder of the values in the tree can be computed using data in Table 4-2. Again, working from right to left, the values for each branch at each node can be determined by subtracting the costs incurred by each of the preceding branches from the total revenue.

5. One of the difficulties in such studies is attributing appropriate shares of these costs to particular development projects in particular locations at particular times. This is the crux of the task of designing appropriate impact fees (see e.g., Nelson 1988; Alterman 1988; White 1996).

6. It is not appropriate to compute the forecast by the Bayesian updating approach of additional sampling (see e.g., Raiffa 1968) because, in general, forecasting does not meet the assumptions of a sampling procedure.

7. A frequent strategy is to make decisions based on a point forecast, such as the mean of the distribution of expected population outcomes. Morgan and Henrion (1990, 307–324) claim that underestimation of demand is more costly than overestimation for many infrastructure capacity questions. Such asymmetry around the ca-

pacity decision means that explicit consideration of the distribution of possible outcomes matters.

5. Plans by and for Voluntary Groups and Governments.

1. This story is based in part on research carried out with Peter Schaeffer (Hopkins and Schaeffer 1985), and some of the details of the story are from a course paper by Lucia Rimavicius. Later parts of the story are based on newspaper reports and interviews conducted by Amy Bridges. The purpose here is a story, not a thorough reporting of the process. Schaeffer and Hopkins (1987) present a formal mathematical treatment of this type of problem from the perspective of a developer.

2. Levine and Ponssard (1977) identified three types of information gathering: secret, unshared, and shared. In secret plans, others do not know that a plan has been made, and they do not know the content of the plan. In unshared plans, others know that a plan has been made, but they do not know the content. In shared plans, others know that a plan has been made and they know the content. The downtown Urbana development story includes examples of all three. The committee knew that the subcommittee was planning but did not know the results even though some actors were using these results to take action (unshared). Others did not even know that the planning was going on (secret). The hiring of a consultant by the city was known by all and the results were announced publicly on completion (shared). Hopkins (1981) presents numerical examples of secret, shared, and unshared forecasts and shows that in certain cases the actors might choose to regulate themselves to require forecasting or to prevent forecasting because of collective good characteristics. In one case, each player is better off if all players are prevented from forecasting, even if they have individual incentives to forecast.

3. There is an extensive literature on collective goods and the variants of toll goods and common pool resources. See, for example, Mueller (1989) for a broadranging theoretical exposition and Ostrom et al. (1994) for theoretical and empirical work on responses to the common pool resource problem in particular.

4. The prisoner's dilemma occurs when two criminals accused of the same crime are being questioned separately. Each is offered leniency for confessing and providing evidence to convict the other. If neither confesses, they will both be tried for a lesser crime and receive one year in prison. If one confesses but the other does not, the confessor gets three years and the other gets ten years. If both confess, they each get eight years because the reduction for confessing is relative to conviction on a bigger charge supported by the evidence provided. As in the example in Game 5-1, each prefers to confess (not join) regardless of what the other does, but if they both confess, they each get eight years when they could each have gotten one year.

5. The diagram structure follows Savas (1982), but the plotting of plans and forecasts is my own and certainly open to argument.

6. A recent study of state-mandated local plan elements by Burby et al. (1997) raises many of the issues of state-mandated local planning, but is limited in its im-

plications by the narrow focus on natural hazards. It concludes that state mandates improve the quality of local plans because these plans meet state guidelines. It is not clear whether such plans are more useful to municipalities or how these plans work. The focus of assessment is on how many different implementation tools were used by a given municipality, rather than on specific ways in which plans work.

6. Rights, Regulations, and Plans

1. The quote from Schmid is an example of observable actions and attempts at explanation based on less observable things (Miller 1987). It also illustrates the difficulty of classifying phenomena without acknowledging distinctions between observable acts and their meanings. Guttenberg (1993) developed the implications of this point for classifying land uses by building type, building function, and several other dimensions. See also Marris (1982).

2. The system in England is based on a distinctly different system of rights. The national government holds the rights to develop land for urban uses. It behaves somewhat like a large corporation in setting policies through which its decentralized agents, the local authorities, may release these rights. These patterns of release may or may not be based on plans. Other policies about housing and jobs, for example, may generate rules for release distinct from urban development plans. Therefore, the British system of development control is not focused on regulation and regulatory justification (e.g., consistency, takings) because government holds the development rights. The situation is thus one of managing the release of land to meet the demand for housing. (See e.g., Bramley et al. 1995.)

3. The opposite side of this timing question and investment dynamics is investment in agriculture or other resource activities on land that may eventually be urbanized. Uncertainty over the timing of conversion may lead dairy farmers prematurely to stop investing in large, fixed facilities, such as barns, silos, and waste treatment lagoons. Thus growth timing information may also increase the efficiency of agriculture. Agriculture districts with specific time limits are one device to fix timing and prevent urban services taxation of agricultural land until development is timely (Bryant and Conklin 1975). Urban growth boundaries might have similar effects, though they are usually implemented with too coarse a timing perspective to matter.

7. Capabilities to Make Plans

1. Two examples of the role of arguments against conventional wisdom of at least a particular group: Krug (1990) argues that acidic lakes in the northeastern United States are in their natural state, not a condition caused by air pollution in the Midwest. The expectation that these lakes would sustain fish is based, in his argument, on an anomaly of the past fifty years caused by extensive clear-cutting around 1900.

Hofer (1997) argues that floods in Bangladesh correlate with rain in the Meghalaya hills just to the north, not with rainfall in the Himalaya of Nepal. He also argues that there is no evidence of change in flood peaks with claimed increases in
cleared land in Nepal. There is increasing support for this view (see e.g., Ives and
Messerli 1989), but it remains an argument against the presumptive explanation.
The ongoing intersubjective process can change the facts. In general, we rely on our
judgments about which people in our own "community" to believe, at least as much
as we rely on our own direct knowledge or understanding when establishing our beliefs, attitudes, and accepted "conclusions."

2. This example is adapted from an example in McKean (1985) reporting on the
work of Kahneman and Tversky. See also Kahneman and Tversky (1984).

3. McGrath (1984, 127) notes that little work has been done on tasks that meet
his strict definition of planning tasks—to find an algorithm or procedure to accomplish a given purpose through a set of actions, which is closest to the strategy aspect.

4. These results argue against the Delphi technique (Dalkey 1969), which provides information about estimates by others but specifically prevents interaction in
groups.

5. The literature on organizations and organizational behavior is vast. March's
introduction to the volume of his collected works is a good tour of the issues (March
1988). The classic economic analysis of firms is Williamson (1975). Alexander
(1992b, 1995) considers these ideas with particular reference to planning. Barzel
(1989) develops the explanations for organizations from concepts of rights.

6. Krumholz and Forester (1990) describe the planning commission's role in the
unusual Cleveland Policy Report and its implied approach to planning. Clavel (1986)
considers the planning commission in relation to the emergence of progressive local
government regimes.

8. Collective Choice, Participation, and Plans

1. Dahl and Lindblom (1953) is one of the classic discussions of a wide range of
possible forms.

2. Merit goods, limited financial resources, and irreversible actions are sometimes included in lists of appropriate government actions. Taking collective action
for any of these reasons involves choosing a common level of provision. For example, if housing is a merit good because I value the quality of housing provided to
low-income households because of my ethical perspective, I can either act privately
or, believing that many others feel similarly, I can try to induce collective action.
Such collective action would be premised on the merit good of low-income housing being a collective good. My ethical beliefs are satisfied if low-income households
have housing, and all others with similar ethical beliefs also benefit. We cannot exclude others from this benefit unless we can keep it a secret from anyone who does
not contribute to the cost. My satisfaction from such housing does not conflict with

the satisfaction of others. Thus consideration of the merit good emerges in the collective action frame because it is a collective good. For present purposes, therefore, we can focus only on decisions about collective goods.

3. Hurley (1989) works from philosophy to consider questions in decision theory and collective choice at an abstract level. Stevens (1993) presents the perspective of neoclassical economics or "public choice" in accessible style. Mueller (1989) is a complete reference on public choice.

4. Elkin (1987) addresses similar issues with his concepts of political equality—absence in bias in content of the agenda—and social intelligence—how well social problem solving works.

5. Hurley (1989) references Elster (1983), chapters 3 and 4. Interpretations of Habermas and the ideas of communicative competence have similar implications. See, for example, Innes (1998) and references therein.

6. Hurley (1989 334) quotes Arrow as equating the cognition view with statistical aggregation.

7. Majority rule is a persuasive decision rule because it makes it equally likely that you will be able to pass a proposal that you wish to pass and to defeat a proposal you wish to defeat (Riker and Ordeshook 1973). Before you know what issues you will face, majority rule is thus a neutral rule for positive and negative votes. For some things that should be hard to do, where you can predict that you would be more concerned about being able to defeat something that you opposed than about winning something you supported, supra majority rules are appropriate. A two-thirds majority, or even unanimity, might be required for changing the rules by which decisions are made. Guarantees of civil liberties by taking them out of the realm of voting may reduce risks of undesired outcomes and thus ease the hurdles to forming a coercive group (Stevens 1993)

8. Individuals are assumed to have only ordinal preferences because within the assumptions of economic theory there is no way to infer intensities of preference that can be compared across individuals. See Mueller (1989) for a complete discussion.

9. This statement of the conditions is from Haefele (1973, 18) based on Arrow (1967).

10. The Danada Farm case (Rubin 1988) describes the packaging of a set of projects for a bond issue for parks in DuPage County, Illinois, based on this strategy.

11. Elkin references John Dewey in general and Lindblom's *Intelligence of Democracy* and *Politics and Markets*.

12. Stevens (1993) references Buchanan and Tullock 1962 as the original source and the discussion in Mueller 1989. Mueller (1989) is the standard comprehensive reference on public choice. Skjei (1973) developed a similar argument using decision analysis to consider the decision to participate in planning activities.

13. The framers of the U.S. Constitution were clearly concerned about the potential dangers of direct, mass democracy and saw representatives as decreasing these dangers. See Stevens (1993), who quotes from Hofstadter (1974) referring to the Federalist Papers. See also Haefele (1973). There is also a presumption that repre-

sentatives will dampen the extremes of individual behavior that might occur in direct democracy because representatives will be better informed and will expect repeat face-to-face encounters with their colleagues in a way the large numbers of citizens voting anonymously would not. The initiative and referendum actions in
western states to limit taxing powers exemplify the different expectations of direct
and representative democracy. Direct democracy for zoning decisions would be
more likely to invade civil liberties and rights of individuals than representative government (see e.g., Caves 1992).

14. For example, see McGurty (1995) and Knowles-Yanez (1997), though neither would accept the Olson argument for group formation as a primary explanation.

15. See, for example, Reardon's (1998) report of work in East St. Louis, Illinois,
or the biography of Saul Alinsky (Horwitt 1989).

16. These differ from Arnstein's (1969) classic "ladder of citizen participation"
but address similar issues.

9. How Plans Are Made

1. Rasmussen et al. (1994) develop an elaborate system for describing processes
within organizations as tasks that can be analyzed in order to create structured, cognitive support systems.

2. The three tasks in the first column are conventional wisdom. I learned it from
Louis B. Wetmore at the University of Illinois at Urbana-Champaign. Sources for
the remaining columns are Patton and Sawicki (1993), Bryson (1995), Black (1990),
and Checkoway (1986).

3. See Alexander (1996) for a similar comparison of these two standards.

4. In his most recent book, Forester (1999, 5–10) frames his own version of how
his views compare with those of other planning theorists.

5. Recent reviews of such work include the symposium in the *Journal of the
American Planning Association*, volume 60, number 1, 1994, and Anas et al. (1998).

6. Neuman's (1997) description of a plan for Madrid might be a counterexam-
ple in which a diagram framed a vision for the south part of the area, which improved the situation of the least-well-off part of the city. In this case, a socialist government was in a position to act, in investment and regulatory terms, for these
interests.

7. Work on implementation of geographic information systems in organizations
and among organizations raises similar issues of whether information technology
is a line department of its own or a staff role to and in other departments (see e.g.,
Budic 1994).

10. How to Use and Make Plans

1. Pitkin (1992) identifies inclusion of an index as one way to increase usability
of a plan, but says little about how such an index might be different from traditional

indexes. The Chicago Plan of 1909 has an index, but it is like the index of any book and not particularly useful for accessing aspects of the plan for decision situations.

2. It is unnecessary to go into detail here about how this should be done in particular situations. One way of accessing large numbers of attributes about each person in either of these sorted orders is to maintain the database stored in one order and create an inverted list, or index to the information in the other order. The computer is likely to use indexes of various kinds to create views. A major advantage of storing only one copy of information rather than storing each view is that it is easier to update and maintain accuracy of one dataset than of many.

3. The plan and original version of the diagram in Figure 10-4 were developed by Matthew Gebhardt, Allison Laff, and Sathyamoorthy Ponnuswamy as a master's project at the University of Illinois at Urbana-Champaign with my guidance and under contract to the City of Taylorville.

4. This example is based on discussions with Dennis Schmidt, Executive Director of the Urbana-Champaign Sanitary District, as well as UCSD documents and local newspaper reports.

5. The *Town Planning Review*, volume 49, numbers 3 and 4 are devoted entirely to papers on use of such methods in British structure planning.

6. The example in Figure 10-5 is from a community meeting in Phoenix, Arizona, discussing transportation issues for the North Black Canyon Corridor. The sketch is courtesy of Cassandra Ecker who was an intern in the City of Phoenix Planning Department in the summer of 1997.

7. Recent examples of such modeling include Landis (1994, 1995), Kim and Hopkins (1996), Klosterman (1997), and Waddell (2000). Westervelt and Hopkins (1999) model animal behavior in a way that at least suggests the possibility of considering what happens to individual persons rather than what happens to land use patterns.

References

Ajzen, Icek, and Martin Fishbein. 1980. *Understanding Attitudes and Predicting Social Behavior.* Englewood Cliffs, NJ: Prentice-Hall, Inc.

Akerloff, George. 1970. The Market for Lemons: Qualitative Uncertainty and the Market Mechanism. *Quarterly Journal of Economics* 84:488–500.

Alchian, Armen. 1950. Uncertainty, Evolution, and Economic Theory. *Journal of Political Economy* 58:211–221.

Alexander, Ernest R. 1992a. *Approaches to Planning: Introducing Current Planning Theories, Concepts and Issues.* 2nd ed. Philadelphia: Gordon and Breach Science Publishers.

———. 1992b. A Transaction Cost Theory of Planning. *Journal of the American Planning Association* 58 (2):190–200.

———. 1995. *How Organizations Act Together: Interorganizational Coordination in Theory and Practice.* New York: Gordon and Breach.

———. 1996. After Rationality: Toward a Contingency Theory for Planning. In *Explorations in Planning Theory*, edited by S. J. Mandelbaum, L. Mazza, and R. W. Burchell. New Brunswick, NJ: Center for Urban Policy Research.

Alexander, Ernest R., and Andreas Faludi. 1989. Planning and Plan Implementation: Notes on Evaluation Criteria. *Environment and Planning B: Planning and Design* 16 (2):127–140.

Alterman, Rachelle, ed. 1988. *Private Supply of Public Services: Evaluation of Real Estate Exactions, Linkage, and Alternative Land Policies.* New York: New York University Press.

Alterman, Rachelle, and Morris Hill. 1978. Implementation of Land Use Plans. *Journal of the American Institute of Planners* 44 (3):274–285.

American Institute of Certified Planners. 1991. AICP Code of Ethics and Professional Conduct. Chicago: American Institute of Certified Planners.

American Planning Association. 1998. *Growing Smart Legislative Guidebook—Phase I and Phase II: Model Statutes for Planning and Management of Change.* Chicago: APA Planners Press.

Anas, Alex, Richard J. Arnott, and Kenneth A. Small. 1998. Urban Spatial Structure. *Journal of Economic Literature* 36 (3):1426–1464.

Andrews, Clinton J. 1992. Spurring Inventiveness by Analyzing Trade-offs: A

Public Look at New England's Electricity Alternatives. *Environmental Impact Assessment Review* 12:185–210.

Arnstein, Sherry R. 1969. A Ladder of Citizen Participation. *Journal of the American Institute of Planners* 35 (4):221–228.

Arrow, Kenneth. 1951. *Social Choice and Individual Values.* New York: John Wiley.

———. 1967. Public and Private Values. In *Human Values and Economic Policy*, edited by S. Hook. New York: New York University Press.

Ascher, William. 1978. *Forecasting: An Appraisal for Policy-Makers and Planners.* Baltimore: The Johns Hopkins University Press.

Ashby, W. Ross. 1956. *An Introduction to Cybernetics.* London: Chapman and Hall Ltd.

Axelrod, Robert M. 1981. *The Evolution of Cooperation.* New York: Basic Books, Inc.

Babcock, Richard F., and Charles L. Siemon. 1985. *The Zoning Game Revisited.* Boston: Oelgeschlaeger, Gunn & Hahn.

Bachrach, Peter, and Morton Baratz. 1962. The Two Faces of Power. *American Political Science Review* 56:947–952.

Bacon, Edmund N. 1974. *The Design of Cities.* Revised ed. New York: The Viking Press, Inc.

Baer, William C. 1997. General Plan Evaluation Criteria: An Approach to Making Better Plans. *Journal of the American Planning Association* 63 (3):329–344.

Bahl, Roy W., Jr. 1963. *A Bluegrass Leapfrog.* Lexington: Bureau of Business Research, University of Kentucky.

Bartholomew, Harland. 1924. *The City Plan of Memphis, Tennessee.* Memphis, TN: City of Memphis, 139.

Barzel, Yoram. 1989. Economic Analysis of Property Rights. Cambridge, England: Cambridge University Press.

Baum, Howell S. 1983. *Planners and Public Expectations.* Cambridge, MA: Schenkman Publishing Company, Inc.

Baumol, William J. 1972. On Taxation and the Control of Externalities. *American Economic Review* 62:307–322.

Baumol, William J., and Wallace E. Oates. 1975. *The Theory of Environmental Policy.* Englewood Cliffs, NJ: Prentice-Hall, Inc.

Beatley, Timothy, David J. Brower, and William H. Lucy. 1994. Representation in Comprehensive Planning: An Analysis of the Austinplan Process. *Journal of the American Planning Association* 60 (2):185–196.

Beer, Stafford. 1966. *Decision and Control.* New York: John Wiley.

Berke, Philip, and Steven P. French. 1994. The Influence of State Planning Mandates on Local Plan Quality. *Journal of Planning Education and Research* 13 (4):237–250.

Black, Alan. 1990. The Chicago Area Transportation Study: A Case Study of Rational Planning. *Journal of Planning Education and Research* 10 (1):27–37.

Blaesser, Brian W., Clyde W. Forrest, Douglas W. Kmiec, Daniel R. Mandelker, Alan C. Weinstein, and Norman Williams, Jr. 1989. *Land Use and the Constitution: Principles for Planning Practice*. Chicago: Planners Press.

Botkin, Daniel. 1990. *Discordant Harmonies: A New Ecology for the Twenty-First Century*. Oxford: Oxford University Press.

Bramley, Glen, Will Bartlett, and Christine Lambert. 1995. *Planning, the Market and Private Housebuilding*. London: UCL Press.

Brams, S. J., and P. C. Fishburn. 1983. *Approval Voting*. Boston: Birkhauser.

Branch, Melville C. 1981. *Continuous City Planning*. New York: John Wiley & Sons.

Brill, E. Downey, Jr., John M. Flach, Lewis D. Hopkins, and S. Ranjithan. 1990. MGA: A Decision Support System for Complex, Incompletely Defined Problems. *IEEE Transactions on Systems, Man, and Cybernetics* 20 (4):745–757.

Bryant, William R., and Howard E. Conklin. 1975. New Farmland Preservation Programs in New York. *Journal of the American Institute of Planners* 41 (6):390–396.

Bryson, John M. 1995. *Strategic Planning for Public and Nonprofit Organizations: A Guide to Strengthening and Sustaining Organizational Achievement*. Revised ed. San Francisco: Jossey-Bass.

Bryson, John M., Paul Bromiley, and Y. Soo Jung. 1990. Influences of Context and Process on Project Planning Success. *Journal of Planning Education and Research* 9 (3):183–195.

Bryson, John M., and Barbara C. Crosby. 1992. *Leadership for the Common Good: Tackling Public Problems in a Shared-Power World*. San Francisco: Jossey-Bass.

Buchanan, James M., and Gordon Tullock. 1962. *The Calculus of Consent*. Ann Arbor: University of Michigan Press.

Budic, Zorica D. 1994. Effectiveness of Geographic Information Systems in Local Planning. *Journal of the American Planning Association* 60 (2):244–263.

Burby, Raymond J., Peter J. May, Philip R. Berke, Linda C. Dalton, Steven P. French, and Edward J. Kaiser. 1997. *Making Governments Plan: State Experiments in Managing Land Use*. Baltimore: Johns Hopkins University Press.

Burnham, Daniel H., and Edward H. Bennet. 1909. *Plan of Chicago*. Chicago: The Commercial Club, 2–4.

Calkins, Hugh W. 1979. The Planning Monitor: An Accountability Theory of Plan Evaluation. *Environment and Planning A* 11 (7):745–758.

Caro, Robert A. 1974. *The Power Broker: Robert Moses and the Fall of New York*. New York: Alfred A. Knopf.

Caves, Roger W. 1992. *Land Use Planning: The Ballot Box Revolution*. Vol. 187, *Sage Library of Social Research*. Newbury Park, CA: Sage Publications, Inc.

Checkoway, Barry. 1986. Political Strategy for Social Planning. In *Strategic Perspective on Planning Practice*, edited by B. Checkoway. Lexington, MA: Lexington Books.

Chicago Area Transportation Study. 1959. Chicago Area Transportation Study,
    Final Report, Volume I: Survey Findings. Chicago: Chicago Area Transporta-
    tion Study.
————. 1960. Chicago Area Transportation Study, Final Report, Volume II: Data
    Projections. Chicago: Chicago Area Transportation Study.
————. 1962. Chicago Area Transportation Study, Final Report, Volume III:
    Transportation Plan. Chicago: Chicago Area Transportation Study.
Chisholm, Donald. 1989. *Coordination without Hierarchy: Informal Structures in
    Multiorganizational Systems.* Berkeley: University of California Press.
City of Chicago Department of City Planning. 1964. Basic Policies for the Com-
    prehensive Plan of Chicago. Chicago: Department of City Planning, City of
    Chicago.
City of Chicago Department of Development and Planning. 1966. The Compre-
    hensive Plan of Chicago. Chicago: Department of Development and Planning,
    City of Chicago.
City-County Planning Commission, Lexington and Fayette County, Kentucky.
    1964. The Nature of Our Community . . . and the Challenge That Lies
    Ahead. Lexington: City-County Planning Commission of Lexington and
    Fayette County, Kentucky.
————. 1973. 1973 Update of a Growing Community. Lexington: City-County
    Planning Commission Lexington and Fayette County, Kentucky.
Clavel, Pierre. 1986. *The Progressive City: Planning and Participation, 1969–1984.*
    New Brunswick, NJ: Rutgers University Press.
Coase, Ronald. 1937. The Nature of the Firm. *Economica* 4:386–405.
————. 1960. The Problem of Social Cost. *Journal of Law and Economics* 3:1–44.
Cohen, Michael D., James G. March, and Johan P. Olsen. 1972. A Garbage Can
    Model of Organizational Choice. *Administrative Science Quarterly* 17 (1):1–25.
Cohen, Stephen S. 1977. *Modern Capitalist Planning: The French Model.* Berkeley:
    University of California Press.
Connerly, Charles E., and Nancy A. Muller. 1993. Evaluating Housing Elements
    in Growth Management Comprehensive Plans. In *Growth Management: The
    Planning Challenge of the 1990s,* edited by J. Stein. Thousand Oaks, CA: Sage.
Costonis, John J. 1974. *Space Adrift: Saving Urban Landmarks through the Chicago
    Plan.* Urbana: University of Illinois Press.
Cronon, William. 1983. *Changes in the Land: Indians, Colonists, and the Ecology of
    New England.* New York: Hill and Wang.
Dahl, Robert A., and Charles E. Lindblom. 1953. *Politics, Economics, and Welfare.*
    New York: Harper and Row.
Dalkey, N. C. 1969. The Delphi Method: An Experimental Study of Group
    Opinion. Santa Monica, CA: The RAND Corporation.
Dalton, Linda C. 1985. Politics and Planning Agency Performance: Lessons from
    Seattle. *Journal of the American Planning Association* 51 (2):189–199.

Dalton, Linda C., and Raymond J. Burby. 1994. Mandates, Plans, and Planners. *Journal of the American Planning Association* 60 (4):444–461.

Darke, Jane. 1979. The Primary Generator and the Design Process. *Design Studies* 1 (1):36–43.

Date, C. J. 1995. *An Introduction to Database Systems.* 6th ed. Reading, MA: Addison-Wesley.

Davis, James H. 1992. Some Compelling Intuitions about Group Consensus Decisions, Theoretical and Empirical Research, and Interpersonal Aggregation Phenomena: Selected Examples, 1950–1990. *Organizational Behavior and Human Decision Processes* 52:3–38.

Dawkins, Richard. 1976. *The Selfish Gene.* Oxford: Oxford University Press.

Demsetz, Harold. 1967. Toward a Theory of Property Rights. *American Economic Review* 57 (2):347–359.

Ding, Chengri, Gerrit J. Knaap, and Lewis D. Hopkins. 1999. Managing Urban Growth with Urban Growth Boundaries: A Theoretical Analysis. *Journal of Urban Economics.* 46:53–68.

Elkin, Stephen. 1987. *City and Regime in the American Republic.* Chicago: University of Chicago Press.

Elster, Jonathan. 1983. *Sour Grapes.* Cambridge: Cambridge University Press.

Faludi, Andreas. 1987. *A Decision-Centred View of Environmental Planning.* Oxford: Pergamon Press.

Feiss, Carl. 1985. The Foundations of Federal Planning Assistance: A Personal Account of the 701 Program. *Journal of the American Planning Association* 51 (2):175–184.

Fischel, William A. 1985. *The Economics of Zoning Laws: A Property Rights Approach to American Land Use Controls.* Baltimore: Johns Hopkins University Press.

Flyvbjerg, Bent. 1998. *Rationality and Power: Democracy in Practice.* Translated by S. Sampson. Chicago: University of Chicago Press.

Foglesong, Richard E. 1986. *Planning the Capitalist City: The Colonial Era to the 1920s.* Princeton, New Jersey: Princeton University Press, 88.

Forester, John. 1989. *Planning in the Face of Power.* Berkeley: University of California Press.

———. 1999. *The Deliberative Practitioner.* Cambridge, MA: MIT Press.

Frank, Robert H. 1988. *Passions within Reason: The Strategic Role of the Emotions.* New York: W. W. Norton & Company.

Freidenfelds, John. 1981. *Capacity Expansion: Analysis of Simple Models with Applications.* Amsterdam: Elsevier North Holland, Inc.

Friend, J. K., and W. N. Jessop. 1969. *Local Government and Strategic Choice: An Operational Research Approach to the Processes of Public Planning.* London: Tavistock Publications.

Friend, John K., and Alan Hickling. 1987. *Planning under Pressure.* Oxford: Pergamon.

Fukuyama, Francis. 1995. *Trust: The Social Virtues and the Creation of Prosperity.* New York: The Free Press.

Garvin, Alexander. 1996. *The American City: What Works, What Doesn't?* New York: McGraw-Hill.

Gaventa, John. 1980. *Power and Powerlessness: Quiescence and Rebellion in an Appalachian Valley.* Urbana: University of Illinois Press.

George, Henry. 1880. *Progress and Poverty.* New York: Appleton.

Godschalk, David. 2000. Montgomery County, Maryland—A Pioneer in Land Supply Monitoring. In *Monitoring Land Supply with GIS*, edited by A. V. Moudon and M. Hubner. New York: John Wiley & Sons.

Goldsmith, Steven. 1998. Neighborhoods: Planning Groups Flex More Muscle. *Seattle Post Intelligencer*, April 28, 1998, B2.

Goldstein, William M., and Jane Beattie. 1991. Judgments of Relative Importance in Decision Making: The Importance of Interpretation and the Interpretation of Importance. In *Frontiers of Mathematical Psychology: Essays in Honor of Clyde Coombs*, edited by D. R. Brown and J. E. K. Smith. New York: Springer-Verlag.

Goulter, Ian C., Harry G. Wenzel, Jr., and Lewis D. Hopkins. 1983. Watershed Land Use Planning Under Uncertainty. *Environment and Planning A* 15:987–992.

Guttenberg, Albert Z. 1993. *The Language of Planning: Essays on the Origins and Ends of American Planning Thought.* Urbana: University of Illinois Press.

Haar, Charles M. 1977. *Land-Use Planning: A Casebook on the Use, Misuse, and Reuse of Urban Land.* 3d ed. Boston: Little, Brown and Company.

Habermas, Jurgen. 1990. *Moral Consciousness and Communicative Action.* Translated by C. Lenhardt and S. W. Nicholsen. Cambridge, MA: MIT Press.

Haefele, Edwin T. 1973. *Representative Government and Environmental Management.* Baltimore: Johns Hopkins University Press.

Hanley, Paul F. 1999. Simulating Land Developers', Sewer Providers', and Land Owners' Behavior to Assess Sewer Expansion Policies. Ph.D., Regional Planning, University of Illinois at Urbana-Champaign.

Harris, Britton. 1960. Plan or Projection: An Examination of the Use of Models in Planning. *Journal of the American Institute of Planners* 26 (4):265–272.

———. 1965. Urban Development Models: A New Tool for Planners. *Journal of the American Institute of Planners* 31:90–95.

———. 1967. The City of the Future: Problem of Optimal Design. *Papers and Proceedings of the Regional Science Association* 19:185–198.

Harris, Britton, and Michael Batty. 1993. Locational Models, Geographic Information and Planning Support Systems. *Journal of Planning Education and Research* 12 (3):184–198.

Helling, Amy. 1998. Collaborative Visioning: Proceed with Caution. *Journal of the American Planning Association* 64 (3):335–349.

Hirshleifer, Jack, and John G. Riley. 1992. *The Analytics of Uncertainty and Information.* In *Cambridge Surveys of Economic Literature*, edited by M. Perlman. Cambridge, UK: Cambridge University Press.

Hoch, Charles. 1994. *What Planners Do: Power, Politics, and Persuasion.* Chicago: Planners Press, American Planning Association.

Hofer, Thomas. 1997. Meghalaya, Not Himalaya. *Himal,* September/October, 52–56.

Hofstadter, Richard. 1974. *The American Political Tradition.* New York: Vintage Books.

Holling, Crawford S., and Michael Goldberg. 1971. Ecology and Planning. *Journal of the American Planning Association* 37 (4):221–230.

Hopkins, Lewis D. 1974. Plan, Projection, Policy—Mathematical Programming and Planning Theory. *Environment and Planning A* 6:419–430.

———. 1979. Quadratic versus Linear Models for Land Use Plan Design. *Environment and Planning A* 11:291–298.

———. 1981. The Decision to Plan: Planning Activities as Public Goods. In *Urban Infrastructure, Location, and Housing,* edited by W. R. Lierop and P. Nijkamp. Alphen aan den Rijn. Netherlands: Sijthoff and Noordhoff.

———. 1984a. Comparative Planning: Looking at Ourselves the Way We Look at Others. *Planning and Public Policy* 11 (3):5.

———. 1984b. Evaluation of Methods for Exploring Ill-Defined Problems. *Environment and Planning B: Planning and Design* 11:339–348.

———. 1999. Structure of a Planning Support System for Urban Development. *Environment and Planning B: Planning and Design* 26 (3):333–343.

Hopkins, Lewis D., E. Downey Brill, Jr., Jon C. Liebman, and Harry G. Wenzel. 1978. Land Use Allocation Model for Flood Control. *Journal of Water Resources Planning and Management ASCE* WR1:93–104.

Hopkins, Lewis D., E. Downey Brill, Jr., Kenneth B. Kurtz, and Harry G. Wenzel, Jr. 1981. Analyzing Floodplain Policies Using an Interdependent Land Use Allocation Model. *Water Resources Research* 17:467–477.

Hopkins, Lewis D., E. Downey Brill, Jr., and Benedict Wong. 1982. Generating Alternative Solutions for Dynamic Programming Models of Water Resources Problems. *Water Resources Research* 18:782–790.

Hopkins, Lewis D., and Peter V. Schaeffer. 1983. Rights in Land and Planning Behavior: A Comparative Study of Mountain Resort Development. Urbana: Department of Urban and Regional Planning, University of Illinois at Urbana-Champaign.

———. 1985. The Logic of Planning Behavior. Urbana: Department of Urban and Regional Planning, University of Illinois at Urbana-Champaign.

Horwitt, Sanford D. 1989. *Let Them Call Me Rebel: Saul Alinsky—His Life and Legacy.* New York: Alfred A. Knopf.

Howard, John T. 1951. In Defense of Planning Commissions. *Journal of the American Institute of Planners* 17 (Spring):89–94.

Howe, Elizabeth. 1980. Role Choices of Planners. *Journal of the American Planning Association* 46 (4):398–410.

Howe, Elizabeth, and Jerome Kaufman. 1979. The Ethics of Contemporary American Planners. *Journal of the American Planning Association* 45 (3):243–255.

Howe, Jim, Ed McMahon, and Luther Propst. 1997. *Balancing Nature and Commerce in Gateway Communities.* Washington, DC: Island Press.

Hurley, S. L. 1989. *Natural Reasons: Personality and Polity.* New York: Oxford University Press.

Innes, Judith E. 1996. Planning through Consensus Building: A New View of the Comprehensive Planning Ideal. *Journal of the American Planning Association* 62 (4):460–472.

———. 1998. Information in Communicative Planning. *Journal of the American Planning Association* 64 (1):52–63.

Intriligator, Michael D., and E. Sheshinski. 1986. Toward a Theory of Planning. In *Social Choice and Public Decision Making*, edited by W. Heller, R. Starr, and D. Starrett. Cambridge: Cambridge University Press.

Irwin, David M., and Jibgar Joshi. 1996. Integrated Action Planning: The Experience in Nepal. In *Integrated Urban Infrastructure Development in Asia*, edited by K. Singh, F. Steinberg, and N. von Einsiedel. London: Intermediate Technology Publications Ltd.

Isserman, Andrew M. 1984. Projection, Forecast, and Plan. *Journal of the American Planning Association* 50 (2):208–221.

Ives, Jack D., and Bruno Messerli. 1989. *The Himalayan Dilemma: Reconciling Development and Conservation.* London: Routledge.

Jacobs, Allan B. 1980. *Making City Planning Work.* Chicago: American Planning Association.

———. 2000. Notes on Planning Practice and Education. In *The Profession of City Planning: Changes, Images, and Challenges 1950–2000*, edited by L. Rodwin and B. Sanyal. New Brunswick, NJ: Center for Urban Policy Research, 49.

Johnson, David A. 1996. *Planning the Great Metropolis: The 1929 Regional Plan of New York and Its Environs.* Edited by G. E. Cherry and A. Sutcliffe, *Studies in History, Planning and the Environment.* London: E & FN Spon.

Johnson, William C. 1989. *The Politics of Urban Planning.* New York: Paragon House.

Joshi, Jibgar. 1997. *Planning for Sustainable Development: Urban Management in Nepal and South Asia.* Kathmandu, Nepal: Lajmina Joshi.

Judd, Dennis R., and Robert E. Mendelson. 1973. *The Politics of Urban Planning: The East St. Louis Experience.* Urbana: University of Illinois Press.

Kahneman, Daniel, Paul Slovic, and Amos Tversky, eds. 1982. *Judgment under Uncertainty: Heuristics and Biases.* New York: Cambridge University Press.

Kahneman, Daniel, and Amos Tversky. 1984. Choices, Values, and Frames. *American Psychologist* 39:341–350.

Kaiser, Edward J., David R. Godschalk, and F. Stuart Chapin Jr. 1995. *Urban Land Use Planning.* 4th ed., Urbana: University of Illinois Press.

Keating, Ann Durkin. 1988. *Building Chicago: Suburban Developers and the Creation of a Divided Metropolis.* Columbus: Ohio State University Press.

Keating, W. Dennis, and Norman Krumholz. 1991. Downtown Plans of the

1980s: The Case for More Equity in the 1990s. *Journal of the American Planning Association* 57 (2):136–152.

Keele, Steven W. 1973. *Attention and Human Performance*. Pacific Palisades, CA: Goodyear Publishing Company, Inc.

Keeney, Ralph, and Howard Raiffa. 1976. *Decisions with Multiple Objectives: Preferences and Value Tradeoffs*. New York: John Wiley & Sons.

Kelly, Eric Damian. 1993. *Managing Community Growth: Policies, Techniques, and Impacts*. Westport, Connecticut: Praeger.

Kelly, Eric Damian, and Barbara Becker. 2000. *Community Planning: An Introduction to the Comprehensive Plan*. Washington, DC: Island Press.

Kent, T. J. 1964. *The Urban General Plan*. San Francisco: Chandler Publishing Co.

Kerr, Donna H. 1976. The Logic of "Policy" and Successful Policies. *Policy Sciences* 7 (3):351–363.

Kim, Hyong-Bok, and Lewis D. Hopkins. 1996. Capacity Expansion of Modeling for Water Supply in a Planning Support System for Urban Growth Management. *Journal of the Urban and Regional Information Systems Association* 8(1):58–66.

King, John. 1990. How the BRA Got Some Respect: Boston's Redevelopment Agency Believes in Doing It All. *Planning*, May, 4–9.

Kirkwood, Craig W. 1997. *Strategic Decision Making: Multiobjective Decision Analysis with Spreadsheets*. Belmont, CA: Duxbury Press, Wadsworth Publishing Co.

Kleymeyer, John E., and Paul Hartsock. 1973. Cincinnati's Planning Guidance System. Planning Advisory Service Report No. 295. Chicago: American Society of Planning Officials.

Klosterman, Richard E. 1980. A Public Interest Criterion. *Journal of the American Planning Association* 46 (3):323–333.

———. 1985. Arguments for and against Planning. *Town Planning Review* 56 (1):5–20.

———. 1990. *Community Analysis and Planning Techniques*. Savage, MD: Rowman & Littlefield Publishers, Inc.

———. 1997. The What If? Collaborative Planning Support System. In *Computers in Urban Planning and Urban Management*, edited by P. K. Sikdar, S. L. Dhingra, and K. V. Krishna Rao. Mumbai, India: Narosa Publishing House.

Knaap, Gerrit J. 1990. State Land Use Planning and Exclusionary Zoning: Evidence from Oregon. *Journal of Planning Education and Research* 10 (1):39–46.

Knaap, Gerrit J., Lewis D. Hopkins, and Arun Pant. 1996. Does Transportation Planning Matter? Explorations into the Effects of Planned Transportation Infrastructure on Real Estate Sales, Land Values, Building Permits, and Development Sequence. Cambridge, MA: Lincoln Institute of Land Policy.

Knaap, Gerrit J., Lewis D. Hopkins, and Kieran P. Donaghy. 1998. Do Plans Matter? A Framework for Examining the Logic and Effects of Land Use Planning. *Journal of Planning Education and Research* 18 (1):25–34.

Knowles-Yanez, Kim. 1997. A Case Study of a Contested Land Use Planning

Process: A Grassroots Neighborhood Organization, A Medical Complex, and a City. Ph.D. Regional Planning, University of Illinois at Urbana-Champaign, Urbana.

Krieger, Martin. 1973. What's Wrong with Plastic Trees? *Science* 179 (February 2):446–455.

————. 1991. Contingency in Planning: Statistics, Fortune, and History, 1991. *Journal of Planning Education and Research* 10 (2):157–161.

Krug, Edward C. 1990. Acid Rain: And Just Maybe . . . the Sky ISN'T Falling. *Champaign-Urbana News Gazette,* June 10, 1990, B-1, B-5.

Krumholz, Norman. 1982. A Retrospective View of Equity Planning: Cleveland 1969–1979. *Journal of the American Planning Association* 48 (2):163–174.

Krumholz, Norman, and John Forester. 1990. *Making Equity Planning Work: Leadership in the Public Sector.* Philadelphia: Temple University Press.

Lai, Shih-Kung. 1998. From Organized Anarchy to Controlled Structure: Effects of Planning on the Garbage Can Decision Processes. *Environment and Planning B: Planning and Design* 25 (1):85–102.

Lai, Shih-Kung, and Lewis D. Hopkins. 1989. The Meanings of Tradeoffs in Multi-Attribute Evaluation Methods: A Comparison. *Environment and Planning B: Planning and Design* 16:155–170.

————. 1995. Can Decision Makers Express Multiattribute Preferences Using AHP and MUT? An Experiment. *Environment and Planning B: Planning and Design* 22 (1):21–34.

Landis, John D. 1994. The California Urban Futures Model: A New Generation of Metropolitan Simulation Models. *Environment and Planning B: Planning and Design* 21:399–420.

————. 1995. Imagining Land Use Futures: Applying the California Urban Futures Model. *Journal of the American Planning Association* 61 (4):438–457.

Lave, Lester B. 1963. The Value of Better Weather Information to the Raisin Industry. *Econometrica* 31:151–164.

Lee, Insung. 1993. Development of Procedural Expertise to Support Multiattribute Spatial Decision Making. Ph.D., Regional Planning, University of Illinois at Urbana-Champaign, Urbana.

Lee, Insung, and Lewis D. Hopkins. 1995. Procedural Expertise for Efficient Multiattribute Evaluation: A Procedural Support Strategy for CEA. *Journal of Planning Education and Research* 14(4):225–268.

Leopold, Aldo. 1949. *A Sand County Almanac and Sketches Here and There.* London: Oxford University Press.

Levine, P., and J. P. Ponssard. 1977. The Value of Information in some Nonzero Sum Games. *International Journal of Game Theory* 6 (4):221–229.

Levinson, D. 1997. The Limits to Growth Management: Development Regulation in Montgomery County, Maryland. *Environment and Planning B: Planning and Design* 24 (5):689–707.

Lewis, Paul G. 1996. *Shaping Suburbia: How Political Institutions Organize Urban*

Development. Edited by B. A. Rockman, *Pitt Series in Policy and Institutional Studies.* Pittsburgh: University of Pittsburgh Press.

Lindblom, Charles. 1959. The Science of Muddling Through. *Public Administration Review* 19:79 88.

Lindsey, Greg, and Gerrit J. Knaap. 1999. Willingness to Pay for Urban Greenway Projects. *Journal of the American Planning Association* 65 (3):297–313.

Lovelace, Eldridge. 1992. *Harland Bartholomew: His Contributions to American Urban Planning.* Urbana: Department of Urban and Regional Planning, University of Illinois at Urbana-Champaign.

Lucy, William. 1988. APAs Ethical Principles Include Simplistic Planning Theories. *Journal of the American Planning Association* 54 (2):147–148.

Lukes, Steven. 1974. *Power: A Radical View.* London: Macmillan.

Mandelbaum, Seymour J. 1979. A Complete General Theory of Planning Is Impossible. *Policy Sciences* 11:59–71.

———. 1990. Reading Plans. *Journal of the American Planning Association* 56 (3):350–356.

Mandelker, Daniel R. 1989. Interim Development Controls in Highway Programs: The Taking Issue. *Journal of Land Use and Environmental Law* 4 (2):167–213.

March, James G. 1978. Bounded Rationality, Ambiguity, and the Engineering of Choice. *The Bell Journal of Economics* 9 (2):587–608.

———. 1988. *Decisions and Organizations.* Oxford: Basil Blackwell, Inc.

Marcuse, Peter. 1976. Professional Ethics and Beyond. *Journal of the American Institute of Planners* 42(3):264–274.

Marris, Peter. 1982. *Meaning and Action: Community Planning and Conceptions of Change.* London: Routledge & Kegan Paul, 73.

Mastop, H., and Andreas Faludi. 1997. Evaluation of Strategic Plans: The Performance Principle. *Environment and Planning B: Planning and Design* 24:815–832.

McGovern, Patrick S. 1998. San Francisco Bay Area Edge Cities: New Roles for Planners and the General Plan. *Journal of Planning Education and Research* 17 (3):246–258.

McGrath, Joseph E. 1984. *Groups: Interaction and Performance.* Englewood Cliffs, NJ: Prentice Hall, Inc.

McGurty, Eileen. 1995. The Construction of Environmental Justice in Warren County, North Carolina. Ph.D., Regional Planning, University of Illinois at Urbana-Champaign, Urbana.

McKean, Kevin. 1985. Decisions, Decisions. *Discover,* June, 22–31.

McLoughlin, J. Brian. 1973. *Control and Urban Planning.* London: Faber.

Mee, Joy. 1998. Seminar on Planning in Phoenix. Champaign, Illinois, October 1998.

Meehan, Patrick. 1989. Viewpoint. *Planning,* September, 55(9):54.

Metro. 2000. *Growth Management.* Growth Management Services Department, Metro, Portland, Oregon, <September 27, 2000 [cited October 2, 2000]. Available from http: www.multnomah.lib.or.us/metro/gms.html>.

Metropolitan Planning Commission. 1966. How Should Our City Grow? Portland, OR: Metropolitan Planning Commission.

Miller, Donald L. 1996. *City of the Century: The Epic of Chicago and the Making of America*. New York: Simon and Schuster.

Miller, Richard W. 1987. *Fact and Method: Explanation, Confirmation and Reality in the Natural and the Social Sciences*. Princeton, NJ: Princeton University Press.

Mintzberg, Henry. 1994. *The Rise and Fall of Strategic Planning: Reconceiving Roles for Planning, Plans, Planners*. New York: Free Press.

Mintzberg, Henry, Duru Raisinghani, and Andre Theoret. 1976. The Structure of "Unstructured" Decision Processes. *Administrative Science Quarterly* 21:246–275.

Mjelde, James W., Steven T. Sonka, Bruce L. Dixon, and Peter J. Lamb. 1988. Valuing Forecast Characteristics in a Dynamic Agricultural Production System. *American Journal of Agricultural Economics* 70 (3):674–684.

Molotch, Harvey. 1976. The City as Growth Machine: Toward a Political Economy of Place. *American Journal of Sociology* 82:309–332.

Moody, Walter D. 1912. *Teachers Handbook, Wacker's Manual of the Plan of Chicago: Municipal Economy*. Chicago: Chicago Plan Commission.

———. 1919. *What of the City?* Chicago: A. C. McClurg & Co, 415.

Moore, Terry. 1978. Why Allow Planners to Do What They Do? A Justification from Economic Theory. *Journal of the American Institute of Planners* 44 (4):387–398.

Morgan, Granger, and Max Henrion. 1990. *Uncertainty: A Guide to Dealing with Uncertainty in Quantitative Risk and Policy Analysis*. Cambridge, United Kingdom: Cambridge University Press.

Mueller, Dennis C. 1989. *Public Choice*. 2nd ed. Cambridge: Cambridge University Press.

Mullen, B., C. Johnson, and E. Salas. 1991 Productivity Loss in Brainstorming Groups: A Meta-Analytic Integration. *Basic and Applied Social Psychology* 12(1):3–23.

Nash, Roderick, ed. 1976. *The American Environment*. 2nd ed. Reading, MA: Addison-Wesley.

Nelson, Arthur C., ed. 1988. *Development Impact Fees*. Chicago: Planners Press.

Neuman, Michael. 1997. Images as Institution Builders: Metropolitan Planning in Madrid. In *Making Strategic Spatial Plans: Innovations in Europe*, edited by P. Healey, A. Khakee, A. Motte, and B. Needham. London: UCL Press.

———. 1998. Does Planning Need the Plan? *Journal of the American Planning Association* 64(2):208–220.

Newby, Howard, Colin Bell, and David Rose. 1978. *Property, Paternalism, and Power: Class and Control in Rural England*. London: Hutchinson.

Nicholson, Walter. 2000. *Intermediate Microeconomics*. 8th ed. Orlando, FL: Harcourt, Inc.

Northeastern Illinois Planning Commission. 1990. Northeastern Illinois Planning Commission Annual Report 1990, Chicago, Illinois. Chicago: Northeastern Illinois Planning Commission.

Nozick, Robert. 1974. *Anarchy, State, and Utopia*. New York: Basic Books.

Ohls, James C., and David Pines. 1975. Discontinuous Urban Development and Economic Efficiency. *Land Economics* 51:224–234.

Olmsted, Frederick Law. 1852. *Walks and Talks of an American Farmer in England*. Vol. 1. New York: George P. Putnam and Company, 133.

Olshansky, Robert. 1996. The California Environmental Quality Act and Local Planning. *Journal of the American Planning Association* 62 (3):313–330.

Olson, Mancur. 1965. *The Logic of Collective Action*. Cambridge, MA: Harvard University Press.

O'Mara, Paul. 1973. The Aurora New Town Story: Who's to Plan the Region? *Planning* December, 39 (12):8–11.

Orfield, Myron. 1997. *Metropolitics: A Regional Agenda for Community and Stability*. Washington, DC: Brookings Institution Press.

Ostrom, Elinor, Roy Gardner, and James Walker. 1994. *Rules, Games, and Common-Pool Resources*. Ann Arbor: University of Michigan Press.

Patton, Carl V., and David S. Sawicki. 1993. *Basic Methods of Policy Analysis and Planning*. 2d ed. Englewood Cliffs, NJ: Prentice-Hall, Inc.

Peattie, Lisa. 1987. *Planning: Rethinking Ciudad Guayana*. Ann Arbor: University of Michigan Press, 112, 148.

Pitkin, S. 1992. Comprehensive Plan Format: A Key to Impacting Decisionmaking. *Environmental and Urban Issues* 19 (4):8–10.

Pressman, N., and Aaron Wildavsky. 1973. *Implementation*. Berkeley: University of California Press.

Pruetz, Rick. 1997. *Saved by Development: Preserving Environmental Areas, Farmland, and Historic Landmarks with Transfer of Development Rights*. Burbank, CA: Arje Press.

Raiffa, Howard. 1968. *Decision Analysis: Introductory Lectures on Choices under Uncertainty*. Reading, MA: Addison-Wesley.

Rapaport, Anatol, and A. Chammah. 1965. *Prisoner's Dilemma*. Ann Arbor: University of Michigan Press.

Rasmussen, Jens, Annelise Pejtersen, and L. P. Goodstein. 1994. *Cognitive Systems Engineering*. New York: John Wiley and Sons, Inc.

Rawls, John A. 1971. *A Theory of Justice*. Cambridge, MA: Belknap Press.

Reardon, Kenneth M. 1994. Community Development in Low-Income Minority Communities: A Case for Empowerment Planning. Paper read at Association of Collegiate Schools of Planning, November 4, 1994, at Phoenix, Arizona.

———. 1998. Enhancing the Capacity of Community-Based Organizations in East St. Louis. *Journal of Planning Education and Research* 17 (4):323–333.

Regenwetter, Michel, and Bernard Grofman. 1998. Approval Voting, Borda Winners, Condorcet Winners: Evidence from Seven Elections. *Management Science* 44 (4):520–533.

Regmi, Mahesh Chandra. 1976. *Landownership in Nepal.* Berkeley: University of California Press.

Reps, John. 1969. *Town Planning in Frontier America.* Princeton, NJ: Princeton University Press.

Richmond, Henry R. 1997. Comment on Carl Abbott's "The Portland Region: Where City and Suburbs Talk to Each Other—and Often Agree." *Housing Policy Debate* 8 (1):53–64.

Riker, William H., and Peter C. Ordeshook. 1973. *An Introduction to Positive Political Theory.* Englewood Cliffs, NJ: Prentice-Hall.

Roelofs, H. Mark. 1992. *The Poverty of American Politics: A Theoretical Interpretation.* Philadelphia: Temple University Press.

Roeseler, Wolfgang. 1982. *Successful American Urban Plans.* Lexington, MA: D.C. Heath.

Rubin, Herbert J. 1988. The Danada Farm: Land Acquisition, Planning, and Politics in the Suburbs. *Journal of the American Planning Association* 54 (1):79–90.

Satz, Ronald N. 1991. Chippewa Treaty Rights: The Reserved Rights of Wisconsin's Chippewa Indians in Historical Perspective. Wisconsin Academy of Sciences, Arts and Letters, Transactions Vol. 79, No. 1.

Saunders, Peter. 1983. *Urban Politics: A Sociological Interpretation.* London: Hutchinson and Co.

Savas, E. S. 1982. *Privatizing the Public Sector.* Chatham, NY: Chatham House Publishers, Inc.

Schaeffer, Peter V., and Lewis D. Hopkins. 1987. Planning Behavior: The Economics of Information and Land Development. *Environment and Planning A* 19:1221–1232.

Schmid, A. Allan. 1978. *Property, Power and Public Choice.* New York: Praeger, xi.

Schultz, Stanley K. 1989. *Constructing Urban Culture: American Cities and City Planning, 1800–1920.* Philadelphia: Temple University Press.

Sedway, Paul H., and Thomas Cooke. 1983. Downtown Planning: Basic Steps. *Planning* 49 (12):22–25.

Segoe and Associates, Ladislas. 1958. Master Plan Supplement: City-County Planning and Zoning Commission of Lexington and Fayette County, Kentucky. Cincinnati, Ohio.

Sen, Amartya. 1992. *Inequality Reexamined.* Cambridge, MA: Harvard University Press.

Shiffer, Michael J. 1995. Interactive Multimedia Planning Support: Moving from Stand Alone Systems to the World Wide Web. *Environment and Planning B: Planning and Design* 22:649–664.

Shipley, Robert, and Ross Newkirk. 1998. Visioning: Did Anyone See Where It Came From? *Journal of Planning Literature* 12 (4):407–416.

Siemon, Charles L., Wendy L. Larson, and Douglas R. Porter. 1982. *Vested Rights: Balancing Public and Private Development Expectations.* Washington, DC: Urban Land Institute.

Silver, Christopher. 1985. Neighborhood Planning in Historical Perspective. *Journal of the American Planning Association* 51 (2):161–174.

Simon, Herbert. 1969. *The Sciences of the Artificial.* Cambridge, MA: MIT Press.

Sipper, Daniel, and Robert Bulfin. 1997. *Production: Planning, Control, and Integration.* New York: McGraw-Hill.

Skjei, Stephen S. 1973. *Information for Collective Action.* Boston: Lexington.

Sniezek, Janet, and Rebecca Henry. 1989. Accuracy and Confidence in Group Judgment. *Organizational Behavior and Human Decision Processes* 43:1–28.

Sonka, S. T., P. J. Lamb, S. E. Hollinger, and J. W. Mjelde. 1986. Economic Use of Weather and Climate Information: Concepts and an Agricultural Example. *Journal of Climatology* 6:447–457.

Steiner, Ivan D. 1972. *Group Process and Productivity.* New York: Academic Press.

Stevens, Joe B. 1993. *The Economics of Collective Choice.* Boulder, CO: Westview Press.

Stevens Thompson and Runyan, Inc. 1969. Tualatin Basin Water and Sewerage Master Plan. Portland, Oregon: Client: Washington County Board of Commissioners.

Stokey, Edith, and Richard Zeckhauser. 1978. *A Primer for Policy Analysis.* New York: W. W. Norton & Company.

Stone, Christopher D. 1973. *Should Trees Have Standing? Toward Legal Rights for Natural Objects.* Los Altos, CA: W. Kaufmann.

Strotz, Robert H. 1956. Myopia and Inconsistency in Dynamic Utility Maximization. *Review of Economic Studies* 23 (3):165–180.

Suchman, Lucy A. 1987. *Plans and Situated Actions: The Problem of Human-Machine Communcation.* Edited by R. Pea and J. S. Brown, *Learning in Doing: Social, Cognitive, and Computational Perspectives.* Cambridge: Cambridge University Press.

Talen, Emily. 1996. Do Plans Get Implemented? A Review of Evaluation in Planning. *Journal of Planning Literature* 10 (3):248–259.

Talen, Emily, and Luc Anselin. 1998. Assessing Spatial Equity: The Role of Access Measures. *Environment and Planning A* 30 (4): 595–613.

Varian, Hal R. 1992. *Microeconomic Analysis.* 3rd ed. New York: W. W. Norton.

Vickers, Geoffrey. 1965. *The Art of Judgement.* New York: Basic Books.

Waddell, Paul. 2000. A Behavioral Simulation Model for Metropolitan Policy Analysis and Planning: Residential Location and Housing Market Components of UrbanSim. *Environment and Planning B: Planning and Design* 27 (2):247–263.

Walker, Robert Averill. 1950. *The Planning Function in Government.* 2nd ed. Chicago: University of Chicago Press, 42.

Warner, Sam Bass Jr. 1978. *Streetcar Suburbs: The Process of Growth in Boston, 1870–1900.* 2nd ed. Cambridge, MA: Harvard University Press.

Weiss, Marc A. 1987. *The Rise of the Community Builders: The American Real Estate Industry and Urban Land Planning.* New York: Columbia University Press.

Westervelt, James, and Lewis D. Hopkins. 1999. Modeling Mobile Individuals in Dynamic Landscapes. *International Journal of Geographic Information Science* 13 (3):191–208.

White, S. Mark. 1996. Adequate Public Facilities Ordinances and Transportation Management. Planning Advisory Service Report No. 465, Chicago: American Planning Association.

Wickens, Christopher D. 1992. *Engineering Psychology and Human Performance.* 2nd ed. New York: HarperCollins Publishers.

Wildavsky, Aaron. 1973. If Planning Is Everything, Maybe It's Nothing. *Policy Sciences* 4 (2):137–153.

Williams, Bruce, and Albert Matheny. 1995. *Democracy, Dialogue, and Environmental Disputes.* New Haven, CT: Yale University Press.

Williams, Cicely. 1964. *Zermatt Saga.* Brig, Switzerland: Rotten-Verlag.

Williamson, Chilton. 1960. *American Suffrage: From Property to Democracy 1760–1860.* Princeton, NJ: Princeton University Press.

Williamson, Oliver E. 1975. *Markets and Hierarchies.* New York: Free Press.

Windsor, Duane. 1979. *Fiscal Zoning in Suburban Communities.* Lexington, MA: D. C. Heath.

About the Author

Lewis D. Hopkins, AICP, is professor of urban and regional planning at the University of Illinois at Urbana-Champaign and was head of the department for thirteen years. He is Chair of the Planning Accreditation Board and was a Fulbright Senior Scholar in Nepal and editor of the *Journal of Planning Education and Research*.

Index

Action
commitment to, 26–27
consequences linked to, 243–49
effects of plan on, in assessment, 48
error-controlled, 18–19, 20, 21
event-driven, 78
expected value, 58–64, 80
generation tasks, 154–55
"hedge" or combination of, 75
lack of, 51–52
in natural systems, 16–17
opportunities for, 29–31
plan-based, 20–21
prediction-controlled, 19–20, 21
role of design prior to, 40–41
system-challenging *vs.* system-maintaining, 159–60
Agenda, 36–37, 225, 235
control of order of voting by, 174
definition, 34, 36
vs. objective, 35
scope of plan and, 242–43
vs. target, 41
use of plan as, 7, 46, 91
Allocation efficiency, 114–18
assumption of mobility of resources, 122
definition, 115
exceptions to, 116–17
Allocation of time, 229
Alternatives
creation by voluntary groups, 83
irrelevant, 173
primary, and bracket, 205, 214
uncertainty with respect to, 65, 78, 83–85
Amenity protection, 128, 129, 134–35
American Institute of Certified Planners
(AICP), 178
American Planning Association, 236
Analysis of interconnected decision areas
(AIDA), 240–41

Anchoring and adjustment bias of a problem,
152–53, 157
Annexation, 1, 3, 8, 123–24, 175–76
Approval voting, 174
Arizona, Phoenix, 131, 201, 245
Arrow's impossibility theorem, 173, 174, 176
Assembly line problem solving, 155–56
Assessment, 46–56
characteristics of good plans, 54
comparison tables, 205–6
diagnostic evaluation, 213–16
different approaches to, 47
four criteria for, 46–47
three observable phenomena in, 52
Attention span, 31, 150–51, 163–64
"Austinplan process," 210
Authority, 10, 108–15
"extraterritorial jurisdiction," 114
within institutions, 172
multi-jurisdiction plans, 1, 2
within organizations, 165, 211
plan decomposition and, 198–99
Availability bias, 153–54

Behavior
alteration by intersubjective knowledge,
146, 148
of construction material suppliers, 73
counterregulatory, 93
equilibrium-seeking, 196
loyalty, 89, 165
plan making, 46, 187, 188–89
rationality, 187, 188, 192–202
reaction to signals, 92–93, 256n.7
signals of commitment, 88
too optimistic or pessimistic, 153
Beliefs, 172, 180, 209
Benefit. *See* Cost-benefit analysis; Net benefit
Bernoulli principle, 73
Brainstorming, 154–55

283